STU

IN

Medieval

&

Renaissance

Music

MANFRED F. BUKOFZER

Professor of Music, The University of California

The Norton Library

W · W · NORTON & COMPANY · INC ·

NEW YORK

ISBN   0   393   00 241   1

Contents

Contents

Illustrations

Preface

"What maketh yow to han al this labour?"
"Ful many a cause . . ."

(The Freres Tale)

ALTHOUGH the studies contained in this volume were written
—with one exception—between 1947 and 1949, they embody
the results of research that has been carried out intermittently over a
period of more than a decade. The course of this specialized research
was interrupted by an altogether different task, that of writing *Music
in the Baroque Era,* and in resuming the study of medieval and Renaissance music I cannot help feeling a little like the prodigal son
coming home. The former book called essentially for a broad interpretation of an entire period and of material already known, and permitted the discussion of particular or new aspects only in so far as
they illustrated larger points of view. These inevitable restrictions
created as the work progressed a wholesome reaction and prompted
the desire to do the very opposite, to reverse the accent by presenting
new source material which in turn may have a bearing on the larger
aspects of the period.

These studies are intended not only as contributions to the ever-
growing research material of musicology, but also as object lessons
of a point of method, namely that specialized topics can be fruitfully
discussed only against the background of a broad perspective. In spite
of the vast difference in subject matter between my previous book and
the present one, my approach has not changed, for it is only a question
of procedure, but not of principle, whether the larger aspects of a
stylistic period are shown through and in the particular ones or vice
versa, so long as their basic interrelation is not lost sight of. Likewise

unchanged is the stylistic orientation, that is to say the concentration on the music itself. However broad or narrow the point of attack may be, and however far specialized research may penetrate into fields that lie at the periphery of the musical orbit, or even completely outside of it, if related to the music itself they enrich it with all the more powerful associations and contribute to a more profound understanding. This is true especially of the liturgical aspects of music to which I have paid special attention. They have been sadly neglected in past musicological writings, with the result that even essential musical points have remained obscure. By innumerable ties musicology is interrelated with such fields as the history of liturgy, art, and literature. The growing specialization, the fate of our departmentalized society, can be overcome only by the co-operation of specialists.

The studies of this miscellany deal mainly with the music of "that solemn fifteenth century which can hardly be studied too much . . . for its positive results in the things of the intellect and the imagination." When he wrote these lines Walter Pater could not possibly have realized how true they were also of music, because in his day fifteenth-century music was practically a *terra incognita*. Only in our century have efforts been made to fill this blank spot on the musical map. Numerous editions have appeared disclosing undreamed-of treasures, but this volume will show that the confines are still far from being fully charted. Musically speaking, the fifteenth century has so far remained the abode of scholars, and while educated persons would be ashamed not to know the works of Leonardo da Vinci, they would be at a complete loss if asked about the nature of the music on which Leonardo exercised his musical talents. Much of the music of the Renaissance is still awaiting its renaissance in the twentieth century; and there is indeed "ful many a cause," as Chaucer says, for devoting a volume to music that is at present very imperfectly known even though it is in no way inferior to the other arts of its time.

The studies collected here are separate but not unrelated, as they circumscribe a well-defined section of music history. They center in a few general ideas prevalent in late medieval and Renaissance music. The accent lies on the presentation of unknown facts, and all studies draw on unpublished manuscripts and materials. Those on the Fountains Fragment and the Meaux Abbey Manuscript discuss for the first time the musical aspects of newly found sources. However, it should not be thought that musical scholarship exhausts itself in the unearthing of musical documents. The studies on the Old Hall Manuscript and on *Caput* investigate compositions that, though available for years, had not been fully appreciated in their historical and musical importance. It will not escape the reader that one question runs like a red thread through nearly all the essays. This is the manner in which a pre-existing melody, be it a plainsong or a secular cantus firmus, was elaborated by the composer and used as an element of musical structure. The *Caput* study demonstrates that the discovery of a single plainsong may lead to a revaluation of an entire group of compositions. It has not always been recognized how fundamental the concept of composition on borrowed material was in medieval and Renaissance music, and if this book helps to correct the perspective on this point it will have fulfilled its purpose.

The first four papers deal with early English music, with which I have been preoccupied for a long time. They are in part the basis of a summary account of English music in the fifteenth century which I wrote for *The New Oxford History of Music*. The restricted space of that contribution made it impossible to give full documentation on several points and to deal adequately with new sources. It will be seen that the research going into the summary is far bulkier than the summary itself, and we have here a beautiful example of the tail wagging the dog—which is perhaps the symbol of all scholarship. The last three studies discuss various aspects of Renaissance music, the emergence of choral polyphony, dance music, and problems of the cyclic Mass. The last study on *Caput,* which should logically stand at the "head" of the series, has been placed at the end, not only for reasons of chronology but also for a more appropriate one which the reader will discover for himself. It is unavoidable, in view of the interrelated topics, that certain problems should come up several times. In order to eliminate repetition numerous cross references have been inserted.

Several of these studies were first publicly presented on various occasions—at a meeting of the Northern California Chapter of the American Musicological Society (1948), the Fourth Congress of the International Society for Musicology in Basel (1949), and in public lectures delivered while I held the Walker-Ames Professorship at the University of Washington (1949). The papers on the Old Hall Manuscript and choral polyphony are the only ones that have previously appeared in print, in *The Musical Quarterly* (1948–1949) and the *Papers* of the American Musicological Society (1940) respectively. With the permission of the copyright holders both are reprinted here, extensively revised and brought up to date. Professor Oliver Strunk of Princeton University has graciously given his consent to including in this volume his valuable Postscript to the Old Hall Manuscript, without which I deem my own study incomplete. I am grateful to him not only for this favor but also for other suggestions. I owe special thanks also to Professor Ernst H. Kantorowicz of the University of California, who with his thorough knowledge of liturgical history cleared up an intricate question of liturgical significance in the *Caput* study. I am furthermore indebted for assistance, advice, and information regarding manuscripts to many persons, of whom I shall name only the following: the Reverend H. C. Chadwick (Stonyhurst College, Lancs.), Professor Otto Gombosi (University of Chicago), Dr. Richard L. Greene (President of Wells College), Professor Wilibald Gurlitt (University of Freiburg), Mr. John H. Harvey (Bookham, Surrey), Professor Erich Hertzmann (Columbia University), Dr. Helen Hewitt (North Texas State College), Dr. R. W. Hunt (Keeper of Western Manuscripts at the Bodleian Library), Dr. Nicholas J. Kelly (Librarian of St. Edmund's College, Old Hall, Herts.), Dr. Gwynn McPeek (University of North Carolina), Professor Walter Rubsamen (University of California, Los Angeles), Mr. Bertram Schofield (Deputy Keeper of Manuscripts at the British Museum), Dr. Egon Wellesz (Lincoln College, Oxford), and my wife. I should like to thank for their courtesy and co-operation the governing bodies of various college libraries in Oxford and Cambridge, the University Library in Cambridge, the Isham Library, the John Rylands Library, the Huntington Library, the Bodleian Library, the British Museum, several Italian libraries, and the Bibliothèque Nationale.

By way of conclusion it may be pointed out that this volume is addressed not only to professional musicologists and to scholars in other fields generally interested in the period discussed, but also to music students who want to learn about the scope and method of musicology, and to those of the general reading public who take an interest in the historical approach to music. Since much of the music discussed is so far unpublished, I have inserted numerous musical examples, including complete compositions whenever called for.

I

Two Fourteenth-Century Motets on St. Edmund

THE FEAST of the English martyr St. Edmund (d. 868), king of East Anglia, was introduced in the English liturgy in the year 1013,[1] and since that time special services have been sung on the day of his death, November 20. The music composed in his honor includes plainchant as well as polyphonic compositions, and an interesting combination of the two is the subject of this essay. MS E Museo 7 of the Bodleian Library contains on flyleaves x–xi two motets of the early fourteenth century:[2] one for three voices, *Deus tuorum militum—De Flore martyrum—Ave Rex gentis,* and one for four voices: *Ave miles—Ave rex patrone—Ave Rex.*[3] Both are transcribed at the end of this study (Exs. 3 and 4). The fragment belonged originally to the monks of Bury St. Edmund's[4] and it is therefore not surprising that it transmits music dedicated to St. Edmund. The liturgical connection between the motets is indicated externally in their being written in direct succession on the same folio. In addition, the tenor

[1] Frere, Introduction to *Grad. Sar.,* xxv; for the historical background to St. Edmund see F. M. Stenton, *Anglo-Saxon England,* Oxford, 1943, 246.

[2] The date of the motets can be inferred from their Petronian notation. It should be noted that the manuscript itself is probably not earlier than the middle of the fourteenth century, as it contains in another part pieces in fully developed *ars nova* notation.

[3] Nos. 9 and 8 of the table of contents given by Besseler, AMW VII, 222. The first motet is unpublished, the second is available in print: the first third in Besseler, *Musik des Mittelalters und der Renaissance,* 172, the remainder in Reese, *Music in the Middle Ages,* 1940, 402. The piece is printed here for the first time with the complete and correct text.

[4] Stainer, *Early Bodleian Music,* 1901, xviii.

17

incipits agree and suggest that the voices draw on the same plainsong. A preliminary comparison of the tenor melodies discloses that they are indeed the same, but only for the first part, after which they go their own ways. Do they draw on the same chant? In order to answer this question it is essential to determine the source of the plainsong.[5] The Vatican reference books leave us in the lurch, as they do not list a chant with that title. For the answer we must turn to the liturgical books of the Sarum use, which in this case as well as in many others prove indispensable for the study of medieval English music. Both the Worcester Antiphonal [6] and the *Antiphonale Sarisburiense* [7] do record an antiphon entitled *Ave rex gentis Anglorum* on St. Edmund which, as will be seen presently, is the source for both tenors. When I copied out the chant I noticed that melody as well as text had a familiar ring, though I was sure I had not previously run across this particular antiphon. Further checking brought to light the reason for this strange familiarity: *Ave rex gentis Anglorum* is identical in music and to a large part in text also with the much better known Marian antiphon *Ave regina caelorum, mater regis*.[8] The Worcester version of *Ave rex* which agrees most closely with the motet tenors is given below (Ex. 1) with both the Edmundian and Marian forms of

Ex. 1. Antiphon: *Ave rex gentis Anglorum* (= *Ave regina*).

A - ve rex gentis An-glo   •   rum, mi-lés re-gis An-ge-lo   •   rum. O Ed-mun-de flos mar-ty -rum
A - ve re-gi-na ce-lo   •   rum, ma-ter re-gis An-ge-lo   •   rum. O Ma-ria   flos vir-gi-num

ve-lut ro - sa vel li- li-um. Fun-de pre -ces ad Do-mi - num pro sa-lu - te fi- de- li-ium.
ve-lut ro - sa vel li- li-um. Fun-de pre-ces ad Do-mi - num pro sa-lu - te fi-de-li-um.

pre - ces   ad Do-mi-num

the text. The version of the *Ant. Sar.* differs in some particulars, and one of its variants, inserted in the transcription in square brackets,

[5] Besseler, *op. cit.*, 172, did not identify the chant but classified it as type six of Gevaert's list of typical antiphon melodies (*La Mélopée antique dans l'église latine*, 1895, 243). However, the melody does not agree too well with any of the variants given by Gevaert.

[6] *Pal. mus.* XII, 405.

[7] Pl. 597.

[8] Chevalier, *Repertorium hymnologicum*, No. 2072; not to be confused with *Ave regina caelorum, ave Domina*, which belongs to the famous set of four Marian antiphons (*Ant. Rom.*, 54–57).

supplements the Worcester version. The variant at *preces ad Do-minum* represents the simplified version of the fifteenth century, as found in Sarum Processionals.[9] The Vatican melody of the Marian antiphon does not concord exactly with any of the Sarum versions, but it need not be given here, as it is easily accessible in print.[10] The basic musical agreement among all known versions of the antiphons is as obvious as their textual similarity. Actually, only a few words of the first lines differ. The adaptation has been made with the least possible change in letters: *rex gentis* corresponds to *regina,* and the names and attributes have been exchanged (*miles* becomes *mater*), but for the rest the words are the same.[11]

Which is the prototype of the two antiphons? As only the Marian form has become famous, it is natural to assume that it must also be the original one. However, the evidence of the sources, incomplete as it is, casts some doubt on this hypothesis. The two Sarum antiphonals which record the Edmundian form only belong to the thirteenth century. The earliest source of the Marian form dates, according to Chevalier, from the fourteenth century, but a two-part setting in the eleventh fascicle of W_1 proves that it existed at least as early as the second half of the thirteenth century.[12] The Marian form rose to prominence with the intensified cult of the Virgin in the fifteenth century and was at that time frequently set in polyphony.[13] Sarum Processionals of the fifteenth and sixteenth centuries transmit only the Marian form, which by this time had far surpassed the other in popularity. However, the Edmundian form is still recorded in the Sarum Breviary of 1531.[14] Moreover, it appears as burden in an English carol of the fifteenth century.[15] It was therefore not yet forgotten in the fifteenth and sixteenth centuries. While lack of adequate documentation does not permit a definitive conclusion, an English origin

[9] See, for example, the Processional of 1519 (Pollard 16235), available in the microfilm series *Books Printed in England before 1600,* University Microfilms, Carton 95.

[10] LU, 1864, and *Proc. Mon.,* 270.

[11] Still a third variant of the antiphon beginning with the words *Ave rex gentis Brivatensium* is listed in Chevalier, No. 35706. The Edmundian form is missing in Chevalier's list.

[12] *An Old St. Andrews Music Book,* ed. by J. H. Baxter, Oxford, 1931, facsimile 194 (fol. 211). The lower voice carries the plainsong in the Sarum version.

[13] There are several anonymous English settings in Bodleian MS Selden B 26; others are by Binchois (Marix, 189), Frye, and Obrecht (see note 161 on p. 310).

[14] Ed. by Procter and Wordsworth, 1879–86, III, 1073. The same source (III, 329) contains also a fourth variant of the antiphon, adapted this time to St. Alban. The text begins *Ave prothomartyr Anglorum,* and continues exactly like the Edmundian form.

[15] See Richard L. Greene, *The Early English Carols,* 1935, No. 312; also lxxxiv.

of the antiphon must at least be considered as a possibility. It may have been composed originally in honor of St. Edmund, adapted later to the more general Marian use, and then introduced on the Continent in its Marian form. This suggestion is supported indirectly by the fact that the latter text has been borrowed in its entirety by a macaronic carol.[16] In addition, the majority of the early polyphonic settings of *Ave regina* stem from English composers. The words of the chant show a fully developed rhyme and can therefore hardly be earlier than the twelfth century. For the two motets under discussion the question of priority is of no consequence, except that if the Edmundian form should prove to be the prototype they would be English even in their underlying plainchant.

Our two compositions are notated in the so-called "Petronian" or "Fauvel" notation current in England about and after 1300. It is characterized by dots marking off the number of short notes that divide the breve. This notation demonstrates the breakdown of strict modal patterns in the upper voices and the turn to a more subtle and diversified rhythm which developed at the same pace as did the division of the breve into smaller units. The four-part *Ave miles* does not go beyond dividing the breve into groups of two or three semibreves and thus proves the more conservative motet in rhythmic respect. In *Deus tuorum* the subdivisions go up to five and six and call for rapid coloratura and parlando in alternation. In both motets, however, the undercurrent of modal rhythm is nevertheless still perceptible, more strongly so in the four-part composition. Harmonically, the motets display the gradual intrusion of the English sixth-chord style in motet writing. The emphasis on contrary motion and perfect consonances at the beginning of each perfection, which characterizes the harmonic style of the thirteenth century, is weakened here by a marked tendency to introduce thirds or sixths, to direct the voices in parallel as well as contrary motion, and to keep them together occasionally by a very conspicuous means: parallel six-three chords. These effectively counterbalance the aim of Gothic music to differentiate and stratify the voices by means of register, color, and, especially, rhythm, which prevailed in France more strongly than in England. English composers with their sensibility to blending intervals and the spell of sheer sonority followed only part of the way and preferred to adhere to what may be called chordal or "harmonic" effects,

16 Greene, *op. cit.*, lxxxv. The Marian form appears also with the unrecorded trope *Funde virgo* (see OS fol. 13), again an English composition.

although they did not entirely shut themselves off from the rhythmic innovations of the Petronian style.

This point is clearly apparent in *Deus tuorum militum,* which apostrophizes St. Edmund in the text of all three voices. The words of the *triplum* [17] paraphrase the well-known hymn *Deus tuorum militum,* which is sung in commemoration of a martyr in the liturgy of today. The melody of the hymn has not been used in the motet, but the textual relations are at times very close, as will be seen from the following passages, which are merely different phrasings of the same thought:

Hymn	Motet
Deus tuorum militum	Deus tuorum militum
. . .	. . .
laudes canentes martyris	laudes extollens martyris
absolve nexu criminis	salvatur nexu sceleris

Before we examine the music it should be understood that, in Fauvel notation, the rhythmic interpretation of the semibreves is a matter of conjecture rather than certainty.[18] It would have been possible and perhaps even preferable to transcribe in straight 3/4 time, as has been done in the four-part motet. This would strengthen the rhythmic pace of the music. The groups of two and three semibreves may be read equally well as simple binary groups and triplets respectively. The unequal interpretation of the group of two, which puts the music into 9/8 time, has been adopted here because the subdivisions of five and six semibreves require a tempo slow enough to make the rhythmic differentiations still perceptible. In the manuscript certain single semibreves in a group of four or more are sometimes marked by an upward *cauda* which transforms them into a minim. To judge from the tentative manner in which they are drawn, the *caudae* are probably later additions [19] which revise the notation in the light of *ars nova* notation.

[17] Owing to the poor state of preservation of the manuscript, three syllables of the text are illegible. Dr. R. W. Hunt, Keeper of Western MSS at the Bodleian Library, was so kind as to check my reading of it with the help of an ultraviolet lamp. His corrections and additions are gratefully acknowledged.

[18] An excellent survey of the problem is presented in Apel, *The Notation of Polyphonic Music,* 1944, 318 ss. The music of the motet is at some places badly rubbed and is not always legible with absolute certainty. The transcription is therefore offered with due reservations.

[19] The musical interpolations in the *Roman de Fauvel* present apparently a parallel case; see Apel, *op. cit.,* 325.

From the rhythmic point of view the *motetus De flore* is the most "modern" part. Only this voice goes beyond the triple division of the breve and contains some lively parlando passages, e.g., m. 14. The *triplum* moves at a more regular pace in conservative manner. The slowest voice is naturally the tenor, which progresses in longs and breves exclusively except in m. 6 (and the corresponding sections of the repeated tenor pattern), where it moves with the other voices in sixth chords.

The treatment of rhythm and plainchant in the tenor calls for some further comment. Above all, this voice is noteworthy for the incipient isorhythmic structure, not shared by the other voices. No more than the first two phrases of the plainchant serve as the melodic foundation of the motet. They are presented faithfully enough, with a slight melodic extension at the cadence. The text, only incompletely given in the manuscript, has been underlaid and completed in square brackets in correspondence with the chant. The composer has cut the melody into three isorhythmic patterns of seven measures each, marked off in the transcription by heavy bar lines. It will be seen that the first ligature recurs in each *talea* very strictly and that only the last measure of the last *talea* is rhythmically not quite exact. The tenor must be repeated once, though the *color* is not expressly called for in the manuscript. The upper voices completely ignore the regularity of the *taleae*, but do observe to some degree the *color* which constitutes the second part of the motet. This is made plainly audible inasmuch as the music of the second part is a freely varied version of the first part. At the beginning of most perfections the respective progressions correspond fairly well to each other if allowance is made for inversions in the position of the voices. Moreover, the last *talea* of the first part is almost literally restated at the end in all voices. Thus the form is skillfully rounded off, as happens not infrequently in motets of the thirteenth century. In its incipient isorhythmic structure and lucid form *Deus tuorum* parallels certain motets of the *Roman de Fauvel* [20] (in which the isorhythmic pattern is likewise as yet confined to the tenor) and foreshadows the rise of strict isorhythmic structure. The *color* of our motet involves a simple repeat; there is as yet no diminution or augmentation, which became the rule only

[20] See Johannes Wolf, *Geschichte der Mensuralnotation,* II–III, Nos. V and VI; DTOe, Vol. 76, 2 (facsimile in Apel, *op. cit.,* 331); and *Historical Anthology of Music,* ed. by Davison and Apel, No. 43.

later in the century with the full establishment of the isorhythmic principle.

The four-part *Ave miles* [21] is less dependent on Continental models and displays a more typically English technique of composition. In their discussion of the motet both Besseler and Reese have already mentioned the role of interchange of voices, this strange device of varied repetition that we meet more often in the medieval music of England than in that of any other country. Trading of parts represents, in fact, the governing structural principle of the composition and leads to some very peculiar and highly absorbing complications with regard to the borrowed plainchant. The motet must be classified as a polyphonic trope paraphrasing the words of the underlying antiphon. The latter could be and probably was replaced in the liturgy by the motet. In our case the upper voices form a trope not only to the antiphon but at the same time to *Benedicamus Domino,* so that the text may be regarded as a double trope. The manuscript contains several "tropical" motets and is only one of several sources that attest to the survival, in English music of the fourteenth century, of the musical trope. The mutual assimilation of the voices by means of textual paraphrase is reinforced musically through interchange of parts, similar movement in all voices, and blending harmonies, such as triads and sixth chords, far more pronounced here than in *Deus tuorum.* The lack of rhythmic differentiation adds even more to the prevailing impression of unified part writing; only the rests and certain sections in hocket bring in an element of diversity.

Ave miles has the appearance of a polytextual double motet, but there is actually only one continuous set of words, spread over the two voices which alternately recite or vocalize. The alternation of melismatic sections and sections with text invariably coincides with the interchange and thus underlines and clarifies the musical structure: all sections of the upper voice provided with text state the music for the first time, while all those of the lower voice repeat the same music with new text in reciprocal imitation. The pair of upper voices has its pendant in a similar pair of tenors. Significantly, the voice

[21] Aside from the completion and correction of the tenor, my transcription differs from Reese's only in minor details: I have read several words differently and corrected a few errors of the scribe and misprints. In addition, I have adopted 3/4 time (one perfection to the measure), because in 6/4 time the major divisions of the piece would fall in the middle of the measure.

above the tenor is not called contratenor but *tenor secundus*—a logical designation because the music of both voices is essentially the
same. Their structural divisions tally, of course, with those of the
upper voices. The motet as a whole falls into five major parts, each
repeated with interchange, and a coda of five measures without interchange or repeat. The schematic outline, with the length of each
section indicated by the number of measures, is simply this:

$$14 \quad 5 \quad 8 \quad 9 \quad 9 \quad 5$$
$$\text{A:}|| \ \text{B:}|| \ \text{C:}|| \ \text{D:}|| \ \text{E:}|| \ \text{F}$$

In our transcription the major parts have been indicated by heavy
bar lines and repeats by vertical dashes above the brace. It should be
kept in mind that the repeats are effected by trading of parts, which
brings variation of timbre. The interchange is in general very strict—
so much so that it permits us to correct scribal errors. Slight deviations appear only at points where the voices switch positions and
where, for the sake of smooth transition, a few notes may be altered.
There is, furthermore, an irregularity at the end of part A. The fourteen measures of the first section are correctly answered by the same
number of measures in interchange, but a fifteenth redundant measure
follows which relates back to the beginning. The rest proceeds in
regular and customary fashion.

All this would not be too remarkable were it not for the pair of
tenor voices. In motets with interchange the tenor must be composed
so as to permit the reciprocation of the upper voices and, if there are
two lower parts, also the sectional interchange of its own music.
These specific conditions can be met best if the tenor is specially composed; and in most works of the kind this is actually the case.[22] If,
however, the tenor is borrowed from plainchant, repeats become unavoidable. Such special cases may be exemplified by two motets of
English origin in the Montpellier MS, *Balaam inquit,* and *Huic
ut placuit.*[23] Here the tenor presents sections from the sequence

[22] This statement is based on the evidence of the following manuscripts: the Worcester fragments (see *Worcester Mediaeval Harmony,* ed. by Dom Anselm Hughes, 1928);
Br. Mus. Add. MS 24198; Bodleian MS 652; Oxford, New College MS 362; Cambridge,
Caius College MS 820/810; and Bodleian Libr., Hatton MS 81. Several of these are as yet
not described, and most of the music is unpublished. I intend to come back to the repertory in a separate study.

[23] Published in Yvonne Rokseth, *Polyphonies du XIIIe siècle,* 1936–1939, Nos. 340 and
341; also in Coussemaker, *L'Art harmonique aux XIIe et XIIIe siècles,* 1865, Nos. 22 and
23. In Oxford, New College, MS 362 the two motets appear as a single continuous piece.

Epiphaniam Domino,[24] and since it is the sole supporting voice it is consistently repeated in correspondence with the interchange of the upper voices. The entire melody of the versicle is restated each time, so that its inner structure remains intact. At the beginning of *Balaam inquit* there is even a short section in which the interchange takes place over the progressing melody of the tenor, but this is possible only because the first two phrases of the versicle happen to be identical melodically. The essential difference between our motet and those in the Montpellier MS is that their tenors do not participate in the reciprocal imitation.

In *Ave miles* the situation is more complex, and for that reason far more interesting. The antiphon *Ave rex* has been taken over in its entirety, but if it had been presented continuously and then repeated the sections would have become excessively long. On the other hand, the chant cannot be used as counterpoint against itself; so there remains no other alternative but to divide the melody into sections, provide each with an independent counterpoint, and repeat them in interchange. This is precisely what the composer has done. As a result, the sections of the plainsong must alternate, whenever the voices switch, with freely composed sections, namely with what was originally the counterpoint to the plainchant. Meanwhile the other voice restates the plainsong section. The switches back and forth have been indicated by arrows which should be self-explanatory. If we designate the various counterpoints by Roman numerals and the sections of the chant by letters, the following diagram results:

Second Tenor: I A II B III C IV D V E VI
Tenor: A I B II C III D IV E V F

The diagram makes clear that the tenor, which starts with the antiphon and carries it through to the end (A-E), is interrupted at regular intervals by interpolated sections (I-V). The whole is a strange composite of borrowed and new material. These interpolations are the

---

[24] The melody has been published by Aubry in *La Tribune de Saint-Gervais* (1910), 9, and by Bannister in *Rassegna Gregoriana*, IV (1905), 6; see also Moberg, *Über die schwedischen Sequenzen*, 1927, No. 15 b. The two motets in the Montpellier MS are not the first works to utilize the sequence. The earliest motet on the versicle *Balaam* is *Balaam, Godalier* (W₂, fol. 197 v; beginning transcribed in Besseler, *Musik des Mittelalters*, 122), which is noteworthy on two counts: it makes some use of interchange of voices and contains several references to England in its text. Among other things the words poke fun at the lover of "good ale" (Godalier!). For other works built on the sequence see Rokseth, *op. cit.*, IV, 185.

solution to the puzzle of why the tenor of *Deus tuorum militum* agrees
with that of *Ave miles* only at the beginning although they draw on
the same chant. They differ, furthermore, in their rhythmic treatment.
Instead of recurrent isorhythmic patterns we find in *Ave miles* very
free and imaginative rhythms which, in striking contrast to so-called
"plainchant rhythm," give the tenor the character of a freely composed mensural melody.

What is perhaps the most remarkable point about the interpolations is the manner in which they divide up the chant. It would be
reasonable to expect the subdivisions to coincide with the phrases of
the melody, so that borrowed and new material would be juxtaposed
as self-contained units. But here we experience a complete disap-
pointment. The composer has consistently disregarded the natural
caesurae and divided the chant arbitrarily into five sections which in
every case straddle the phrase divisions. That this arrangement was
quite deliberate is not only implied in the internal evidence of the
music but also externally expressed in the distribution of the text.
The scribe supplied the tenor not with the complete set of words
but merely with cues which in themselves were unintelligible so long
as the plainsong remained unidentified. In our transcription the missing words have been inserted in brackets in accordance with the
melody. It will be seen that the tenor keeps, in general, close to the
plainchant and that this fact is emphasized by the position of the cues
in the manuscript. At first glance they seem to be distributed at ran-
dom, but closer examination reveals that they appear precisely where
called for by the melody. The transcription reproduces the cues
exactly as they stand in the manuscript, except for the syllable *ad*
[*Dominum*]. The latter comes too late in the manuscript; it stands
here directly before *Dominum,* one measure before part E. Since the
agreement between tenor and chant is less satisfactory in this passage
than at any other place, it may be assumed that the composer has used
a somewhat different variant. The accurate location of all other cues
proves that even the scribe was aware of the derivation of the tenor
from plainsong.

The sections of the chant, arbitrary as they are, progress regularly
in interchange except, again, in part E, where the switch back to
the plainsong comes one measure too early. The connection between
the trading voices is made by the interpolation of one or two notes
not belonging to the chant. After the last switch in part E the plain-

song has run its course, and it could be assumed that the unrepeated coda F is freely composed. However, the scribe was careful to add *Evovae* to the tenor, and even this little section turns out to be a correctly designated piece of plainsong: it is one of the *differentiae* of the *seculorum amen* formula in the first psalm tone. It is very curious that this formula actually forms an integral part of the motet.

It follows from the above analysis that the motet represents a strange combination of cantus-firmus treatment and interchange of voices, two techniques usually regarded as mutually exclusive. Although they have both been applied consistently, they do not, in the final analysis, assert themselves with equal musical force. Obviously, interchange prevails over cantus firmus. Even a person well acquainted with the plainsong will not be able to follow it in actual performance. Its melodic outline is obscured if not obliterated by four factors. The first of these is the division of the chant into sections which alternate with freely composed counterpoints. That each of the sections is restated at once in the other tenor is, of course, the result of the interchange, but the repeats destroy the continuity of the melody. The second factor is the arbitrary nature of the division. The sections break off at all but the logical places and go over imperceptibly into the free music before the listener has realized it. Thirdly, the frequent use of voice crossing between the two tenors makes it difficult to distinguish the parts even if they are set off by different timbres. Neither one can be said to be the lowest-sounding part for any length of time. If they would keep consistently to one register, this difficulty would be obviated. There are, finally, numerous rests in both voices and at times pronounced hocket effects, for example at the beginning of part B. Although the chant is clearly stated in one voice, it is transformed by the hocket into a new melody quite dissimilar to the chant. This can be seen in the following excerpt (Ex. 2), in which the chant

Ex. 2. Plainsong and motet tenor compared.

is compared with the actual effect of the passage which combines the discontinuous tones of the two voices into a single line as the ear perceives it. Aside from the hocket, the rests in the cantus firmus further obfuscate the line because wherever they occur the intruding counterpoint is inadvertently accepted as the continuation of the chant. The line of the cantus firmus is therefore split up not only by the sections in interchange but also *within* the sections by whatever note sounds while the tenor pauses.

These observations will leave no doubt that it is not the presentation of the chant as an audible and continuous entity that the composer was striving for. The tones of the borrowed melody are no more than pegs to hang the tenor on, or mere raw material for its structure. Obviously, the chant cannot be perceived by the listener, from the outside as it were. This circumstance ought not to be criticized as a shortcoming of the composition. To demand that the structural voice should be clearly perceptible would mean to force modern standards on a piece of medieval music and would represent a serious mistake in method. The motet is not composed to be heard from without, from an external perspective. There is only one person that can follow the structure of the tenor without difficulty: the singer who carries the part. To him the hockets, voice crossings, and rests do not obscure the chant. The music is premised on an "internal perspective" like certain medieval paintings and reveals itself only to the participants, not to an "audience." It is music to be heard from within—singer's music. The only concessions toward an external perspective are the blending sonorities and the somewhat chordal texture of the music which represent elements of unification but which, on the other hand, prevent the tenor from standing out.

The structural features of the motet are, as far as is known today, very exceptional if not unique. The entire repertory of compositions with interchange should be re-examined for similar examples. The trading of parts, in itself a concrete and audible device, is superimposed in *Ave miles* on a strangely abstract cantus-firmus treatment. The structural rationality of the work may perhaps be compared with that of the isorhythmic principle, which at first glance seems to be something entirely different. However, the latter device applies to rhythm what the former does to melody. With its mechanical divisions and non-liturgical repeats the chant almost loses its identity and becomes a rational, if not mechanical, means of structure. To the medieval composer it does not matter that it cannot be heard from without. To him it is indeed true that "heard melodies are sweet, but those unheard are sweeter." The main point is that the chant exists in the music. It provides the sacred ground on which the human mind can erect its rational artifices.

Ex. 3. Motet: *Deus tuorum militum.*

Ex. 4. Motet: *Ave miles celestis.*

de- vo- ta ti-bi cog- no-ve- ris

Clau-dis gres-sum pre- ce re- sti- tu - is le- pras sa-

ro - sa

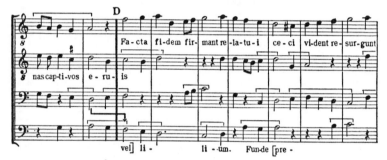

D

Fa- cta fi-dem fir- mant re- la-tu- i   ce- ci vi-dent re- sur-gunt

nas cap-ti-vos e- ru- is

vel] li - li -um. Fun-de [pre-

mor- tu- i.

Ho-stes ar-ces iu - sto iu- di-ci- o   ser-vis par-cis cor- de pro-

- ces] ad

E

Tan-ti re-gis ful- ti suf- fra- gi - o   Be- ne-di-ca-

pi- ti- o

Do-mi-   - num pro sa- lu - te

mus de- vo - te Do - mi - no

Fac no - bis mar-tyr in vi - te ter - mi - no dig -

fi - de - li - um.

nas lau- des re- fer - re Do - mi- no.

E - vo - vae

II

The Music of the Old Hall
Manuscript

1. THE EDITION

THE MUSIC of the Old Hall MS (OH) has at last been made available, and by printing the three impressive volumes the Plainsong and Mediaeval Music Society has fulfilled an obligation of long standing toward musicology in general and English music in particular. Ever since Barclay Squire published his brief study of the manuscript with a thematic catalogue,[1] the crucial position of the codex in the development of English music has been known, but it has taken more than a generation for its treasures to be made accessible to the general public. It will not be necessary to dwell on the significance of the music or the value of OH as a source. Not only is it the largest manuscript of English music in the early fifteenth century, but it is the first one to acquaint us with the names of numerous English composers. It is therefore gratifying to see that the manuscript has been published almost in full, though the idea of selecting merely the most valuable pieces from the rather uneven repertory must have been a tempting one.

The edition appeared between the years 1933 and 1938 and was entrusted originally to the Reverend A. Ramsbotham, who transcribed all the compositions except those that foiled him because of their

[1] Barclay Squire, "Notes on an Undescribed Collection of English 15th-Century Music," in *Sammelbände IMG*, II (1901), 342.

intricate notation. His premature death prevented him from seeing the first volume through the press; the co-editors, H. B. Collins and Dom Anselm Hughes, took over, completing the rest, revising the existing transcriptions, and adding helpful introductions. Originally, it was planned to print only complete compositions, but fortunately this policy was changed to include those fragments that give more or less complete settings of at least certain sections.

The compositions in OH are arranged according to a simple plan: sections of the Mass are grouped together under one heading—Gloria, Credo, Sanctus, or Agnus—while motets and conductus-like settings have been inserted more or less arbitrarily between the main groups. This order has not been strictly maintained in the edition, where all fragments, scattered throughout the manuscript, have been collected in an appendix. A condensed index of the contents and an index of composers (both in Vol. III) permit us to locate each piece. Several (but not all) incipits of pieces not printed in the edition are given in the prefaces to Vols. II and III. To go through all the compositions in their original order the reader has to turn to four or five different places: the thematic catalogue of Barclay Squire, the main text of the edition, the appendix, the prefaces, and, in addition, the annotations and corrections in Vol. III, without which the first volume in particular should not be consulted. All this is a rather cumbersome and confusing business, but perhaps it is the inevitable result of joint editorship and the gradual process of clarification in the course of publication. By and large it cannot be said that the editors have maintained the high level of scholarship that distinguishes the edition of *Polyphonia Sacra* by Charles van den Borren, published only a year before OH by the same society. Unlike that edition, the present publication contains no formal critical commentary (instead, there are some footnotes), no list of concordances, and no collation with other manuscripts which give sometimes a better, sometimes even the only complete, version of the composition; the sole exception is the newly discovered Fountains fragment (British Museum, Add. MS 40011 B), which, however, has been collated only superficially, so that three important compositions have passed unnoticed so far. Moreover, the music in OH has not been analyzed sufficiently to guarantee a definitive transcription. This is true especially with regard to the isorhythmic compositions. As a matter of fact, the editors, evidently not familiar with isorhythmic tech-

nique, failed to notice the returns of identical rhythmic patterns in
the upper voices, and as a result the editorial conjectures with regard
to missing notes are most unsatisfactory.

Before we go into details, it may be well to point out that the
numbering of the compositions in the thematic list of Barclay Squire
must be revised because he sometimes erroneously regarded unrelated
voices as belonging to one composition and completely overlooked
other pieces. Since they are usually quoted by numbers in musicological literature, it is best to retain the original numbering and merely
modify it by letters. The following corrections should be incorporated:

3.   Anon.   *Gloria* (III [6]) stands on fol. 2 and 2v, not on fol. 3.
3a. Anon.   *Gloria,* fol. 3, fragmentary at the beginning, does not belong
             to No. 3, as Barclay Squire supposed. The opening of the
             fragment is printed in Vol. III, xix, but incompletely; see
             the comment at the end of this list.
4.   Anon.   *Gloria* (III, [8]) stands on fol. 3v, not fol. 4.
4a. Anon.   (III, [11]), last section of a fragmentary *Gloria.*
8.   Damett   *Gloria* (III, [13]), fol. 7b only, not 8.
8a. Anon.   (III, [16]), last section of a fragmentary *Gloria,* fol. 8.
39. Anon.   . . . *veniae,* end only of a conductus motet [not printed].
42. Anon.   fol. 37 fragmentary conductus motet . . . *et propitia* [not
             printed]. What seems to be a continuation on the same folio
             is actually a new piece, namely No. 42a.
42a. Anon.   [*Salve mater*] *Salvatoris, salve salutifera.* This text is known
             from a composition by Dunstable.[2] Only the section begin-
             ning with *Venter tuus* has been printed (III, [54]). The
             words, incidentally, are in part identical with those of an
             English Sanctus trope.[3]
43. Anon.   fol. 37v. The first words may conjecturally be restored as
             [*Salve Mater*] *Salvatoris, te celestis stilla roris.*[4] Beginning of
             text similar to 42a, but different continuation. Neither text
             is listed in Chevalier's *Repertorium.* Only the section begin-
             ning with *Vas virtutum* (III, [56]) has been printed.
45. Anon.   fol. 38. This is the incomplete beginning of the antiphon
             Nesciens mater, as Barclay Squire pointed out. The first
             words are missing. Only the section *Ipsum Regem* (III, [58])
             has been printed.

[2] See the references in Bukofzer, *Acta Musicologica*, VIII (1936), 114.

[3] J. Wickham Legg, *The Sarum Missal,* 1916, p. 543.

[4] See the similar text of the motet *Salve mater salvatoris, vas electum, vas honoris,* by
Jean Mouton, published in Glareanus' *Dodecachordon* (1547), ed. by Bohn, 1887, 417.
This sequence appears also in the *Sarum Missal,* p. 521; music in *Les Proses d'Adam de
Saint-Victor* (Misset-Aubry), Paris 1900, 302.

70. Leonel *Credo* [not printed, except for incipit, II, xv], fol. 61v only, not 62. Only the cantus part is extant. Does not belong to the following item; see list of concordances.

70a. Anon. fol. 62, two lower parts of another *Credo* (see list of concordances below).

121a. Anon. *Agnus Dei* (III, 102), fol. 101v.[5]

121b. Anon. *Agnus Dei* (III, 104), fol. 101v–102.

121c. Anon. *Agnus Dei* (III, 106), fol. 102.

126. Leonel *Agnus Dei* (III, 118), fol. 104v only.

126a. Anon. *Agnus Dei* (III, 120), 104v; see list of concordances.

135. Anon. fol. 109v only, *Carbunculus*, single voice (treble) of an isorhythmic motet. Does not belong to the following item.

135a. Anon. *Mater mundi* (motetus) and *Mater Sancta Dei* (tenor), fol. 110; two lower voices of an isorhythmic motet.

This list contains ten compositions not catalogued by Barclay Squire and brings the total to 148. No. 3a calls for some comment. The editor lists on p. xix of Vol. III after No. 3a "another Gloria" of which only a complete contratenor part is extant. Since this part directly follows the preceding Gloria, which began originally on the opposite page, now lost, the whereabouts of the other voices complementing the contratenor are rather mysterious. The mystery is solved by the discovery that the contratenor is not an isolated part of another composition, but forms the fourth voice of the fragmentary Gloria. It has taken some time to puzzle out the exact place where the fourth and textless part comes in. However, the result shows how smoothly the voices fit together (Ex. 1).

Ex. 1. Anonymous: Gloria No. 3a with fourth voice added.

5 This item and the next two have been erased and have therefore been discounted by Barclay Squire, who lists fols. 101v–102 as blank. The music is, however, just barely legible and has been deciphered by Mr. Collins.

As the contratenor is the only extant part that is complete, we are now able to determine exactly how much of the music is lost. Gloria No. 3a, which increases the number of four-voice compositions in OH, is written in a most peculiar manner: three voices in score and one voice separately. It is unlikely that the fourth voice was added later, because the manner in which the rests alternate in the various voices suggests that the piece was conceived from the outset as a four-part composition. The reason for the inconsistent manner of notation is possibly that the scribe did not want to write a score of four staves (a four-part Agnus on fol. 106v is written in identical fashion). The Gloria listed in the introduction (III, xx) as a fragment for fol. 11v is not an independent piece but belongs to the Gloria by Cook, correctly printed in Vol. I, 33.

The repertory of OH has been thought to be the product of a "provincial" English school which had little or no contact with the more famous English composers abroad. This position can no longer be maintained without qualifications. Four concordances with Continental sources have already been known for some time,[6] and eight others can now be added. The complete table of concordances, including those from the Fountains fragment (LoF), comprises at present eighteen compositions:

OH

14, fol. 13v–14	Byttering	*Et in terra*	= Ao 175, anon.[7]
26, fol. 24v–25	Rowland	*Et in terra*	= Br. Mus. Add. MS 40011 B (LoF), 9v. anon.
28, fol. 26v–27	Jervays	*Et in terra*	= Bologna, Liceo Mus. 37 (BL), 22v–23, Gervasius de Anglia.
30, fol. 28v	Anon.	*Et in terra* (fragment)	= BL 86v–87, Zacar (complete for three voices); Munich, MS mus. 3232a, 37v–38v, Zacharie.
31, fol. 29	Anon.	*Et in terra* (fragment)	= LoF, 10v, anon. (two voices only) and LoF, 13v–14, anon. (complete for four voices)

[6] See Besseler, AMW VII (1925), 225.

[7] The Aosta MS has been indexed by de Van in *Musica Disciplina* II (1948), 5. Neither in this list nor in his index to BL (*ibid.*, 231) do any of the correspondences to OH appear. The list of correspondences will undoubtedly continue to grow. As this book is going to press Dom Anselm Hughes kindly informs me that he has found in Oxford, Univ. Coll. MS B 192, fragments of two correspondences to OH 69 and 89, both Patrems by Damett.

63, fol. 55v–56	Anon.	*Veni sancte spiritus*	= Trent 1537, Dunstable; Modena, lat. 471 (ModB), 106v–108, Dunstable; Munich, MS mus. 3224, 8, anon.
64, fol. 56v–57	Forest	*Qualis est dilectus*	= ModB 108v–109, Polumier; Trent 1049 and 1829, anon.

It should be noticed that the last two compositions stand in OH and ModB in the same order.

65, fol. 57v	Forest	*Ascendit Christus* (Beginning of treble only)	= ModB, 96v–97, Dunstable. (complete, see DTOe, Vol. 76, 53)

The last three motets, Nos. 63, 64, and 65, have been added to OH by a later hand.

70, fol. 61v	Leonel	*Patrem* (treble only)	= Ao 173, anon. (complete)
70a, fol. 62	Anon.	*Patrem* (fragment)	= Trent 949 and 1780, anon. (compl.), Oxford, Univ. Coll. B 192 (frgm.)
79, fol. 70v–71	Leonel	*Patrem*	= BL 110v–111, de Anglia.
86, fol. 77v	Anon.	*Patrem*	= LoF 13, anon.

Both sources preserve only two parts each, which fortunately complement each other and form the complete piece.

97, fol. 84v	Anon.	*Sanctus*	= LoF 11v, anon.; Brit. Mus. Lansdowne 462, fol. 1v, anon. (tenor only)
112, fol. 94v–95	Leonel	*Sanctus*	= Trent 79, anon.; Ao 184, anon.

In the last composition there are some interesting variants in the use of *musica ficta*.

117, fol. 99	Excetre	*Sanctus*	= Lansdowne 462, fol. 1v, anon. (tenor only)
122, fol. 102v	Anon.	*Agnus Dei*	= LoF 12, anon. Variants with regard to rhythm and accidentals.
126a, fol. 104v	Anon.	*Agnus Dei*	= LoF 12v, anon. Has a written-out third Agnus lacking in OH.
132, fol. 107	Anon.	*Agnus Dei*	= Ao 176, anon.

Several items of the above list have not been printed in the edition because of their fragmentary state, and others have been published

but lack notes for certain sections, as, for example, No. 112. All of
these can now be completed from other sources, so that the new evidence for which Dom Anselm Hughes hoped in his preface to Vol. II
has come to light for at least a sizable number of compositions. It
would be most desirable if the supplementary fourth volume which
he envisaged there would eventually be published; it should include
the complete compositions and the various readings from other
manuscripts and, in addition, all the remaining fragments, which
even in their present state can tell us much about the musical style
of the period. No doubt the most interesting of the concordances is
the anonymous and fragmentary Gloria No. 30 from OH, which appears in BL complete under the name of Zacar. This Italian composer, who is represented fairly frequently in BL, is either Zachara
de Teramo or Zacharia Cantor N.D.P. who was a singer at the Papal
Chapel in 1420 and the last great representative of Italian *trecento*
music.[8] At any rate, in this particular Gloria survivals of Italian
ars nova music are quite unmistakable. In BL the contratenor is
supplied with the troped text *Gloria, laus et honor,* which is lacking
in OH. The beginning of the piece is given in Ex. 2.

Ex. 2. Zacharia: Gloria No. 30 after BL.

The importance of the concordance lies in the fact that it supplies
the first and so far the only definite proof of a direct exchange between Italian and English repertories, a relationship that up to now
could be suggested only on the basis of stylistic analysis as a strong
"Italian influence." The concordance that confirms our stylistic evidence with unhoped-for exactitude was discovered only after this
study had been completed. The paragraphs of section 3 below dealing with Italian influence have been left unchanged, although in the

[8] Perhaps the two names refer to the same composer, as is claimed by Korte, *Studie
zur Geschichte der Musik in Italien,* 1933, 77.

light of the new evidence they could now be formulated somewhat more emphatically.

The other concordances with BL and Ao testify to a fairly wide distribution of the pieces in OH. The appearance of a Gloria by Byttering in Ao proves in addition that the group of English composers known abroad was greater than suspected. Another surprise is the occurrence of two OH tenors in the Lansdowne MS of the British Museum, a Sarum Gradual with a few flyleaves of mensural music. The tenors here are anonymous; they are written as monophonic *cantus fracti*.

The sources do not always agree as to the author of a particular composition. For No. 64 the ascription to Forest in OH—an English source—seems more trustworthy than that to Polumier in ModB, an Italian manuscript, and this is also borne out by stylistic considerations, because the other motets by Forest in ModB are similar to *Qualis est dilectus,* and unlike the works by Polumier or Plummer (Plomer). If the ascription in OH can be trusted also with respect to No. 65, Forest and not Dunstable must be regarded as the author. It is interesting to note that in both cases one manuscript errs as to the name of the composer, but not as to his nationality. We do not know why the scribe of OH never finished copying *Ascendit Christus,* but its fragmentary state does not necessarily reflect on the reliability of the ascription. The tenor of the piece is based on the antiphon *Alma redemptoris,* which breaks off quite arbitrarily at *Virgo prius.* An anonymous Credo by "Anglicanus" in the Trent Codices [9] adopts the same antiphon in the same voice in a very similar manner, and what is even more striking, it interrupts the Gregorian melody at exactly the same place. These similarities suggest a common author for the Credo and *Ascendit Christus,* but they cannot help us decide whether he is Forest or Dunstable. Stylistic analysis, the last resort in these matters, does not furnish us with tools reliable enough to separate very clearly the individual from the general features of the English school. It must be noted, however, that both *Ascendit Christus* and *Qualis est dilectus* have in common a very loose and airy texture, and that they both end with subtly spun melodic sequences, not typical of Dunstable. Merely on stylistic grounds, therefore, Forest may very well be the composer of the two motets as well as the Credo.

[9] DTOe, Vol. 61, 92.

In their transcriptions the editors have adopted modern clefs throughout. This practice has sometimes been criticized as unscholarly, but insistence on old clefs strikes me as an unnecessary formalism, provided, of course, that the original clefs are indicated, as they are in Vols. II and III of this edition (the clefs lacking in the first volume are summarized in a table in Vol. III). However, the method of transcription calls for some remarks. The editors waver between practical and scholarly considerations. While the clefs have been modernized in keeping with the practical purpose of the edition, the original values of the notation are rendered in modern symbols without reduction, apparently because this method of transcription was thought to be more scholarly than any other and perhaps also because it presented the least difficulty to the transcriber. Actually, it makes the reading cumbersome, at least to the average reader, no longer used to thinking in longs and breves; and from the scholarly point of view unreduced transcriptions of fifteenth-century music are not more desirable (or accurate) than reduced ones, since the meaning of our values of notation has changed considerably during the past centuries. The aim of a scholarly edition should be to give the best possible idea of the actual rhythm and enable the reader at the same time to reconstruct the original from the transcription, a task that can well be combined with a practical purpose. In the present edition the ligatures are indicated by slurs (which have been inexplicably omitted in Vol. I, pp. 76 to 123), but no effort has been made to mark by appropriate means the frequent coloration of notes. Indications of ligatures only or of colored notes only do not suffice to give a clear picture of the original, especially if the notation is as intricate as it is in many compositions of OH. Fortunately, the most complicated piece with red and blue notation has been printed in color facsimile. It is regrettable that for financial reasons the only other example of double coloration (a Gloria by Leonel, I, 65) could not be reproduced likewise. Except for minor blemishes, both pieces have been correctly rendered.

As to the accuracy of the transcriptions, it can be stated that they are reliable in general, but that there are a great number of minor and several major errors. The first volume is weakest in this respect and betrays very patently the drawbacks of amateur scholarship. Ramsbotham mistook the fermatas or pauses above the notes for erasures and consequently transcribed the notes at what he believed to be the original, but what is actually the wrong, pitch. His outstanding errors and his arbitrary changes, often not even indicated in the score, have been corrected by Collins in the introduction to Vol. III, the careful study of which is indispensable before the reader makes use of Vol. I. Those who want to make a specialized study of the notation or the dissonance treatment must refer to the original anyway, so that it is not necessary to list here all the minor errors. It would go beyond the scope of this study and hardly be worth the trouble to record minutely where accidentals or ligatures have been omitted in the score, because they do not essentially change the music. It must suffice to illustrate by means of a few selected passages the various kinds of faulty transcription. One of these occurs in a Credo by Leonel (II, 185) which is also known from BL. The treble of this piece is notated in major prolation *diminutum,* that is to say in notes twice their actual value, the other voices being in ordinary *tempus perfectum.* In the edition the values of two lower voices have been doubled throughout, whereas, conversely, the treble, which alone has a highly figural line, should have been halved in order to match the lower voices. The same procedure applies also to Leonel's Sanctus (III, 58), which presents an analogous case. In addition, the passage *ex Maria Virgine* (p. 189) of the Credo has been incorrectly transcribed in the middle voice. The rhythm is not so abstruse as the printed version indicates, but should be read, as is confirmed by the Bologna MS, in triplets (Ex. 3).[10]

Ex. 3. Leonel: Credo No. 79.

Another type of error occurs in an anonymous Credo (II, 125). Here the first longa of the upper voice has been cut off almost completely, but enough remains to make pitch and stem recognizable. The rest inserted by the editor at the beginning departs from the

---

10 Our transcription gives the Bologna version, which differs from OH only in the fact that the *g* in m. 3 of the middle voice is repeated as an eighth note.

original unnecessarily, since the subsequent duets use exactly the same type of dissonant syncopation that the editor tried unsuccessfully to avoid at the beginning. In Ex. 4 the original version of the

Ex. 4. Anonymous: Credo No. 72; and Leonel: Gloria No. 18.

manuscript has been restored and juxtaposed with a Gloria by Leonel (I, 60), in which the notes with fermatas are incorrectly reproduced in the edition. The two compositions have several features in common. Both begin with two voices only, both consistently alternate between duets and four-part sections, both reach their climax in a five-part conclusion, both use a somewhat similar initial motive or motto in tenor and treble, both come to a halt on fermatas, and both use the same set of clefs and accidentals. These similarities strongly suggest that the two pieces were composed by the same author, and if this conclusion is correct the Credo can be ascribed to Leonel. Possibly the two settings form a related pair of Mass compositions, such as became common at the beginning of the fifteenth century. In OH the pairing of Mass movements is not yet clearly established, but we shall have occasion to point out two similar instances below (p. 60).

In the very first Gloria of the manuscript (III, [1]), the first three measures of the Amen are omitted by an oversight. The following measures should therefore be inserted on p. [2], line 4, after m. 2 (Ex. 5).

Ex. 5. Anonymous: Gloria No. 1.

Still another type of error occurs in an anonymous Credo (II, 176), the first part of which has been erased and is barely legible. Here the first few notes of the first and second sections of the *cantus secundus* are missing because of the removal of initials in the manuscript. They have been conjecturally restored by the editor, but he overlooked the fact that the *cantus secundus* is nothing but a slight elaboration of the familiar plainsong. The missing notes must therefore be supplied in accordance with the chant, and they fit the other voices very well. The first two notes of the treble should be changed to *a* and *b,* and the beginning of the second section should read probably as suggested in Ex. 6.

Ex. 6. Anonymous: Credo No. 78.

Finally it may be said that nobody will reproach the editors for not having recognized two cases of unspecified canon, recently discovered by Professor Strunk (see the Postscript to this study). His ingenious and brilliant solution calls for a completely revised transcription which alone discloses the compositions in their true importance.

2. CANTUS-FIRMUS TREATMENT

As it is impossible to deal with all aspects of the OH repertory, we shall consider here only two outstanding ones: the treatment of cantus firmus, and the different styles of Mass composition, with particular emphasis on the isorhythmic Masses.

The treatment of the plainsong in the compositions of OH is of great musical and historical interest. Dom Anselm Hughes has devoted to this question an important section of the introduction to Vol. III dealing with the Sanctus and Agnus Dei settings. The comparative table which he submits reveals that the compositions in question are grouped, apparently, according to the festal and ferial chants. Furthermore, he observes that the plainsong is treated occasionally with great freedom as regards transposition and melodic elaboration, and that it is at times even presented by more than one voice. The latter practice is far from being an isolated instance of curious cantus-firmus treatment. The Old Hall MS is in fact the first large source to contain a considerable number of compositions in which the plainsong wanders from one voice to another in succession. This wandering or "migrant" cantus firmus, as it may be called, represents a distinct type of cantus-firmus treatment, which has not been thoroughly investigated and whose historical importance has not been recognized. It must suffice at present to draw attention to it and to state that early examples of it can be found in several fourteenth-century sources, which, significantly, are of English origin. A chordal conception of music is inherent in the English "sixth-chord style," and it is only in such a homogeneous style that the idea of migrant cantus firmus could originate, because here the voices were regarded no longer separately as superimposed parts or lines, but as a unified whole. The adoption of migrant cantus firmus affords unmistakable evidence of the fact that the successive composition of superimposed voices, the traditional medieval technique of polyphonic composition, was nearing its end, and that composers were beginning to turn to simultaneously conceived parts. Consequently the chant was no longer invariably bound up with a single voice and its melodic substance could pervade the entire setting.

According to the evidence available up to now, there remains little doubt that migrant cantus firmus originated in England; the study of the ramifications of this technique and its eventual spreading to the continent, to which a Kyrie by the Flemish composer Liebert attests,[11] would yield valuable results. It may be remarked parenthetically that migrant cantus firmus continued to be popular in English music throughout the fifteenth century. We find it in several compositions of Oxford, Bodleian MS Selden B 26 and even as late as the Pepys MS (Cambridge, Magdalen College, MS 1236). By the time the Old Hall MS was compiled, migrant cantus firmus was a well-established practice, as can be gathered from the subjoined table of all compositions in which a plainsong can clearly be traced. The voice or voices in which it appears are indicated each time, also the source of the chant. In several items the identification of the plainsong was too doubtful to be included here, but a few borderline cases have been noted. The list is divided into Mass compositions and antiphons,

[11] DTOe, Vol. 53, 1; see also Besseler, *Musik des Mittelalters und der Renaissance*, 233.

but observes otherwise the order of the manuscript, not that of the printed edition.

MASS SETTINGS

No.			C.F.		Source of C.F. Sarum	Roman
4	(III, [8])	Anon.	*Gloria*	middle	5	V
17	(I, 55)	Excetre	"	treble	5	V
53	(II, 1)	Anon.	*Credo*	middle	1	I
54	(II, 8)	Anon.	"	treble (and middle?)	1	I
55	(II, 15)	Anon.	"	middle	1	I
57	(II, 30)	Anon.	"	migrant? treble at beginning, later middle and treble?	?	IV?
59	(II, 44)	Typp	"	migrant, middle and treble (many variants after the first phrase)	1	I
78	(II, 176)	Anon.	"	*cantus secundus*	1	I
91	(III, 4)	Typp	*Sanctus*	migrant, all voices	1	II
92	(III, 7)	Leonel	"	middle	1	II
93	(III, 9)	Lambe	"	"	2	VIII
94	(III, 12)	Typp	"	migrant, middle and tenor	2	VIII
95	(III, 15)	Leonel	"	" " " "	3	IV
96	(III, 18)	Anon.	"	" " " "	3 [12]	IV
97	(III, 20)	Anon.	"	" " " "	5	XVII
99	(III, 24)	Anon.	"	middle	9	XII
100	(III, 26)	Anon.	"	"	4	XI
101	(III, 28)	Anon.	"	"	4	XI
102	(III, 30)	Typp	"	"	6	XIII
103	(III, 32)	Anon.	"	"	8	XV
104	(III, 34)	Chirbury	"	migrant, all voices	7	—
105	(III, 36)	Leonel	"	middle	10	XVIII
106	(III, 38)	Typp	"	"	10	XVIII
110	(III, 55)	Sturgeon	"	only intonation, remainder is freely composed	1	II
111	(III, 58)	Leonel	"	migrant, treble and middle, freely treated	1	II
112	(III, 66)	Leonel	"	treble, freely treated	2	VIII
113	(III, 70)	Leonel	"	treble	3	IV
114	(III, 76)	Leonel	"	tenor	5	XVII
115	(III, 81)	Oliver	"	treble (and middle?), freely treated	2	VIII
116	(III, 86)	Oliver	"	treble, freely treated	5	XVII
117	(III, 90)	Excetre	"	treble?	?	?
118	(III, 94)	Tyes	"	tenor	5	XVII
119	(not printed, fol. 100v)	Pycard	"	treble	3 [12]	IV
120	(not printed, fol. 101)	Anon.	*Agnus Dei*	middle	1	XII

[12] The Benedictus is troped; plainsong of the trope in *Grad. Sar.*, Pl. 17ˣ.

MASS SETTINGS

No.			C.F.		Source of C.F. Sarum	Roman
121	(III, 100)	Anon.	*Agnus Dei* middle		1	XII
121a	(III, 102)	Anon.	" "		2	IV
121b	(III, 104)	Anon.	" "		3	XIV
121c	(III, 106)	Anon.	" "		3	XIV
122	(III, 108)	Anon.	" "		6	II
123	(III, 111)	Anon.	" "		5	I
124	(III, 113)	Anon.	"	migrant, middle and tenor	4	VI
126	(III, 118)	Leonel	"	middle	—	XVII
126a	(III, 120)	Anon.	" "		9	XV
127	(III, 122)	Typp	" "		8	—
128	(III, 125)	Anon.	" "		8	—
129	(III, 128)	Leonel	"	migrant, middle and tenor	7	VII
130	(III, 132)	Leonel	"	middle	10	XVIII
131	(III, 133)	Añon.	"	*cantus secundus* (contratenor)	10	XVIII
133	(III, 136)	Leonel	"	tenor, freely treated	—	XVII
134	(III, 141)	Oliver	"	treble, " "	6	II

CONDUCTUS SETTINGS OF ANTIPHONS

No.			C.F.		Source of C.F.	
38	(III, [51])	Anon.	[*Maria* or *Exsult*]*a laude genitrix*	middle ?	Not identified	
40	(I, 151)	Leonel	*Ave regina cae-lorum*	middle	*Ant. Rom.*	55
41	(I, 153)	Anon.	*Regina caeli*	"	*Ant. Rom.*	56
45	(III, [58])	Anon.	[*Nesciens Mater*]	"	*Ant. Sar.*	55
46	(I, 156)	Leonel	*Beata progenies*	"	*Ant. Sar.*	518
47	(I, 157)	Byttering	*Nesciens Mater*	migrant, all voices	*Ant. Sar.*	55
48	(I, 159)	Fonteyns	*Regali ex progenie*	middle	*Ant. Sar.*	526

In several compositions one of the voices is occasionally subdivided into two lines, one of which is written in red notes. The first Gloria (No. 4) is a case in point. Here the editor has failed to indicate such division in the middle voice on p. [10], line 4, m. 4; he has transcribed only the supplementary red notes of the middle part, but not the essential black ones. Ex. 7 gives the passage in its complete form. That the black notes represent the main voice can be proved by the fact that they carry the plainsong. There is, however, a difficulty inasmuch as the cadence of the plainsong falls on *d* while the red note in the same voice reads *c'*; it should probably be corrected to read *d'*, as suggested in Ex. 7, even though the resulting cadence is very uncommon.

Ex. 7. Anonymous: Gloria No. 4.

Inspection of the above list makes it very plain that the gymel influence is predominant in compositions with cantus firmus. Most often the borrowed melody appears as the middle voice, which means that the underlying structure of the setting is a gymel. The voice presenting the chant was naturally written first, then the supporting tenor, and finally the treble. The parallel fifths that frequently occur between the two upper voices point to the subsidiary function of the treble in these settings, and conversely, the two lower voices come often to the essential sixth-octave cadence which proves their structural function. Thus the repertory of OH emphatically underlines the important position of the gymel in English polyphony.

Among the compositions without gymel influence migrant cantus firmus occurs more frequently than any other type. In only a few pieces does the plainsong affect all voices, and whenever it does they were probably composed simultaneously. More often it is restricted to only two parts, usually the middle and tenor. It is of particular interest that compositions with the chant in either tenor or treble are the least numerous. The opposite could be expected in view of the improvisatory practices of English discant and fauxbourdon. The scarcity of English discant is especially striking because most of the treatises describing it stem from precisely the time of OH, the early fifteenth century. However, the compositions of OH are examples of *res facta,* and the improvised polyphonization of plainsong may have been practiced without being written down. The scarcity of fauxbourdon, on the other hand, can be explained by the fact that the manuscript was written before the Continental fashion of fauxbourdon had reached England. We need only compare OH with the Meaux

Abbey Manuscript (Br. Mus. MS Egerton 3307), the most recent addition to our knowledge of English sources,[13] to see how fundamental a change in the technique of composition the arrival of fauxbourdon effected.

The compositions of OH deal with the chant in a highly variegated manner. The most retrospective settings are written in score in conductus arrangement, especially the Sanctus and Agnus compositions. Even those notated in choir-book manner show the background of the conductus style, as does, for example, Leonel's four-voice Sanctus (III, 76).[14] The conductus settings of the Sanctus and Agnus are often no more than simple "harmonizations" of the chant with no melodic coloration whatever. They present the plainsong at times mechanically in breves throughout, set off against the livelier rhythms of the freely composed voices (e.g., Nos. 122, 123, 126a, and 128). Lambe's Sanctus (No. 93) and several other compositions keep so close to the plainsong that even its original ligatures are retained in the polyphonic setting.

While the great majority of compositions with borrowed plainsong belong to the conductus type, there are also a few others that treat the cantus firmus in the free treble style of the secular song. The preoccupation with the figural melody in the highest voice naturally induced the composers to put the chant into the treble, as we can see in Nos. 112, 115, and 116. As is to be expected, we find in this type the greatest freedom with regard to melodic embellishments of the cantus firmus. On the other hand, the Gloria by Excetre (No. 17) which belongs to this group is noteworthy for scanty coloration and the archaic style of the setting. Van den Borren[15] has already drawn attention to this composition, but he overlooked the fact that the treble is borrowed from the chant; what he analyzed as a case of melodic variation is actually the design of the plainsong itself. It goes without saying that this plainsong, like nearly all others in OH, adheres to the Sarum rather than the Roman version.

[13] See Schofield and Bukofzer in MQ XXXII (1946), 509, and XXXIII (1947), 38; also "Holy-Week Music and Carols at Meaux Abbey" in this book.

[14] The printer's error in this piece, p. 77, should be corrected; m. 4 of the contratenor has a rest for the entire measure.

[15] Van den Borren, *Etudes sur le XVe siècle musical*, 1941, 96. Only after the completion of the present study did Mr. John H. Harvey identify the composer from the Wardrobe Books of the English kings, which list him with his full name, William Excestre, in the years 1393 and 1402 as clerk of the Chapel Royal. These early dates certainly justify our characterization of his style as "archaic."

This is not the place to analyze in detail the methods of plainchant harmonization. Suffice it to say that a melody with many repeated phrases like the Gloria is harmonized differently each time and also treated with some rhythmic variation. When the plainsong ends with a repeated note we sometimes find unusual six-four chord cadences, as for example in the antiphons of Leonel and Credo No. 53. In many settings the cantus firmus appears transposed to the fourth or fifth, occasionally also to the second, and even to such an exceptional interval as the third, e.g. Leonel's Sanctus (III, 36). In all of these the transposition is strictly maintained throughout the composition. Far more remarkable and noteworthy, however, are pieces in which the plainsong is transposed successively to different intervals, e.g. Nos. 47, 59, and 91. It does not seem to be a coincidence that these are compositions with migrant cantus firmus which greatly facilitated or possibly even prompted such shifting transpositions. The principle according to which the sections of the migrant cantus firmus were distributed among the various voices was apparently fairly flexible and not necessarily dependent on the range of the given melody. In Leonel's Agnus (III, 128), for example, the tenor presents only the low notes of the plainsong, and here the register seems to have been the determining factor. However, this does not hold true in compositions with shifting transpositions. Other compositions without these shifts prove that the migrant cantus firmus followed purely musical principles. An anonymous Agnus (No. 124, III, 113) harmonizes the same low notes at the word *miserere* the first time in the tenor, the second time in the middle and the lowest voice; obviously the distribution of notes cannot have anything to do with range in this case.

The great number of compositions with embellished cantus firmus permits us to draw some conclusions concerning the use of cantus firmi in general and to discuss various theories held about this subject. We should mention here first an article by Dom Anselm Hughes [16] because it has a direct bearing on the music of OH. He tentatively suggests that the compositions by Roy Henry that have no cantus firmus were written originally on an embellished plainsong and that in a "second edition" by a later scribe this plainsong voice was replaced by a freely composed one. Hughes makes this rather

[16] Hughes, "Background to the Roy Henry Music, An Essay in Reconstruction," in MQ XXVII (1941), 204.

far-fetched assumption because he believes that the plainsong can be fitted after a fashion to Roy Henry's Gloria and Sanctus as an additional or substitute part, provided it is properly "arranged" by means of inserted notes and rests. This method is too speculative and arbitrary to warrant any definite conclusion, and is moreover so vague that it does not lend itself to verification. It is at any rate clear that the method as such is doubtful because it gives us leave to link many absolutely unrelated plainsongs to almost any Mass composition in OH.

Somewhat different ideas of cantus-firmus treatment have been entertained by Ficker [17] and Handschin; [18] they have tried to show that the chant was freely paraphrased in the upper voices of the Tournai Mass, the English setting of the Gloria trope *Spiritus et alme* in the Coussemaker fragment, the Credo of Machaut's Mass, and other Continental and English compositions. Their claims have not been generally accepted, [19] and the more our knowledge of cantus-firmus treatment in the period increases the more doubtful they become. The authors were able to construct certain melodic correspondences between the composed voice and the plainsong only by selecting notes arbitrarily, by disregarding the difference between structurally important notes at the cadences and merely ornamental ones, by assuming transpositions whenever necessary, by drawing on isolated notes from another voice if convenient, and by postulating at times even cancrizans motion. Here again, the method of such "proof" is questionable in itself; given a certain mode and the restrictions of melody writing of the time, almost any melody can be forcibly derived from plainsong of the same mode simply because there are only seven notes in each and correspondences result merely from fortuitous agreement. The ostensible "derivation" of *God Save the King* from plainchant, perhaps the most preposterous example of its kind, may serve as a warning. [20] The compositions of OH and, incidentally, of the Apt MS also, give an entirely different picture of what real cantus-firmus treatment looked like, and even when they depart from the plainsong with freely inserted melismas the connec-

[17] Ficker, *Studien zur Musikwissenschaft*, VII and XI.

[18] Handschin, *Zeitschrift für Musikwissenschaft*, X, 513, and *Kirchenmusikalisches Jahrbuch*, XXV, 75.

[19] See Wagner, *Gregoriusblatt*, XLVIII; Besseler, *Zeitschrift für Musikwissenschaft*, XI, 3; and Bukofzer, *Geschichte des englischen Diskants und Fauxbourdons*, 116.

[20] E. A. Maginty, "The National Anthem: Its Evolution," in *Musical Times*, LXXIII (1932), 27.

tion between figured elaboration and its model is never as tenuous as it is in the above-mentioned examples. The settings with migrant cantus firmus especially, in which the danger of being carried away by vague analogies is always very close at hand, bear witness that the composers, although they transposed the plainsong to different intervals within the same composition, respected its structure sufficiently so as not to obliterate its cadences and essential notes. Until new evidence can prove that the alleged cantus firmi are not mere figments of the imagination, we must assume that compositions like the Tournai Mass were freely composed and must restrain the desire to read into them principles of construction that they actually do not follow.

3. STYLISTIC CLASSIFICATION

One of the most remarkable features of the Old Hall repertory is the unsuspected variety of musical styles. The strong English cast of the music notwithstanding, there are unmistakable signs of direct contact with Italian and French music. The English style is most prevalent in the conductus settings of the Marian antiphons, hymns, and sequences,[21] all of which are written in the traditional score arrangement which even as late as the Pepys MS had not yet fallen into disuse. The four groups of Mass settings also contain a group of conductus Masses which have been placed, significantly, at the beginning of each section. These form the "old layer" of the OH repertory. The majority of the Sanctus and Agnus compositions belong to this type, including the melodious and graceful Sanctus by Roy Henry (III, 1). It should be noted that most of the conductus Masses are founded on plainsong, except for the Gloria series, in which so far only one composition could be connected with the chant.

Continental influence prevails in Mass sections fashioned after the model and in the style of other forms, such as the *caccia*, the French secular song, and the motet. The Italian *caccia* Mass is characterized by strongly imitative duets or even strictly canonic con-

---

[21] The term "motet," which the editor applies somewhat loosely to these compositions, must be qualified by a reference to conductus style. Several compositions of this type are three-voice hymns and sequences. For example, *Stella celi extirpavit* (I, 168) is a processional hymn seeking protection against the plague. The text of Damett's *Salve porta paradisi* (I, 166), which does not appear in Chevalier, can be identified as the second stanza of the sequence *Salve virgo sacra parens*, which belongs to the Sarum use (see Legg's *Sarum Missal*, 530). The fact that only the second stanza has been set in polyphony indicates that the odd-numbered stanzas were sung in plainchant.

nection between the parts, either (and more commonly) the upper or the lower voices. An outstanding example of the first possibility is the five-voice Credo (II, 82) in which the three upper voices move in canon; although not expressly called for in the manuscript, there seems to be little doubt that canon is intended despite the harsh dissonances that often result. An anonymous Credo in similar style (II, 101) is especially noteworthy as an example of an unusually complex mensuration canon. Mr. Collins' ingenuity in solving the really exceptional intricacies of notation [22] deserves the highest praise. A five-voice Gloria by Pycard (I, 119) is also canonic, but here only two upper voices moving in vigorous rhythm form the canon, while the other parts clash with them in startling dissonances. Dissonant style and emphasis on intricate mensural problems seem to be the trademark of Pycard's music, and it may not be too venturesome to suggest that he is also the author of the Credo with mensuration canon which has been made anonymous only by the removal of the initial and which directly precedes another composition by him in the manuscript.

The other possibility, canon between the lower voices or what van den Borren has fittingly called *caccia à rebours,* can be found in Pycard's Gloria (I, 84). Professor Strunk has discovered that the upper voices, too, form an unspecified canon, so that we have here one of the rare cases of double canon. Mass sections with freely imitative duets which lean toward the Italian motet style are also not infrequent, e.g. Byttering's Credo (II, 203), or Pycard's Credo (II, 135), in which the two upper voices alternate in the lively recitation of the words.

Masses in free treble style, usually though somewhat narrowly termed "ballade Masses" after their secular model, the French chanson, constitute the largest group of the repertory and indicate that the English composers practiced extensively this principal French Mass type. A Gloria (I, 65) and Credo (II, 167) by Leonel stand out for the ostentatiously difficult mensural and proportional complexities in which the generation of composers around 1400 took special pride. They signify the Indian summer of the *ars nova*. The decline of an epoch manifests itself also with regard to harmony, in

[22] See the discussion in Apel's *Notation of Polyphonic Music,* 432, where certain emendations and corrections of the transcription are proposed. It should be noted, however, that the variant proposed for m. 37 ff. involves some awkward unison passages.

the liberal and somewhat freakish use of accidentals.[23] These give the music unexpected color by what can be called "accidentalism" in contradistinction to our modern term "chromaticism," which implies something quite different. The Gloria of Roy Henry (I, 34) and several other ballade Mass sections by Chirbury (III, 116), Leonel, and others contain such purple patches, often involving such progressions as tritones and augmented fifths; the editor very often suggests, especially in Vol. I, the omission of accidentals, assuming a mistake of the scribe in the insertion of sharps, but many of them are no doubt intended, as can be gathered from the two versions of the Gloria by Rowland (I, 104 and III, [63]), which agree not only in their accidentals but also in their playful and bouncing hocket sections with some extremely harsh dissonances. That sustained clashes such as f against f-sharp or b against b-flat (I, 85, m. 3) were intentional is unlikely, and here one voice should be adjusted even if it involves a melodic dissonance like an augmented interval. We should, however, be wary of establishing any *a priori* rules of what was and what was not possible harmonically at the time. A similar clash of b against b-flat (I, 130, m. 3) does not seem to call for an adjustment, because the notes are introduced at different times and the progression in each voice is logical in itself.

The ballade Mass sections can be grouped in two categories as regards their rhythm. The first retains the rhythm of major prolation, which by the beginning of the fifteenth century was on the wane. It prevails in what must be considered the older group. The compositions of Byttering (I, 47; II, 149), Roy Henry (I, 34), and Excetre (II, 158) may be quoted as illustrations, and it is not by coincidence that so many of the old-fashioned conductus settings of Masses and antiphons adhere to this rhythm. The second group is characterized by a smooth and flowing *tempus perfectum,* which rose to dominance in the first part of the century. This rhythm appears in OH in a rather crude form, and is not yet so elegantly polished as is customary in Continental works, but the trend is unmistakable. It may be significant that these compositions are inscribed in the manuscript as a rule after those in major prolation. They include a Gloria by Cooke

23 See Lowinsky, "The Functions of Conflicting Signatures in Early Polyphonic Music," in MQ XXXI (1945), 246. In this study the author gives an illuminating account of the various types of cadences, drawing in part also on the music of OH. It lies in the nature of his approach that he does not stress the numerous instances where the accidentals have a coloristic, that is to say non-cadential, function.

(I, 138), notable for the fact that its first section is restated at the end with different words as a clear *da capo,* a Credo by the same composer (II, 252), and Mass sections by Damett (I, 132; II, 261) and Byttering (I, 39). It goes without saying that triple rhythm obtains also in compositions with treble cantus firmus, which Leonel in particular handled in his late compositions with great ease; of all the compositions in OH his Sanctus (III, 66) comes closest to this mature style.

Several Mass sections stand off from the rest by the deliberate contrast of duet passages with a full four- or five-voice *tutti* in consistent alternation. Pairs of voices contrast with each other, as they do in Italian compositions of the early fifteenth century. Examples of the type with group contrasts include the paired Gloria and Credo that we have ascribed to Leonel (I, 60 and II, 125 [anon.]), a Credo by Pycard (II, 114), and a Gloria by Cooke (I, 124).

The most modern type of composition in OH appears, significantly, not in the main body of the manuscript, but only in the later additions. It is represented by the two non-isorhythmic motets (Nos. 64 and 65), both ascribed in OH to Forest. The first one, *Qualis est dilectus,* leans toward the declamation motet, and the second, *Ascendit Christus,* is a motet with double structure which elaborates in its tenor the antiphon *Alma redemptoris.*[24] The advanced style as regards texture and, especially, dissonance treatment bears out what can also be gathered from such external features as the handwriting, namely, that these compositions belong stylistically to a later period.

4. ISORHYTHMIC COMPOSITIONS

The greatest surprise of the Old Hall repertory is unquestionably the prominent role of isorhythmic technique, which is irrefutable proof of a strong French influence. The manuscript contains altogether eleven motets (we do not count here the antiphons in conductus style or "conductus-motets," which occupy an intermediate posi-

[24] Double structure means that the composition is built on two structural elements, tenor and treble. The term does not necessarily imply double cantus firmus, which is only a special case of double structure. In the motet under discussion the treble is freely composed in song style; Handschin's claim (see the second of the quoted articles) that it paraphrases the antiphon *Ascendit Christus* is based on evidence much too slender to be convincing. The motet *Ascendit Christus* and the isorhythmic motets and Mass sections have not been included in our table of compositions elaborating plainsongs (see section 2) because they employ only sections of the chant in a different, purely constructive, fashion.

tion between motet and conductus). Three of the motets are later
additions (Nos. 63–65, fols. 55–57v) which have been inserted between the conductus and the motet settings of the Credo and thus
separate, perhaps not accidentally, the old layer from the more recent
one. The eight motets of the original repertory are without exception strictly isorhythmic, as is, of the later ones, Dunstable's *Veni
sancte spiritus* also. Unfortunately, three motets at the end of the
codex (Nos. 135, 135a, and 138) are fragmentary and have therefore
been excluded from the publication, but the extant voices reveal
isorhythmic structure. The Fountains fragment, which, as we have
seen, duplicates six pieces from OH, contains also a number of
isorhythmic motets, and although none of these appear in OH, they
further confirm the French influence on English music of the time.
We may add here that the little-known fragment British Museum,
Cotton MS Tib. A. VII preserves on fol. 38v in white notation two
voices of a presumably four-voice Gloria which is likewise strictly
isorhythmic and ends with a lively hocket section. The absence of
rhythmic complications in this piece points to a date slightly later
than that of the Old Hall repertory.

Convincing evidence for the influence of the isorhythmic motet
on Mass composition comes to light in the motet Mass sections, many
of which are strictly isorhythmic while others are so only in their
tenor. The isorhythmic Mass sections actually outnumber the isorhythmic motets proper in OH; the prevalence of isorhythmic technique is perhaps the most significant and most interesting feature
of the entire repertory, both historically and musically. That this
point has escaped the editors represents one of the greatest weak-
nesses of the edition. In an isolated case, Pycard's Gloria (I, 92), Mr.
Collins (III, xxiv) did notice that the rhythmic patterns return
not only in the tenor but also in the upper voices. Yet he did not
realize the structural function of the return, and at two other places
he takes pains to point out that the tenor is divided into "symmetrical
halves" as if this were a peculiar trait of only these compositions. It
needs no reiteration here that all these tenors have regularly at least
two isorhythmic patterns (*taleae*) or occasionally even three or four,
and in one case as many as ten. Had the return of the same rhythmic
schemes in the upper voices been noticed, the missing notes—the result
of the vandalism of cutting out illuminated initials for bookmarks
and similar purposes—would have been filled in more accurately.

As they stand now most of the numerous editorial conjectures must be corrected according to the analogous sections of the composition.

In view of the musical importance of isorhythmic technique, all compositions of this type will be briefly discussed here in the order of their appearance in the manuscript. Particular attention has been devoted to finding the Gregorian source of the tenors, and in nearly all cases the search has been successful. In the isorhythmic motets proper and several isorhythmic Mass sections the tenor carries a short textual motto which usually permits identification, but numerous Mass sections are founded on unnamed tenors whose design sometimes precludes a Gregorian origin. While the isorhythmic motet was, as a rule, founded on a section of a plainsong, many other compositions of the time, especially Italian ones, were built on freely composed tenors. The presence of such tenors in OH may be taken as an additional indication of Italian influence. The fact that the tenor carries no designation does not, of course, necessarily prove a non-Gregorian origin, because unreliable sources do sometimes omit the words. The Old Hall MS belongs, however, to the group of reliable sources in which the words are carefully given, and here undesignated tenors are as a rule specially composed for the occasion.

In the following, the measures of the isorhythmic periods are represented by numbers, the repeat by :||, and each time the number of *taleae* in the tenor is noted.

1. Tyes, Gloria (I, 50), 32 (℃ C):|| 16 (℃ C):||. Tenor not designated; two *taleae*, repeated in diminution. The semibreve *d'* added by the editor in m. 4 of p. 53 should be inserted instead before the preceding minim *d'*, to conform with m. 13 of p. 51. Note that the isorhythmic period is divided into two sections of contrasted rhythms.

2. Leonel, Gloria (III, [23]), 56 (℃ C):|| 28 (℃ C):||. Tenor not designated; two *taleae*, repeated in diminution. The composition resembles the preceding one in its subdivision of the isorhythmic period into two sections of major prolation and imperfect time respectively, but it is composed on a much larger scale for four voices. The words are presented in alternation by the duet of the upper voices. The editorially restored notes in m. 13–14 can be emended after the corresponding period, but the continuation cannot because here both

periods are fragmentary. The editorial conjectures on p. [25], however, must all be corrected according to m. 1 ff. of p. [28].

3. Anon., Gloria (III, [32]), 46 (C):|| 16 (O):||. Tenor not desig-
nated; twice two *taleae*. This tenor is noteworthy because the first
two *taleae* are not, as is customary, restated but are followed by two
different ones, so that we have a continuous melody without repeat
—a rather unusual occurrence in the literature of isorhythmic construction. What appears to be a melodic return to the beginning
(*color*) is suggested in m. 3 of p. [35]. However, the repeat is varied
rather than literal, and at the end the tenor melody does not conform
to the regular *color* of an isorhythmic tenor; if this apparent repeat
is really a deliberate variation and not merely an accident, it would
be a unique combination of melodic variation with the complicated
overlapping of *color* and *talea*, although the *color* cannot be carried
out very strictly because of the variation. That the *taleae* are strictly
observed throughout while at the same time the *color* is used in
a singularly vague fashion seems inconsistent and thus appears to
favor the conclusion that the repeat may after all not have a structural function; but it is too strange an occurrence to be passed over
in silence. The editorial suggestions in the transcription concern
only the first isorhythmic period and should therefore all be emended.
The beginning, which lacks the first notes in the treble,[25] should read,
according to m. 47, like Ex. 8. Thus restored, the beginning of the

Ex. 8. Leonel (?): Gloria No. 21.

Gloria resembles that of a Credo by Leonel (II, 194) discussed below as No. 8. Quite possibly they form a related pair of Mass com-

[25] The editor overlooked in his restoration of the beginning not only the isorhythmic
correspondence, but also the fact that the semibreve *g* in m. 2 is at least partially visible
in the manuscript.

positions like the Gloria [26] and Credo to which we have referred above (see Ex. 4). A third analogous case can be discovered in a Sanctus and Agnus by Leonel (III, 76 and 136). These two are clearly akin by virtue of their cantus firmus (both stem from Mass XVII of the *Grad. Rom.*), the placement of the cantus firmus in the tenor, its similar treatment in sustained notes, and the four subdivisions of the whole piece by exactly the same time signatures. It may also be significant that in all these compositions Leonel is involved as the author of at least one setting of the pair. The Gloria of Ex. 8 can be ascribed to Leonel with great probability for the following reasons: (1) the beginning is similar to the Credo by Leonel; (2) the piece stands in the manuscript in the middle of a whole series of compositions by Leonel; (3) both compositions are isorhythmic; (4) the tenor of the Credo has no melodic repeat, not even the vague one of the Gloria; (5) the two compositions have exactly the same clefs and the same conflicting key signatures; (6) the tenors of both pieces differ from all other isorhythmic compositions in that they are composed not in the uniformly ponderous tenor style with sustained notes but in a very flexible rhythm, especially in the short duet sections in which the tenor is not rhythmically differentiated from the other voice; and (7) there is a similarity in style, in the treatment of duets, fermatas, and rests, and the division of the words between the two upper voices. The last point, admittedly, does not weigh very heavily —it may be due merely to stylistic similarity of the school—but taken together, the points confirm Leonel's authorship at least as strongly as in the case of Ex. 4.

4. Pycard, Gloria with trope, *Spiritus et alme* (I, 92), 12:|| 12:|| 8:|| 12:|| (the time signatures of the tenor and the upper voices conflict and have therefore not been indicated). Tenor: *Johannes Jesu care* (add these words to the transcription), two *taleae* of six (or four) measures each, stated eight times in various diminutions in the ratio of 12:9:8:12 or 4:3:2:4. The two contratenors also follow the isorhythmic scheme.

The identification of the tenor presented great difficulty. The words recur in a cantilena of MS Egerton 3307, but the melody is different from the beginning (upper voice) of Pycard's composition,

---

[26] This piece should be compared with a Gloria, of very similar texture, by Cooke, I, 124.

and not, as Schofield [27] and Hughes claim, "virtually the same." The only similarity, downward motion, is too general a trait to warrant the conclusion that the two compositions are musically related. After a long search I could identify the tenor as a section from the sequence *Johannes Jesu Christo multum dilecte,* which Schubiger has published in *Die Sängerschule St. Gallens* (App. p. 3) and Moberg in *Über die schwedischen Sequenzen,* No. 26 (see also *Variae Preces,* 82). The words and melody of the tenor are taken not from the beginning but from the very end of the sequence, and this is the reason why the words proved so elusive. Schubiger's version reads *Johannes Christi care* (not *Jesu*), and the melody to these words also deviates somewhat from Pycard's tenor. Further search in the different versions of the sequence has revealed that Pycard adopted a specifically English variant, which can be found only in the liturgical sources of the Sarum use. The end of the sequence appears with the words *Johannes Jesu care* and exactly the same melody as Pycard's in an unpublished English Gradual of the fifteenth century (fol. 9v) which belongs to the private library of Mr. Otto Ege of Cleveland, who kindly permitted me to make a copy of his manuscript.[28] A similar version of the sequence can be found in Cambridge, Univ. Lib. Add. MS 710, fol. 44v. The identification of the tenor proves that the tenor of the cantilena is not related to the upper voice of Pycard's Gloria. Hughes and Schofield were right in suspecting musical relations, but they compared the wrong voices. Actually the upper voice of the cantilena quotes at the words *Johannes Jesu care* (end of the stanza) the first five notes of the plainsong, which agree with Pycard's tenor.

Pycard's composition has been analyzed in the preface to Vol. III (p. xxiv). Collins points out a number of misprints and errors in the transcription which must be noted. I should add that the rest supplied by the editor in m. 2 of p. 95 in the second voice must be deleted and the note a' be sustained throughout the measure, as is proved by m. 3 of p. 93. I cannot agree that the c''-sharps on pp. 96 and 103 are not authentic; on the contrary, the resulting cadence in consecutive fifths is often expressly indicated in the music of the *ars nova.*[29] The difficulty arises in Pycard's Gloria only from the *alius contratenor,* which must be altered in order to fit the treble even if

[27] Schofield, MQ XXXII (1946), 525.

[28] MS 20, listed in De Ricci-Wilson, *Census,* 1940.

[29] Compare the accidentals in the Mass of the Meaux Abbey MS, MQ XXXIII (1947), 41, m. 4–5.

there results a chromatic progression—rare but not entirely unknown at this time. The reader may refer to the Agnus by Chirbury (III, 116), which begins with a deliberate chromatic progression *c'–c'*-sharp. On the other hand, what seems to be the same progression in m. 3 of I, 121, is not chromatic because here the sharp placed between the two *c'*'s applies apparently to both.

The outstanding characteristic of the piece lies in highly imitative duets, sometimes even approximating canon, which set off the upper voices against the supporting parts. Pycard fuses here in novel fashion the Italian duet technique with the strict isorhythm of the French motet. Collins claims that the tenor and contratenor are only a broken-up version of the *solus tenor* and regards the piece as in four parts. Actually, it is the other way around: the *solus tenor* was composed last, as a substitute part contracting tenor and contratenor into one voice. The piece is therefore essentially in five parts, which can be reduced optionally to four. Whenever it occurs in fourteenth-century motets the *solus tenor* is invariably a substitute part. That tenor and contratenor were first conceived singly can be proved by the fact that they are usually isorhythmic, while the *solus tenor* is not. The latter part could not easily be isorhythmic because it combines two different patterns. The plainsong melody itself furnishes additional proof. In most cases only the tenor agrees with the plainsong, while the *solus tenor* combines the lowest notes of contratenor and tenor and can therefore not state the Gregorian melody in its original form. In this particular composition the combination of the two voices does not, for once, result in a different melody, but it does in item No. 11 below. In the canonic Gloria by Pycard (I, 84) the *solus tenor* is obviously a substitute part because it destroys the canon between the two lower voices.

5. Queldryk, Gloria with trope, *Spiritus et alme* (I, 109), 18 (C):‖ 9 (C):‖. Tenor not designated, two *taleae*, repeated in diminution. The contratenor has the same structure, but does not always strictly observe the rhythmic pattern. The two upper voices recite the text alternatingly in dialogue fashion.

6. Anon., Gloria (III, [37]). This is a ballade Mass section which does not belong to the isorhythmic compositions proper; however, the last portion (p. [43]) consists of four isorhythmic periods of five

measures each. The partial adoption of isorhythmic technique is quite unique in the OH repertory.

7. Dunstable, *Veni sancte spiritus* (II, 66), 45 (O):|| 22½ (C):|| 15 (O):||. Tenor: *Mentes tuorum visita;* two *taleae,* stated three times in diminution of 3:2:1. Origin of the tenor: the second and third lines of the hymn *Veni creator spiritus*. The barring for the middle part of the motet (pp. 72–74) distorts the rhythm. Here the editor should have allowed three imperfect breves to the measure according to the *modus perfectus*. Dunstable's famous motet has often been analyzed,[80] and little needs to be added here. The three related, but different, sets of words bear eloquent witness to the close relationship between trope and motet, a relationship that has been preserved in the medieval motet literature of England more faithfully than in that of any other school. One interesting trait of this piece relating to cantus-firmus treatment has remained unnoticed thus far: in the introductory duets of each isorhythmic period the treble states successively the entire melody (not just the first phrase) of the hymn *Veni creator spiritus* in slightly embellished form although the text is taken from the sequence *Veni sancte spiritus*. We have here a double use of the same plainsong—as far as I know the only example of the kind in the isorhythmic motet. The tenor presents the chant as cantus firmus in protracted notes, the treble as a flowing melody whenever the tenor pauses for three longs. The continuity of the plainsong is thus never broken, though different sections of it are stated in alternation. Just as the words are liturgical or a trope to the liturgical text, the music keeps as closely as possible to the liturgical melody. In this work Dunstable was striving for a rapprochement between the isorhythmic motet and the new type of liturgical motet that arose at the beginning of the century with the active participation of Dunstable and his fellow composers. The use of plainsong in the treble invalidates Riemann's analysis of the piece,[31] in which he tried to show that the second and third periods were merely melodic variations of the first. Although he did not realize it, his analysis actually implies the absurdity that the second half of the hymn *Veni creator* is a variation of the first half.

---

[80] See Reese, *Music in the Middle Ages,* 415; and Ficker, *Studien zur Musikwissenschaft,* VII, 33.

[31] Riemann, *Handbuch der Musikgeschichte,* II:2, 111 ff.

8. Leonel, Credo (II, 194), one period of 54 measures, stated three times. Tenor not designated; three *taleae*. That this motet is isorhythmic easily escapes attention because there is no repeat in the tenor and there is only one unusually long period even though all voices adhere to it with very few deviations. The Credo apparently makes a pair with Gloria No. 3 of this list. The text is presented in duet form and alternates between the two upper voices, as in the Gloria, which is probably also by Leonel. The tenor of the Credo is a strictly continuous melody without any suggestion of *color*, and, again as in the Gloria, it contrasts with other isorhythmic tenors by virtue of its free rhythm. It should be noted that Nos. 3 and 8 are the only two isorhythmic compositions of OH built on a continuous tenor without the customary repeat.

9. Byttering, Credo (II, 203). This is not an isorhythmic composition proper, but only strongly influenced by isorhythmic technique. An imitative duet of the upper voices is supported by two lower voices which form a rhythmic *ostinato* of seven measures. After two introductory measures the lower voices come in with a rhythmic configuration that is strictly isorhythmic as regards the rests and less rigidly so as regards the notes. The pattern is stated eighteen times, and is followed by a coda of four measures. The upper voices, too, are organized in a pattern of seven measures, which begins invariably with a rest of one measure. This rest alternates regularly between the second voice and the first so that the complete pattern comprises fourteen measures. It is stated nine times and overlaps that of the two lower voices. The loose handling of isorhythmic technique that characterizes this composition can be found also in several Italian compositions, and serves as further proof of the Italian influence on the OH repertory. The imitative dialogue of the upper voices points in the same direction. The extensive hocket section on Amen at the end should be noted.

10. Swynford, Credo (II, 213), 54:|| 27:||. Here the tenor only is isorhythmic; its *taleae* are repeated with different time signatures so that the upper voices must needs have a different rhythm. Tenor not designated; two *taleae*, stated first in ℂ (54 measures), repeated in C. Then the same *taleae* are restated in diminution (27 measures) again in ℂ and C. This type of partially isorhythmic motet can also

be found in Italian sources, and Swynford probably follows an Italian model. The text of the Creed is broken up in motet fashion and different sections of it are recited simultaneously by the voices, as in several other compositions of OH (see II, 185, 252, and 261). These telescoped versions appear frequently in English compositions of the time, but they are not an exclusively English feature, as has been claimed by Ficker.[32] The Turin MS (Tu B), which dates from about the same time as OH, contains a motet-like telescoped Gloria (fol. 29), and so long as it cannot be proved to be English or to have been written under English influence we must assume that this method of abbreviation was practiced, if rarely, on the Continent also.[33]

11. Typp, Credo (II, 224), 32 (©):|| 32 (©):|| 8 (©):||. Tenor: *Benedicam te Domine* (these words are missing in the transcription), four *taleae,* twice repeated in increasing diminution in the ratio 12:8:3. Note that each isorhythmic period corresponds to two *taleae* of the tenor (16 measures). Origin of the tenor: the antiphon *Benedicam te (Ant. Sar.,* 107), which is no longer in current use. The editorially supplied notes must be corrected. This is another example of telescoped Mass setting. The motet is remarkable for suggestions of isomelic returns by means of which the rhythmic periods are made similar to one another melodically so that they can be actually perceived by the ear. At certain places there are even direct repeats, for example measures 13–16 and 45–48.

12. Queldryk, Credo (II, 232), 58 (℃ C):|| 29 (℃ C):||. Tenor not designated; two *taleae,* repeated with diminution. Each isorhythmic period falls here, as in Leonel's Gloria (No. 2 of this list), into two contrasting sections. The two compositions are similar also as regards the treatment of the text; the voices recite the words in alternation and the textless sections are probably instrumental.

---

[32] Ficker, *Studien zur Musikwissenschaft,* XI, 42; see also Hughes, Introd. to *Missa O quam suavis,* xxxiii.

[33] Unlike the telescoped setting, the dialogue or duet setting does not actually shorten the length of the composition, as the voices sing the text in alternation only (see, for example, Nos. 2, 3, 5, 8, 12, and 13 of our list). However, very rapid and close alternation leads at times to overlaps of different words and thus approaches the telescoping method, as may be seen in a Gloria by Loqueville (*Polyphonia sacra,* 134). The dialogue setting was well known on both sides of the Channel.

13. Pennard, Credo (II, 241), 80:||. Tenor: *Te iure laudant,* ten *taleae,* repeated without diminution. Origin of the tenor: the now obsolete antiphon *Te iure laudant* (*Ant. Sar.,* 293). We have here an interesting specimen of isorhythmic and isomelic combination. The *solus tenor* can be ignored, since it is a substitute part; it merely contracts the two lower voices into one, thereby, however, obliterating the plainsong, which is stated note for note in the tenor. The two lower voices form *taleae* of eight measures which appear ten times in different melodic form, but always in identical rhythm. The upper voices are partially isorhythmic in a very peculiar fashion. They present the words alternately in eight-measure phrases which coincide with the *taleae* of the tenors. The phrases with text are freely composed, but the textless ones observe an isorhythmic pattern that begins and ends with a breve rest. Both voices are therefore alternately isorhythmic and free in their eight-measure sections. In m. 81 the second part begins with a repetition of not only the lower voices but also the textless sections of the upper voices. The sections with text, however, form an isomelic variation of the first part of eighty measures. In the last thirty-two measures both upper voices vary the corresponding section of the first part by means of a huge hocket section in which the isorhythmic pattern of the upper voices is no longer retained. Although the two gigantic parts of Pennard's Credo employ the longest single isorhythmic period of the entire repertory, it is not the longest motet because it contains no more than one repeat.

14. Anon., Credo (III, [68]), 36 (𝄴), stated thrice; 12 (𝄵), stated thrice. Tenor especially composed with a descriptive "canon," three *taleae* to be read three times; first in forward movement, then backwards (cancrizans), and then as at first; after which the entire tenor is repeated in diminution. The prominence given to the number three, the "perfect number," is striking—three *taleae,* three statements, and the number of measures in each major period is a multiple of three—and may not be a coincidence, in view of the strongly speculative bent in medieval music. The piece begins with an introductory duet in canon of the two upper voices. The editor has devoted a great deal of ingenuity to finding a supporting part for the first voice because he finds it "very improbable that the treble should be left for eight bars without any accompanying voice." These efforts

are unfortunately wasted, because such introductory sections in canon (without accompaniment) are a stereotyped feature of the isorhythmic motet, particularly the most sumptuous and representative examples. They can be found several times with Dufay and are often designated as *"introitus."* They usually stand, as in our motet Mass section, outside of the isorhythmic scheme. I doubt also that the second voice of the canon should, as the editor suggests, be changed because of parallel fifths. The awkward dissonances the editor deplores are not worse than in many other compositions of OH. Of particular interest is a comparison of the first with the third isorhythmic period, which reveals in the upper voices one of the most prominent cases of isomelic variation. The corresponding periods four and six, however, resemble each other much less closely. It should also be observed that the end of each isorhythmic period is made audible and emphasized by pronounced hocket writing, as was the custom in this form. By and large, this composition is more closely akin to the isorhythmic motet proper than any other Mass section of OH. It is accurately transcribed except for a few oversights: the *f* in the tenor, m. 18, p. [71], should be replaced by a rest, and in the contratenor m. 6–7 of p. [69] and m. 16–17 of p. [72] should have the same rhythm as m. 1–2 of p. [71].

15. Damett, *Salvatoris Mater pia* (III, 40), 36 (O): || 18 (C): || 18 (O): || 6 (O): ||. Tenor: *Benedictus Mariae Filius qui ve,* two *taleae,* stated four times in increasing diminution. The tenor belongs to the Gregorian Sanctus, Sarum No. 3 (*Grad. Sar.,* Pl. 15^x), in which the Benedictus appears in its regular form. The Benedictus of our tenor is, however, troped and corresponds exactly with the Benedictus trope [34] as given in the *Grad. Sar.* Pl. 17^x. This is apparently an English trope, which gives a melodic elaboration of the version of Sarum No. 3. Now, it should be noticed that the last word of the tenor in our motet appears incompletely in the manuscript, although the editor has written it out as *venit,* assuming probably an error of the scribe. It is, however, far from being an error, because the plainsong ends exactly with the notes for the syllable *ve-* and does not bring the note for *nit.* To mention such ostensibly trifling mistakes may seem like dealing pedantically with points "verging on the moot,"

---

[34] The trope has also been used with the same plainsong in a conductus setting of a Sanctus (No. 96, III, 18).

but the discussion of item No. 17 will show that this is not the case, that there is in fact more to the fragmentary syllable than meets the eye. The motet stands out for its smooth and flowing rhythm in triple meter and represents Damett's style at its best. It may be pointed out that the words of the *triplum* are taken from a sequence, probably of English origin, which forms part of the Sarum Missal,[85] but the topical references in the motet to King Henry are unique here.

16. Cooke, *Alma proles regia* (III, 46), 27 measures in 6/2 (but more accurately 18 measures in 9/2):‖ 18 (C):‖ 12 (C):‖. Tenor: *Ab inimicis nostris defende nos Christe,* two *taleae,* stated three times in increasing diminution ☉, O, and C.[86] The source of the tenor was again hard to determine because this plainsong is now obsolete. It is an optional part of the litany of the Rogation days, the three days before Ascension Day, sung only during wartime, *in tempore belli.* It occurs in the Sarum Processional, of which, unfortunately, no musical edition has ever been published. I have found the melody, in the same form as in the OH tenor, in various English processionals of the fifteenth and sixteenth centuries. The plainsong has also been used in a composition of the Pepys MS—a three-voice setting of *Ab inimicis nostris* in which the plainsong appears as tenor in English discant style. Judging by the liturgical function of the plainsong, we can safely conclude that Cooke's motet was composed during wartime, but this helps us little in fixing the exact date. The motet text also implies a war, since it is a prayer for the intercession of St. George.

As the editor himself admits, he should have allowed nine minims to the bar in his transcription of the first two isorhythmic periods (the first fifty-four measures), because in the present transcription all cadences fall in the middle of the measure. In the last two isorhythmic periods the meter of the tenor and that of the upper voices conflict throughout, and should have been represented in the transcription by independent barring, imperfect time in the tenor, and major prolation in the upper voices.

17. Sturgeon, *Salve mater Domini* (III, 51), 30 (O):‖ 16 (O):‖ 9 (O):‖ (the number of measures does not reflect the exact propor-

---

[85] Legg, *op. cit.,* 528.
[86] In the reproduction of the tenor in the edition the last C appears by an engraver's mistake as O.

tion, because the editor has adopted, not without justification, irregular barring). Tenor: *It in nomine Domini,* two *taleae,* stated three
times in increasing diminution ⊙, O, and ℂ. The notation of the
tenor presents considerable difficulty, but the problem has been correctly solved by the editor. In his comments Collins points out what
he believes to be an inconsistency of the notation. The long of the
first ligature should be worth twenty-seven minims, but the two
following semibreve rests (worth three minims each) must be deducted, which reduces the long to twenty-one minims. The music,
however, will allow only a long of eighteen minims, as Collins correctly transcribes it without being able to account for the discrepancy.
The tenor is, however, correctly notated because the very first semibreve rest, which is clearly set off by a *punctum syncopationis,* must
also be deducted from the long that forms with the two rests after
the ligature one perfect *modus minor,* expressly indicated in the inscription of the tenor. Thus the value of the long is reduced to
eighteen minims, as is called for by the music. The passage proves
that in essentials like these the writing of the Old Hall MS is by and
large rather accurate, although there are, as in every manuscript, a
number of mistakes.[37]

The identification of the rather mysterious tenor brought a surprising result. The strange *it* at the beginning is not a medieval spelling for *id,* as one could possibly assume, but the second half of the
word *venit.* The plainsong belongs to [*Benedictus qui ven*]*it in
nomine Domini* of Sarum No. 3 (*Grad. Sar.* Pl. 15ˣ), that is to say,
it is the exact continuation of the Sanctus used by Damett in his
motet *Salvatoris Mater* (item No. 15). Although Damett transposes
the melody a tone below and Sturgeon presents it at its original pitch,
there can be little doubt that Sturgeon deliberately continued Damett's
tenor. Damett carried it to *ve* and Sturgeon continued with [*n*]*it* (the
letter *n* got lost in the shuffle), so that the quoted section of the
melody is quite complete although divided between two separate,
but distinctly related, works. It is of course impossible to tell whether
Damett and Sturgeon composed the motets at the same time, or
whether Sturgeon, who succeeded to Damett's post at the Chapel
Royal in Windsor, composed his later, thus literally taking up where

---

[37] Apel (*op. cit.,* 366) agrees with our interpretation of the tenor rhythm but assumes,
unnecessarily I believe, a clerical error in the use of mensuration signs. He claims that
only a reversal of the last two time signatures makes understandable the table of note
values that Collins offers in the preface to Vol. III (p. xxviii).

his predecessor had left off. It has been overlooked thus far that the
first four measures of the treble in the first four isorhythmic periods
have exactly the same rhythm in the two works—a feature that con-
nects them even more closely. It is hard to believe that all this should
be a coincidence. The position of the motets in the manuscript should
also be noted. They appear in the middle of the Sanctus section dividing the settings in conductus style from those in ballade style.[38]
The insertion of the motets by Damett and Sturgeon in the Sanctus
group is highly appropriate because they are based on the plainsong
of the Sanctus and can therefore be regarded as elaborately troped
settings of the Sanctus. In view of the kinship between trope and
motet it is hardly a coincidence that the texts of both motets begin
with the syllable *Sa.*[39] The motet by Cooke, however, seems out of
place because no connection whatsoever exists between the Litany
and the Sanctus. Like Damett's motet, Sturgeon's is noteworthy for
its flowing rhythm in spite of its mensural intricacies.

18. Anon., *Carbunculus ignitus* (not printed, fol. 109v). Only the
triplum of this motet in honor of St. Thomas of Canterbury has been
preserved. It consists of three isorhythmic periods, ⊙, ₵, and C, each
of which is stated three times.

19. Anon., *Mater mundi* (not printed, fol. 110). Only *motetus* and
tenor are extant. The *motetus* contains two isorhythmic periods C, O
stated twice each. Tenor: *Mater sancta Dei,* two *taleae,* repeated in
diminution. The words of the tenor are probably the same as those
of the missing *triplum;* they are, at any rate, not traceable to a liturgical
source. The motet has been omitted by mistake from the summary
list of contents (III, xxxvii ff.),[40] probably because Barclay Squire
regarded it as part of the preceding item.

[38] The solitary conductus setting of the Sanctus by Sturgeon which directly follows the
motets on fol. 92v was not written by the original scribe A who wrote the bulk of the
conductus and ballade Mass sections.

[39] It is interesting to note that the illuminator of the MS made a telling mistake on
fol. 89v, where Damett's motet appears. In the preceding Sanctus settings the pieces begin
with two large initials S for treble and tenor, placed one directly beneath the other because of the score notation. These two initials can be found also on fol. 89v although
only one is needed in choir-book notation.

[40] The list contains, incidentally, a number of misprints: The page numbers for fol.
11v and 34v should be corrected to III, [18] and [44] respectively; for nearly all incomplete compositions printed the page numbers have been omitted.

20. Byttering, *En Katherinae solemnia* (III, 145), 27:|| 9:|| 9:||.
Tenor: *Sponsus amat sponsam,* two *taleae,* stated three times in increasing diminution. Source of the tenor: the respond for St. Catherine *Virgo flagellatur* (*Proc. Mon.* 214), the *versus* of which begins
with *Sponsus amat sponsam.* As Dom Anselm Hughes reports in the
introduction, I have suggested that this motet may possibly be associated with the marriage of Henry V with Catherine of Valois in 1420.
The reason for this conjecture is not only the coincidence of names,
which would not prove anything by itself, but especially the selection from the Catherine respond of only those words that could be fittingly sung at a wedding, "the groom loves the bride." The words of
the motet refer exclusively to the saint and give no further clue.

21. Mayshuet, *Arae post libamina* for five voices (III, 150), 21:||
7:|| 3 1/2:|| 3 1/2:||. Tenor: *Arae post libamina,* two *taleae,* stated
four times in diminution. The contratenor, too, is isorhythmic. The
tenor is not of Gregorian origin, since it carries the same words as the
triplum. It should also be noted that it is not written in ligatures. The
two *taleae* consist of two musically identical strains differing only in
their endings. The secular character of the tenor tune is very pronounced. The motet text, a *Benedicamus Domino* trope, refers to a
French musician who may be the author of this motet, as the words
practicus Gallicus . . . hunc discantavit cantum imply. Possibly,
discantavit means that he only sang the work and did not write it.
At any rate the Frenchman is said to have turned a French motet into
Latin deemed "more agreeable to the English." The consistent use
of extreme dissonances—they are not of the chromatic type like those
in Machaut, but mostly diatonic (seconds and sevenths)—puts the
work into a specially archaic class; it may very well have been composed in the fourteenth century. This lends emphasis to the identification of Mayshuet with Mayhuet de Joan of the Chantilly MS. The
motet is remarkable also for hints of isomelic repeats in the first
isorhythmic period, and for the close relations between the third and
fourth major periods, which are linked through interchange of voices
at the beginning, while the lower voices are almost exact repeats.

22. Anon., *Post missarum solennia* (not printed, fol. 112v.; for the
beginning see III, xix). Only the cantus and contratenor are extant;

one or probably two voices are missing. The cantus, the words of
which are a *Benedicamus* trope like *Arae post,* contains three isorhythmic periods, each of which is repeated once. The tenor had
probably the same isorhythmic construction as the contratenor,
namely two *taleae,* stated three times in diminution. As far as one
can judge by the fragmentary state of the music, this motet resembles
in style the one by Mayshuet. The words of the motet have a close
parallel in a fourteenth-century motet of the Ivrea MS, *Post missarum solempnia,* although the music is not the same.[41] Here we have
for once a definite literary contact with the *ars nova* which can be
supported by numerous stylistic peculiarities of the music.

Looking back on the list of isorhythmic compositions, we can draw
a few general conclusions. It easily escapes notice that the seven
Credos, items 8–14 of our list, stand in the manuscript in direct succession (as Nos. 80–86 of the thematic catalogue) entered by the oldest hand, scribe A. This fact is of great significance because it proves
that the scribe fully realized the import of isorhythmic technique
and deliberately grouped all isorhythmic compositions of the Credo
together. He obviously followed a definite plan by dividing the
whole Credo section into three groups: (1) the conductus settings,
most of which are based on a cantus firmus (after this first group a
few extraneous motets were later inserted); (2) a large group of ballade
Mass sections and non-isorhythmic motet and *caccia* Mass sections;
and (3) the isorhythmic motet Mass sections. The Gloria group, on
the other hand, was not as carefully planned, because the five isorhythmic Glorias do not form a special section. The isorhythmic
motets proper appear as an insertion in the Sanctus group (three
motets, Nos. 15–17) and at the very end of the manuscript (Nos. 18–22).

That about a seventh of the entire repertory is isorhythmic is in
itself a sign of Continental influence. We have seen that this technique appears in its strict French and in its looser Italian form, but
the application of both to Mass compositions rather than to motets
proper in the Continental fashion bespeaks the strong liturgical attitude of English medieval music. If we can trust the rather fragmentary picture that the sources of English music in the fourteenth

[41] Besseler, AMW, VII, 225. The motet of the Ivrea MS is not isorhythmic in the
upper voices.

and fifteenth centuries present, the isorhythmic motet held second place beside the motet Mass, and it was in the Mass that the isorhythmic technique was extensively cultivated. The proportion of motets and motet Mass sections, which runs in OH heavily in favor of the latter, is due primarily to the liturgical purpose of the collection, but it seems to reflect at the same time a general trend. Several compositions make conspicuous use of hocket after the orthodox fashion at the end of isorhythmic periods.

All this points to a thorough acquaintance of the English musicians with Continental practice, although the motets sometimes show in their harmonic language such English characteristics as full triads and sixth chords. Great freedom of dissonance treatment obtains particularly in the many-voiced compositions and is more pronounced in the motets and motet Mass sections than in the conductus Mass sections, which make much greater use of sixth-chord style, but even here we do not find so much extensive parallel motion as we do, for example, in the Passion of the Meaux Abbey MS,[42] which dates from c. 1450. Although the handling of dissonances is often very suggestive of *ars nova* practice, the rhythmic flow of the compositions in triple meter makes it unlikely that the music was composed prior to the first decades of the fifteenth century, with the possible exception of such archaic motets as *Arae post libamina* by Mayshuet and *Post missarum*.

5. THE DATE OF THE MANUSCRIPT

The last remarks bring us to the much-debated question of the date of the manuscript. We must distinguish here between two points of time which do not necessarily coincide: when the repertory was composed and when it was actually assembled in the manuscript. The latter date can only be fixed by such external features as handwriting, illuminations, etc. These suggest a date of c. 1420, but it is well known that it is impossible to narrow down strict palaeographical evidence to a period of one or two decades, because the scribe may have been old and may therefore have retained the palaeographic characteristics of say, 1410, when he was actually writing about 1440 or even later. The date of the repertory can be determined mainly by three factors: (1) the stylistic internal evidence and comparison

42 MQ XXXIII (1947), 43.

with parallel sources, (2) the type of musical notation employed, and (3) historical dates for composers or particular compositions.

Stylistic evidence is the least precise as far as exact determination of the date is concerned, especially if a national school like the English is involved, a school that was habitually slow in taking up stylistic innovations and equally slow in abandoning them. On the other hand, stylistic features can be fairly accurately defined; and these furnish most valuable evidence, if not for the exact date, at least for the period in general and the relative position of English music.

The dissonance treatment of which we have repeatedly spoken conforms in the last two motets of the manuscript and in several of the *caccia* Mass sections to the standards of the *ars nova,* and even other compositions, which seem to be of somewhat later date and have fewer and less harsh clashes, show that the composers were as yet not concerned about the preparation of dissonances. The systematic use of prepared dissonances arose in English music in what I have called the "panconsonant" style of the generation of Dunstable and Pyamour (d. 1431), which cannot be dated before c. 1420–30. The only compositions written in this advanced style are the motets by Dunstable and Forest, but these do not belong to the original repertory of OH, as has been pointed out above. Disregarding these additions, we can distinguish six types of composition: (1) conductus settings of Mass sections and antiphons, (2) Mass sections in *caccia* style, (3) Mass sections in free treble style, (4) Mass sections with group contrasts, (5) isorhythmic Mass sections, and (6) isorhythmic motets proper. These types do not by themselves give any definite clue to the date, for they were probably used side by side by the composers of the Chapel Royal. It should be noted, however, that all of the types were known as early as the late fourteenth century, and the preoccupation with hocket effects to which many compositions of OH attest is also a characteristic of the *ars nova,* becoming obsolete during the first half of the fifteenth century.

Several types differ fundamentally in respect to rhythm. The majority of the conductus settings make relatively little use of minims; that is to say, the movement proceeds essentially in breves and semibreves with many ligatures, as a glance at almost any page will disclose (see, for example, the frontispiece to Vol. III). This is the most conservative rhythmic scheme of the OH repertory. The greatest rhythmic complications, with extensive use of minims, occur in the *caccia* and motet Mass sections, while the ballade Mass sections waver between complex rhythms and evenly progressing motion in *tempus perfectum*, which became the principal meter in the first half of the fifteenth century. We find analogous Mass compositions of the conductus type in the Apt MS, which has been edited in a regrettably unreliable manner by Gastoué,[48] and of the isorhythmic type in both the Ivrea and Apt MSS. The repertory of the former belongs to the first half and middle of the fourteenth century, that of the latter to the last third. The two sources approximately indicate at what time those types of composition originated in European music. That the Old Hall compositions should be as early as the two Continental manuscripts is out of the question, because English fourteenth-century music looks quite different. Apt and Ivrea are therefore not strictly parallel but analogous sources to OH. The OH repertory is stylistically not coeval with the *ars nova* manuscripts but comes later, and for this reason we have used such terms as "archaic" and "conservative." The first two decades of the fifteenth century represent the most probable date at which this conservative attitude could still prevail before the Franco-Flemish innovations took root in England.

A further point of stylistic evidence is the fact that OH gives as yet no hint of the unified Mass cycle which appears only in the late works of Leonel and Dunstable and which was not fully established before the middle of the century.[44] Even its earliest manifestation, the pairing of no more than two movements as seen in TuB and BL, is not reflected in the external order of compositions in OH. We have found that certain movements of Gloria and Credo, or Sanctus and Agnus, were composed possibly in pairs, but these are exceptional in OH and by no means very clear. In no case do these pieces have a tenor cantus firmus in common, as do the Masses from such later sources as the Aosta and Trent MSS. The absence of cyclic Masses and the on the whole conservative style of the compositions suggest that OH contains only the works of Leonel's early and middle period. The circumstance, moreover, that a manuscript of such dimensions does not include a single work by Dunstable in the original body of the collection suggests that Dunstable had not yet reached his full stature by the time the manuscript was put together. His possible absence from England would not contradict the argument,

---

[48] *Publications de la Société française de Musicologie,* 10.

[44] Compare our study *Caput,* especially the first section.

because the concordances show a lively give and take between Italy and England.

The type of musical notation in OH corresponds very closely to that of a number of late *ars nova* manuscripts, notably the Chantilly codex; Paris, Bibl. Nationale, f. ital. 568; Turin, Bibl. Naz. J II 9; and Modena, Bibl. Estense, lat. 568. They all indulge in deliberately involved mensural puzzles and syncopations, draw extensively on red notes, and employ specifically the *dragma,* the semibreve with an upward and downward tail. All these characteristics appear also in the Old Hall notation. The Continental sources can be dated between the last decades of the fourteenth century and the early ones of the fifteenth and thus support a date not later than 1420–30, which applies to Old Hall as well as to the Turin MS, which was written in Cyprus. Both sources stand outside of the central development and represent two late offshoots of the same type of notation. The repertory of the Turin Codex is as yet untouched by the music of Dufay's generation, which gradually abandoned mensural sophistications.

Since the publication of the Old Hall MS several new historical dates have come to light, largely through the research of Mr. John H. Harvey, who very kindly placed his findings at my disposal.[45] It is generally accepted that Thomas Damett and Nicholas Sturgeon can be identified with the two canons of Windsor active 1430–36 and 1441–54 respectively. It can now be added, thanks to Mr. Harvey, that the last wills of both composers have been found.[46] They were probated in 1437 and 1454 respectively, which means that each composer's last year in office was also the last year of his life. If we allow about sixty years as an ordinary life span, we may assume that they were born c. 1370 and 1390 respectively. We now know that Damett was presented by Henry V to the prebend of Rugmere in St. Paul's Cathedral in 1418, and Nicholas Sturgeon received a pension from the same monarch in 1419. These two dates are important with regard to the "Henrician" question because they prove irrefutably that the two masters who directly participated in or supervised the compilation of our manuscript were associated with Henry V.

Aleyn and Mayshuet have been identified with Johannes Alanus and Mayhuet de Joan of the Chantilly MS, which can be dated be-

[45] For particulars refer to John Harvey, *Gothic England,* 2nd ed., London, 1948, 86–89.
[46] The text of Damett's will has been printed by Harvey, *op. cit.,* 181.

cause of its political references to the late fourteenth century (the extant manuscript is a copy made in the early fifteenth century). The general stylistic similarity between the repertory of Chantilly and OH, referred to above, corroborates the identification, and, moreover, there is conclusive evidence that Alanus was English because his motet *Sub Arthuro plebs* [47] lists by name numerous English composers about whom next to nothing is known otherwise. Dom Anselm Hughes has tentatively suggested that the Aleyn of OH was the same person as John Aleyn, canon of Windsor, who died in 1373. This early date would be out of line with the other dates of OH, and the identification cannot in fact be maintained. One of the composers listed in Alanus' motet is Richard Blithe (or Blich), who is known to have been a clerk of the Chapel Royal in 1419. If the canon Aleyn really were the composer, there would be a discrepancy of at least forty-six years if we assume that the motet was composed shortly before Aleyn's death. This seems rather far-fetched, and it is therefore much more likely that the composer was still living around 1400. If so, he could very well be identical with Jean Alain, who was in the service of the Duke of Lancaster in 1396. This may be the same John Aleyn who became Minor Canon at St. Paul's Cathedral in London in 1421 and died in 1437. New dates are available also about John Pyamour (Piamor), Master of the Children of the Chapel Royal in 1420. He belonged in 1427 to the retinue of the Duke of Bedford—it will be recalled that Dunstable, too, was in the Duke's service—going overseas. Pyamour died in (or before) 1431, when he is mentioned as deceased. The only extant motet known to be by him is preserved in the Modena MS, Estense lat. 471, and its style is at least as advanced as that of Forest's motet *Qualis est dilectus*. I include these references here because they permit us to date the advanced, panconsonant style of English music c. 1430 at the latest. This style appears in OH only in the pieces that were added by hand; the main repertory belongs to the preceding phase of English music.

It is noteworthy that Pyamour, who definitely belonged to the Chapel Royal, is not included in the manuscript, while Leonel, who appears here more frequently than any other composer, has no traceable connection with Windsor. However, it would be wrong to assume that all composers of the Chapel Royal were associated with

47 Facsimile in Wolf, *Schrifttafeln*, Pls. 30–31; transcription in DTOe, Vol. 76, 9.

St. George's Chapel at Windsor Castle. Mr. Harvey has pointed out to me that music historians since Barclay Squire have confused the general institution of the Chapel Royal, which was not fixed to any one place, with the particular one at Windsor. The repertory of OH is not restricted to composers active in Windsor.

Certain composers have not yet been definitely identified. There is a record of one John Forrest who held a prebend in Lincoln Cathedral in 1394, became archdeacon of Surrey in 1414, Dean of Wells in 1425, and died in 1446. John Tyes of the manuscript may be identical with John Dyes, organist of Winchester in 1402, as has been pointed out by Dom Anselm Hughes.[48] There were at least two clerks in the Chapel Royal by the name of John Cooke, one who is mentioned in 1414 and 1417, and who died in 1419, and another who received grants in 1430, 1440, and 1455. According to Dom Anselm Hughes there are also references in the Windsor archive to Rowland, Robert Cherbury, and Pycard in 1454, 1455, and 1461 respectively, but he stresses the fact that we have no proof of sure identification, and the last date especially is highly improbable in view of Pycard's close adherence to *ars nova* style.[49] A date of great importance is the death of Leonel Power on June 5, 1445.[50] This places the leading composer of the Old Hall MS somewhat before Dunstable's mature phase, which seems very likely from the stylistic point of view also, as I have suggested elsewhere.[51]

Let us now weigh the dates with regard to the question whether Roy Henry was Henry V or Henry VI. In the first published version of this study I tried to show on the basis of circumstantial evidence that Henry V was the more likely alternative. In the meantime Mr. Harvey has come forth with new discoveries which furnish conclusive proof for dating the Old Hall MS in the reign of Henry V (d. 1422) and confirm our stylistic conclusions and circumstantial inferences by historical facts in most welcome fashion. The Wardrobe Books

[48] "The Music in the Chapel of Henry VI," in *Proceedings of the Musical Association*, LX (1933), 27.

[49] Lowinsky, MQ XXXI, 248, holds that Pycard's music "cannot have been written much before 1450" because of its sonorous chord combinations. But these have a venerable ancestry in English music; besides, the two compositions to which he refers are not contemporary with the last layer of the manuscript, as he implies. Single stylistic characteristics, such as harmony and the use of accidentals, must be seen in the stylistic whole and are in themselves insufficient criteria for the date.

[50] So given in Moser's *Musiklexikon* (2nd ed., 1943, 1098), according to a reference in an unpublished book by the late Johannes Wolf.

[51] *Acta Musicologica*, VIII (1936), 106.

of the royal household, so far unpublished, list as clerks of the Chapel Royal no less than six composers from OH, namely Thomas Damett, Nicholas Sturgeon, John Cooke, John Burell, Robert Chirbury, and William Excestre. A certain John Aleyn is also listed in 1421 as minstrel, but it is rather unlikely that he should be the same person who became Minor Canon of St. Paul's in the same year. Excestre appears in the Wardrobe Books even before the reign of Henry V, while Damett, Sturgeon, Cooke, and Burell are mentioned in 1413,[52] that is to say the very year Henry V acceded to the throne. Chirbury occurs first in 1421 [53] and is then listed with the others for some time. The disappearance of the names from the lists before and shortly after 1450 probably indicates the death of the composers, as we know for certain in the cases of Damett and Sturgeon. We have here the largest group of composers from OH so far discovered, definitely active in the first decades of the fifteenth century and associated directly with Henry V. In view of these facts Dom Anselm Hughes has reversed his former stand and no longer sees any reason to connect the manuscript with Henry VI at all. It is a great pleasure to see a controversy on a vital point concluded in unanimous agreement.

With the authorship of Henry V generally accepted, the chronicler's specific report about the monarch's musical interests gains new significance and reveals itself as trustworthy information. Roy Henry's Sanctus, which was thought to be a later insertion, actually belongs to the old layer, as the handwriting shows. The motet *En Katherinae solemnia* by Byttering very probably points to the wedding of Henry V and must therefore be dated in the year 1420. Damett's motet *Salvatoris mater,* in which "Henricus" is mentioned, must have been composed before 1422; [54] this date may possibly also apply to Sturgeon's *Salve mater,* which continues the tenor of Damett's motet. All these dates concord agreeably with the general style of the music, the palaeographic evidence, and the notation. We may conclude, then, that the Old Hall MS was written during the lifetime of Henry V and that only late sections, if any, were completed under Henry VI before the latter came of age. It was therefore not necessary to make a distinction in the source between the composer Henry V

52 Public Record Office, E.101/406/21.

53 E.101/407/4.

54 It could not possibly refer to the marriage of Henry VI in 1445, as Hughes once tentatively suggested, because the composer died about nine years before the event.

and the child Henry VI. The virtues and accomplishments of Henry V, which have been drawn into the brightly colored limelight of the cinema, can now be added to by a new and real one, that of a composer.

6. A POSTSCRIPT

[Upon publication of the first version of this essay, in the *Musical Quarterly* (Vols. XXXIV, 1948, and XXXV, 1949), Professor Oliver Strunk called my attention to a group of canonic pieces discussed only briefly in my essay, which, as stated before, could not deal with all aspects of the Old Hall repertory. I was glad to have his valuable observations appended to my study and welcomed their publication, in the form of a postscript, in the *Musical Quarterly* (Vol. XXXV, 1949). The postscript is included here in its original form.]

With the settling of the controversy over the date of the Old Hall MS it at last becomes possible to relate it to the general scene. Particularly helpful from this point of view are the additional concordances with Continental MSS, which show that the Old Hall repertory was rather more widely diffused than formerly supposed, and the demonstration that the MS itself contains at least one additional piece of Continental origin. Significant, too, is the bearing of the date of the MS upon the date of Leonel Power's removal from England to Continental Europe.

As published in the edition, the Old Hall MS contains five canonic settings of texts belonging to the Ordinary of the Mass—three Glorias by Pycard (I, 76, 84, and 119) and two anonymous Credos (II, 82 and 101). For the solution of the canons in all but one of these pieces the MS itself gives explicit Latin directions. In the one case remaining (II, 82) there is no direct indication that canonic writing is involved, but an attempt to score the three voices found in the MS shows unmistakably that something is missing. Mr. H. B. Collins offers a brilliant and altogether convincing solution of this piece— as a three-part canon with two accompanying voices—in the second volume of the Plainsong and Mediaeval Music Society's edition, and in a note printed with his transcription he remarks that at several points within the piece the written cantus part has two sets of words

—at *Genitum non factum* the second set begins with *Qui propter nos,* while *Et in Spiritum* is similarly combined with *Qui cum Patre,* and *Confiteor* with *Et exspecto.* At the corresponding points in his transcription, Collins adapts the upper lines of text to the voice beginning the canon and to the first of the two voices that follow it, leaving the lower lines to the second of the consequent voices. In effect, the result is not unlike that seen in the familiar "telescoped" settings of Gloria and Credo.

Thanks to Mr. Collins and his remark about the double set of words in his anonymous Credo, it is not difficult to add a new item to the list of canonic settings in the Old Hall MS and to show that another item, already on this list, is not a simple canon, as indicated in the MS, but a double one. For, once it is recognized that a single voice-part provided with a "telescoped" double text may in itself be an indirect indication of the presence of canonic writing, the rest is easy and the surprising thing is that the obvious conclusions were not drawn long ago.[55]

The first of the two pieces in question is a Gloria by Byttering (I, 47)—No. 15 in Barclay Squire's thematic list of contents. This is a setting in three written parts, with vocal cantus and instrumental tenor and contratenor. Here the "telescoped" double text runs without a break from the first measure of the cantus part to the last, the upper line giving the beginnings of the successive clauses, the lower line the endings. If one approaches this piece with the possibility of unspecified canonic writing in mind, the solution leaps to the eye—in the first section (*tempus imperfectum cum prolatione majore*) the consequent voice enters at the unison after four measures (Ex. 9).

[55] After Professor Strunk had told me of his discovery I checked the manuscript again for indications of canon that might possibly have been overlooked. The customary *signum congruentiae* is indeed lacking, but there is nevertheless a direct hint. In Byttering's Gloria (I, 47) the final word "Amen" is written down twice in full, and, what is more, the Amen of the consequent voice is not placed directly below the music of the antecedent voice, but is shifted back for three measures, the exact time interval of the second section of the canon. Correspondingly, the Amen is written three times in the two Credos with three-voice canon (II, 82 and 101; for the latter see the color facsimile in Vol. III), and again the words are placed at the correct time interval! All this is certainly no coincidence, because the scribe feels obliged to write out the word "Amen" several times only in compositions with canon; in all other pieces he spreads the word out melismatically like this: A. . . . .men. It follows that each voice of the canon should sing Amen only once, not several times, as the edition now indicates. The point is minute, but fully confirms that the pieces in question are indeed canons. We have here again an object-lesson of the well-known fact that certain hints escape detection so long as the point they hint at is not understood. [M.F.B.]

Ex. 9. Byttering: Gloria No. 15 with canon.

Not only does the consequent voice fit perfectly with those given in the MS, it also supplies the missing fifths and thirds for a number of incomplete triads and fills in occasioinal gaps in the texture. With three voices only, the sudden cessation of movement in measures 5 and 6 of the tenor and contratenor has an awkward appearance; with four voices, it is seen to be a deliberately calculated refinement. Indeed, it is no exaggeration to say that without the fourth voice the piece makes no real sense at all.

In the second section of Byttering's Gloria (*tempus perfectum*, with the contratenor in *tempus imperfectum* at the beginning) the entrance of the consequent voice is again at the unison; a nice stroke is the reduction of the time interval from four measures to three for this, the final section of the piece (Ex. 10).

A particularly attractive feature of Byttering's little piece is the carefully planned co-ordination of words and music. As a result of the canonic structure, the first section falls into periods of four meas-

Ex. 10. Byttering: Gloria No. 15, second section.

ures, the second into periods of three. In dividing the liturgical text between antecedent and consequent, Byttering follows this over-all periodization exactly, with the result that in each period the consequent voice completes the clause left unfinished by the antecedent, echoing the notes that have just been sung, while the antecedent voice is simultaneously propounding the first half of the clause that follows. A further result, characteristic of many canonic and quasi-canonic settings of the Gloria text, but unusually well worked out in this one, is the symbolically simultaneous declamation of the appeals to Father and Son: while the consequent voice is singing *Deus Pater omnipotens,* echoing the *Domine Deus Rex caelestis* that has just been heard, the antecedent voice is already beginning the *Domine Fili unigenite.* Similarly, but with another shade of meaning, *Domine Deus, Agnus Dei,* and *Jesu Christe* are heard at the same time.[56]

We ought now to be ready to assume that any voice provided with a "telescoped" double text is a potential canonic antecedent, and meeting with one more such voice among the Glorias of the Old Hall MS we shall naturally put it to the test. This time (I, 84) the composer is Pycard, by whom we have two other canonic Glorias (I, 76 and 119) and—if Professor Bukofzer's attribution is accepted—a canonic Credo (II, 101); his piece is No. 24 in Barclay Squire's thematic list. There are two vocal parts, one with a "telescoped" text that is alternately single and double (as in the Credo transcribed by Mr. Collins), the other with the complete text in the usual form.

[56] Compare the comments of Friedrich Ludwig on a similar treatment of the Gloria text in Modena 568 ("Die mehrstimmige Messe des 14. Jahrhunderts," in AMW VII [1925], 423).

Accompanying them is an instrumental tenor with the direction: *Tenor et contratenor in uno, unus post alium fugando quinque temporibus.* The manuscript has also a "solus tenor" part which may be substituted for the canonic tenor and contratenor if a reduction in the number of voices is desired. As it stands, then, the piece appears to be for four voices (or for three, if the "solus tenor" is used). But the "telescoped" text below the one cantus part suggests that it is actually for five voices (or for four), and an attempt to apply the tenor's rule to the cantus confirms this. In Ex. 11 (four five-measure

Ex. 11. Pycard: Gloria No. 24 with double canon.

periods from the concluding "Amen"), the alternative "solus tenor" is omitted. As in the Gloria by Byttering, the added consequent voice fills out a number of incomplete triads. What is more striking, it also completes the hockets: the construction of the antecedent voice, which sings alternately after and on the beat in the corresponding measures of the successive five-measure periods, is now seen to be a deliberate and ingenious calculation. Once again the piece becomes fully intelligible only when the unspecified canon is resolved; it is this canon that is the truly essential one—not the specified canon of tenor and contratenor, whose omission the composer expressly sanctions. Pycard's canonic Gloria is doubtless somewhat earlier than Dufay's familiar *Gloria ad modum tubae* and is in any case one of the very few multiple canons that we have from the time before Josquin and the later Okeghem.

Surely it is significant that of the six canonic pieces in the Old Hall MS four are Glorias, while only two are Credos. Throughout the earlier fifteenth century the Gloria text is the preferred text for canonic treatment: we have no Credos to offset the canonic Glorias of Modena 568,[57] of Arnold and Hugo de Lantins,[58] of Trent 925 and 927, of Dufay.[59] It is also significant that of the six canonic pieces in the Old Hall MS only the two Credos involve three-part canonic writing. For their time, these six pieces constitute the largest known group of their kind. And they follow too closely on the heels of the pair in Modena 568 to justify the assumption of a direct borrowing from Italy; it is at least equally possible that the application of the canonic principle to the Ordinary of the Mass began independently and more or less simultaneously on both sides of the Channel.

[57] An anonymous dialogue-like setting with accompanying instrumental canon (fol. 2v), published in part by Handschin in *Zeitschrift für Musikwissenschaft*, X (1927–28), 552–55, and an accompanied canon ("Fuga," fol. 9v) by Matteo da Perugia, cantor at the Milan Cathedral from 1402 to 1414.

[58] Charles van den Borren, *Polyphonia sacra* (1932), pp. 10 (the canon broken off at "Laudamus te") and 118.

[59] The Aosta MS contains another canonic Gloria for four voices (No. 150) which is probably of English origin. Mention should be made also of a canonic Kyrie by John Benet (Tr 107–108), listed in the thematic catalogue erroneously as a three-voice composition because the editors overlooked the canon. These pieces do not increase the number of canonic Credos, but one by Chierisy (*Polyphonia sacra*, No. 10) is at least partially canonic. [M.F.B.]

III

The Fountains Fragment

1. CONTENTS AND NOTATION OF THE MANUSCRIPT

VERY FEW complete manuscripts of polyphonic music in medieval England have withstood the vicissitudes of time. If we had no other than complete sources at our disposal, our knowledge of the state of medieval music in England would be extremely restricted and lack perspective as to the general repertory. A flourishing musical life is attested to not only in many literary and historical documents but also in a surprisingly large number of musical fragments. Most of the large musical manuscripts of which we have today some indirect record or even some direct remains suffered destruction during the Reformation. However, such planned destructive policies were pursued not only in that period but also, if for different reasons, in the monasteries of the fourteenth and fifteenth centuries. Musical manuscripts considered outdated at the time were cut up and used in bindings of non-musical books. Well concealed as flyleaves or protective covers of fascicles, they weathered the storm of centuries and can now be removed from their hiding places, many of which may as yet have remained undiscovered. It is mainly from such mutilated and isolated leaves that we, like a palaeontologist who reconstructs from a few scattered bones an extinct species, can piece together a fairly comprehensive picture of medieval English music. Although the fragments may be small and not necessarily revealing in themselves, taken together they sketch the outline of a large body of music and give us evidence in much the same manner as the visible part of an iceberg does of its total dimensions.

The method of integrating a fragment in the known repertory may be shown by a discussion of the newly found "Fountains fragment," which supplements in welcome fashion our knowledge of English polyphony in the early fifteenth century. Mr. Bertram Schofield, Deputy Keeper of MSS in the British Museum, discovered the manuscript in the binding of a memorandum book of Fountains Abbey (Yorkshire) which records events between the years 1446 and 1460. It was subsequently removed from the binding and is now listed as Add. MS 40011 B.[1] The fragment, which may be briefly designated as LoF, has been alluded to several times in musicological literature,[2] but its contents have not yet been discussed as a whole. It commands a very special interest because of its relations to the music of the Old Hall MS, which Mr. Schofield was the first to notice. It will be seen below that his list of concordances can be substantially enlarged.

In its present form Add. MS 40011 B consists of two parts. The first is made up of eight narrow parchment strips with minute fragments of motets [3] of the early fourteenth century. These remnants are too small to be very informative or to warrant a description here. It may only be added that in spite of their extreme mutilation one of them could be identified as belonging to the motet *Rota Katerine/ Orbis dominatio,* which occurs in fragmentary state also in two other sources, Add. MS 24198 of the British Museum and Bodleian MS 652.[4] The second part of LoF, which alone interests us here, consists of six paper leaves, now numbered fols. 9–14, with part music in black-void or "white" notation and occasional solid black notes indicating *color.*[5] The leaves are not consecutive, so that several compositions at the beginning or end of a leaf are now incomplete; fortunately, however, the fragment forms three separate pairs of leaves

---

[1] *British Museum, Catalogue of Additions to the Manuscripts, 1916–1920,* London, 1933.

[2] *The Old Hall Manuscript,* The Plainsong and Mediaeval Music Society, London, 1938, III, xxix; some of the particulars stated here are inaccurate. See also Schofield, "A Newly Discovered 15th-century Manuscript of the Chapel Royal, Part I," in MQ XXXII (1946), 510, and the essay in this book, "The Music of the Old Hall MS."

[3] Not "certain items of Plainsong," as is stated in the preface to the edition of OH.

[4] Bukofzer, *Sumer is icumen in, A Revision,* University of California Publications in Music, Vol. 2, No. 2, Berkeley, 1944, 97.

[5] In the preface to OH the notation is erroneously described as black-full.

each of which is continuous in itself—fols. 9–10, 11–12, and 13–14. The subsequent thematic catalogue departs from convention in giving the incipits of the compositions in transcription [6] rather than original notation in order that they may serve at the same time as musical examples. The contents are listed in the present order with all known concordances. While all compositions are anonymous in LoF, one can be ascribed definitely to Rowland because of a concordance, and No. 1 tentatively to Pennard for reasons that are explained below. Unless the contrary is expressly noted, the voices are written in choir-book form or *cantus collateralis*.

LoF

1. Gloria [Pennard ?], fol. 9, four voices (Plate 1)
2. Gloria, fol. 9 v = OH 26, Rowland (Rowlard), three voices; printed in OH I, 104, and according to LoF in OH III, [62]

3. Gloria, fol. 10, four voices
4. Gloria, fol. 10 v, superius and tenor only of a four-voice composition, = LoF 16 (see below) = OH 31

[6] The original note values have been reduced by four.

5. Sanctus, fol. 10 v, three voices in score, last few measures lacking; first part printed below as Ex. 1

Et in ter - ra pax ho-mi-ni - bus bo - ne vo - lun-ta - tis

6. Gloria, fol. 11, single voice (complete) of a four(?)-voice composition

Sanc - tus

Sanc - [tus]

7. Sanctus, fol. 11, three voices in score

Sanc - tus

Sanc - - - - tus

8. Sanctus, fol. 11 v, three voices in score

9. Sanctus, fol. 11 v, three voices in score = OH 97. Tenor voice only also in Brit. Mus. MS Lansdowne 462, fol. 1 v; printed in OH III, 20, and according to LoF in OH III, [76]

Ag - nus De - i

Qui tol - - - lis

10. Agnus Dei, fol. 11 v, three voices in score

11. Agnus Dei, fol. 12, three voices in score
12. Agnus Dei, fol. 12, three voices in score = OH 122; printed in
    OH III, 108

13. Agnus Dei, fol. 12 v, three voices in score
14. Agnus Dei, fol. 12 v, three voices in score, last three measures
    missing = OH 126a; printed in OH III, 120
15. Credo, fol. 13, alto and contratenor only of a four-voice composi-
    tion (the other two voices are preserved in OH 86); printed
    in OH III, [68]

16. Gloria, fol. 13v–14, four voices = LoF 4 (two voices only), and
    OH 31 (alto and contratenor only, fol. 29)

17. Motet, fol. 14, *Humane lingua organis*
                  Supplicum voces
   Tenor [*Deo gratias*] and contratenor, four voices with **an alter-**
   native *solus tenor* for three-voice reduction

18. Motet, fol. 14v, *Alme Pater pastor,* superius and tenor only, orig-
    inally for four (?) voices

Of the eighteen compositions in LoF no less than seven (Nos. 2, 4,
9, 12, 14, 15, and 16) recur in OH. In view of the fragmentary state
of LoF, the percentage of overlap is remarkably high and suggests
that the repertory of the composers of the Chapel Royal was taken
over almost bodily in Fountains Abbey. That the manuscript actually
reflects the music at York seems fairly certain, as, according to information kindly supplied by Mr. Schofield,[7] it was incorporated in
the binding as early as the fifteenth century, perhaps already in 1446
when the book was begun. The extended parallelism of a locally
restricted group of compositions at two rather distant places is unique
in the annals of English medieval music and all the more striking
because of the differences in liturgical use between Salisbury and
Fountains Abbey.

   [7] He has furthermore pointed out to me that the names of two composers in OH may
possibly establish a relation to Fountains Abbey. They are Fonteyns [Fountains] and
Queldryk. Now, at Fountains Abbey there was an estate known as Queldrike. It is impossible to say whether or not the identity of names is more than a coincidence.

The only variant copy outside of OH is preserved in Lansdowne MS 462 of the British Museum. Well known as a noted Sarum Gradual,[8] it contains on its flyleaves (vellum) some little-known mensural music in black notation. The additions consist of a series of tenor voices from three-part Masses and other liturgical compositions. Notated in direct succession with no space left for the supplementary parts, the extant voices were destined apparently for monophonic performance or possibly to be sung as counterpoints to plainsongs. The concordance with LoF 9 and OH 97 convincingly proves that they are not themselves plainsongs, as several authors—myself included—have believed,[9] but freely composed music, and this fact is confirmed furthermore by a second concordance, the Sanctus by William Exce(s)tre which only OH transmits. The circumstance that one composition in LoF has come down to the present day in three different sources indicates that certain compositions were distributed more widely than one would assume.

What is the date of the Fountains fragment? Its extensive overlapping with the repertory of OH leaves little doubt that the two manuscripts must date from about the same period. It is now generally agreed that OH originated in the first decades of the fifteenth century. If LoF actually belonged to the binding in 1446, it must have been written even earlier, because it would not otherwise have been used for such purposes. We arrive therefore at a date of c. 1420–30. The handwriting seems to bear out this conclusion. Apparently, then, LoF is contemporary with OH.

There is, however, one serious obstacle to the acceptance of this early date, namely the white notation of the music, which is usually dated after 1450.[10] An additional difficulty is that the more recent form of notation made much slower progress in England than in other countries. Therefore we must digress for a moment and briefly consider the development of notation in the various European countries. The change from black to white notation did not occur in all countries simultaneously but originated in Italy, where, as Ludwig [11] has pointed out, it coincides with a change in writing material, the

[8] Its version of the Ordinary is reproduced in facsimile in the appendix of *Grad. Sar.* 1ˣ–19ˣ.

[9] Davey, *History of English Music*, 2nd ed., 1921, 64, and Bukofzer, *Acta Musicologica* VIII (1936), 109.

[10] Johannes Wolf, *Geschichte der Mensuralnotation*, 1904, I, 396; *Handbuch der Notationskunde*, 1913, I, 382. Apel, *The Notation of Polyphonic Music*, 2nd ed., 1944, xxii.

[11] Quoted by Besseler in AMW VII, 244, where the question is more fully discussed.

increased use of paper instead of parchment. The ink of solid black notes was apt to eat through the paper and mar the other side of the leaf. Since parchment manuscripts were immune to this hazard, they continued to be written in black notation. In the case of MS 37 (Q 15) of the Liceo Musicale in Bologna (BL),[12] the black notation has destroyed the paper and made many folios practically illegible. The MS contains numerous compositions that Bodleian MS Can. Misc. 213 (O) transmits in white notation, also on paper. The fascicles of O were written at different times; the oldest ones contain certain political compositions that fall between 1400 and 1413.[13] They confirm Besseler's contention [14] that the old gatherings of O were begun in the first part of the century. Wolf [15] regarded O as a late transcription in white notation of an earlier source in black notation and placed the manuscript in the second part of the century merely because he took white notation as *ipso facto* proof of the date. However, it will be seen below that Wolf never actually proved his premise. Moreover, it is contradicted by the evidence of the handwriting in this particular case. Wolf's general date for the change of notation is a little too rigid, as it does not allow for the earliest documents of white notation before 1450, though it remains true that white notation became the main form of writing music only after 1450. Its final establishment was associated with the emergence of a new repertory,[16] and the change of notation has here a stylistic reason— it coincides with the turn to High Renaissance music,[17] which is only rarely written in black notes. From this time on, white notation prevails even in parchment manuscripts.

The situation in England is somewhat more complicated owing to the conservatism of English scribes, reluctant to abandon black notation. The huge choir books in Lambeth Palace, MS 1 and MS 667 of Caius College, Cambridge, which contain Masses of the Fairfax period, prove that black notation was current in England as late as the end of the fifteenth and the beginning of the sixteenth century. Significantly, these sumptuous codices are written on parchment. It goes without saying that black notation is used also in major manu-

12 See the analytical list by de Van in *Musica Disciplina*, II, 231.

13 Pirro, *Histoire de la musique de la fin du XIVe siècle à la fin du XVIe siècle*, 1940, 58.

14 AMW VII, 244.

15 *Mensuralnotation*, I, 185–6.

16 Besseler, AMW VII, 245.

17 Bukofzer, MQ XXX (1944), 118.

scripts of the second half of the fifteenth century, such as the well-known Bodleian MS, Selden B 26 (c. 1450); [18] the Meaux Abbey MS, Egerton 3307 (c. 1450); [19] and Cambridge, Pepys Libr. MS 1236 (c. 1480). Of these the first two are written on parchment, the last on heavy parchment paper.

But this is only one side of the story. Granted the predominance of black notation in English sources of the time, there are nevertheless several noteworthy exceptions. That the use of paper was not necessarily a decisive consideration for the choice of notation is proved by Bodleian MS Ashmole 191.[20] This paper manuscript employs black notation, yet it dates from the second part of the century, as it contains the fragment, here textless and anonymous, of the English chanson *So ys emprinted* by Walter Frye, whose compositions occur only in manuscripts of the late fifteenth century. We may conclude, therefore, that in England black notation was used on paper after 1450. On the other hand, there is evidence that white notation on parchment as well as paper was known in England even before 1450. A decisive document in this respect is a parchment leaf with white notation in the Bodleian Library, MS lat. theol. d 1,[21] which fortunately indicates 1436 as the year of its writing. Although it records only a musical cipher and is therefore not a source of actual music, it proves nevertheless the existence of white notation in England before 1450. There are in addition three or four other sources in white notation which, though their date cannot be determined with the precision of the foregoing example, belong in all likelihood to the first part of the century by virtue of their handwriting, repertory, and musical style.

The first of these is an isolated vellum leaf in the British Museum, Cotton Tib. A VII, fol. 38 v, which preserves two voices of an isorhythmic Gloria.[22] Written in a somewhat finer hand than the two manuscripts subsequently discussed, it agrees in style so closely with the isorhythmic Mass compositions of OH (and LoF) that it would be difficult to assign a much later date to it. The handwriting of the text, too, points to the first half of the century.

The second source in white notation is a collection of English,

[18] *Early Bodleian Music*, ed. by Stainer, 1901, I, Pls. XXXVII–XCVII.
[19] Compare the study in this book, "Holy-Week Music and Carols at Meaux Abbey."
[20] *Early Bodleian Music*, Pls. XXX–XXXVI.
[21] *Ibid.*, Pl. XXIX.
[22] See p. 109.

French, and Latin songs, formerly in the library of Lord Howard de
Walden and now in Cambridge, Univ. Libr., Add. MS 5943,[23] fols.
161–169. Written on paper, it is bound up with tables of eclipses
ranging from 1414 to about the middle of the century. Since these
tables were usually compiled for the future, they must have been
written about 1414. It is likely that the musical part, too, originated
in the first part of the century, because it is written by a contemporary
though different hand. More important than this external evidence
are the stylistic findings. The rather primitive idiom of the music
can hardly be later than the early fifteenth century, and this date is
supported by a concordance which has remained unnoticed so far. The
French song *Esperance,* which does not differ in style from other pieces
of the collection, belongs to the repertory of the late *ars nova.* It recurs in MSS Paris, f. ital. 568, fol. 7, and Prague, Univ. XI E 9, fol. 5,[24]
both of which transmit secular pieces of the *ars nova* in black notation.
As it is improbable that this fourteenth-century song should have been
recorded in England after 1450,[25] we must assume that the Cambridge
MS was compiled in the first part of the century.

Similar to the Cambridge MS in notation and handwriting are several separate parchment leaves, Bodleian MS Douce 381,[26] to which
Nicholson has assigned the date of c. 1425 with the approval of the
palaeographer Sir E. Maunde Thompson. The leaves are written by
different scribes, mostly in white notation; one which is written in
black notes differs from the rest in that it is done in a more elegant
hand. The music in white notation consists again of English songs in
early fifteenth-century style. They resemble those of Add. MS 5943
not only externally in the poor handwriting but also internally with
regard to style and even repertory. The song *I rede that thou be*[27]
occurs with the identical music in both collections, and there is no
cogent reason why they should differ in date and why c. 1425 should
not be correct. Wolf, who was unaware of this, was forced, in order
to be consistent with his theory, to question the verdict of Nicholson

[23] Published in facsimile and a very unreliable, often useless transcription by S. L.
M[eyer], *Music, Cantelenas, Songs,* 1906.
[24] Kammerer, *Die Musikstücke des Prager Kodex XI E 9,* 1931.
[25] It is true that many medieval manuscripts were compiled long after the music they
preserve was written, e.g. the famous Squarcialupi codex, the origin of which is due to a
certain antiquarian interest. The Cambridge MS, however, was destined for practical
use.
[26] *Early Bodleian Music,* Pls. XXII–XXV.
[27] Carleton Brown and R. H. Robbins, *Index of Middle English Verse,* 1943, No. 1347.

and Thompson.[28] He nevertheless agrees with them in dating Bodleian MS Selden B 26 at c. 1450. The latter manuscript furnishes, in fact, one of the main arguments in support of his claim that white notation originated after 1450. He asserts that the collection presents black and white notation side by side and thus indicates the approximate point of time when the change-over occurred. Now, it is very strange that Wolf, careful scholar that he was, should be in error on this crucial point. Actually, the manuscript is written in black notation throughout, void notes are used only for *color,* and the only evidences of white notation are short scribbles added in the sixteenth century which obviously have no bearing on the point in question. Thus, one of the main pillars of Wolf's proof breaks down.

Black and white notation co-existed in England for a much longer period than Wolf realized. The famous vellum roll of carols, Cambridge, Trinity Coll. O 3.58 [1230] [29] belongs probably also to the first half of the century by virtue of its handwriting and musical style and must be regarded as the fourth English source in white notation before 1450. It contains polyphonic carols in a rather archaic form and must therefore be somewhat older than the Selden MS. The latter and later source transmits in black notation several carols that the Trinity Roll presents in white notation, the well-known Agincourt Song, for example. Here we have indeed an overlap of black and white notation, with the latter appearing in the presumably earlier source—but not in the same manuscript.

We may conclude from this digression that white notation on paper as well as parchment was known in England sometime before 1450 and that it ran parallel with black notation to the end of the century. While it remains true that English scribes were in general conservative and preferred to employ the old form of notation, a number of exceptions must be recognized which do not lag behind the practice in other countries.

To return now to the Fountains fragment: It will be seen that its notation no longer presents a serious argument against dating

[28] Wolf, *Mensuralnotation,* I, 395. For the same reason he placed Cambridge, Add. MS 5943 in the second half of the century (*Notationskunde,* I, 452). His theory would make the *Lochheimer Liederbuch* (1455) one of the oldest documents of white notation, and Wolf actually draws this very unlikely conclusion in his *Notationskunde,* I, 384.

[29] Fuller-Maitland, *English Carols of the XVth Century,* 1891. The transcriptions and the preface are out of date. For further discussion of the date of the MS see p. 166.

it in the first part of the century. Rather it should be added as a new item in the list of early English sources in white notation. It stands in the same relation to OH as does O to BL; in other words, OH presents in black notes and on parchment the same compositions that appear in LoF in white notes and on paper. Thus LoF tends to confirm Ludwig's observations, though, as we have seen above, the writing material cannot be taken as an infallible criterion. Were we to date LoF in the second part of the century, we should have to make the unlikely assumption that OH and LoF, which convey a well-defined repertory of the early fifteenth century, were separated by the span of a generation.

The handwriting of the text in LoF is executed in a much less formal style than in OH and betrays signs of haste. The musical hand is rather rough and scrawling, especially in the oblique ligatures, which can be read at times only with difficulty as to their exact pitch. There are some interesting peculiarities of notation, such as the joining together of several ligatures *cum opposita proprietate* and the unorthodox combination of normally single notes with a ligature, e.g. ⊓⊔⊓. In one composition (No. 17) single semibreves are sometimes marked by what looks like a dovetailed caret: ⋄. It indicates alteration of the note in perfect time, not, as it sometimes does in other sources, correction of pitch.[30] This special mark is superfluous for those familiar with the rules of alteration, and its use bespeaks a provincial attitude toward mensural notation. Apparently the scribe, putting little trust in the singers' acquaintance with mensural notation, wanted to make doubly sure that they did not miss the alteration. In other English manuscripts of the time, for example in Cambridge, Pembroke Coll. Inc. C 47 and Br. Mus., Lansdowne 462, the number 2 is added below certain semibreves for the same purpose —a usage that persists even as late as the Lambeth MS. The caret goes back to the fourteenth century. Hanboys and Tunstede ascribe it in their treatises [31] to the English theorist Robert de Brunham, and though they flatly reject his innovation LoF shows that it was nevertheless followed in practice for a long time. Another interesting peculiarity is the sign for the rest of a perfect semibreve in major prolation, which, contrary to common usage, is drawn across the line of

---

[30] Wolf, *Notationskunde*, I, 431.
[31] Coussemaker, *Scriptores*, I, 43, and IV, 271 [= III, 349].

the staff like this —┼—. Only English theorists, such as Anonymous IV, Hanboys, and Tunstede, record this practice,[82] so that in this respect also the manuscript cannot deny its English origin.

Although a small fragment of a larger manuscript, LoF circumscribes a repertory that can be fairly well estimated by analogy with that of OH. Some of the leaves betray a planned order of compositions. With the Masses exceeding the motets by 16 to 2, the original collection was probably arranged like OH, in groups of Mass settings with motets inserted between the main headings of the Ordinary. The gathering of Masses under one heading is observed less rigidly than in OH, but it was nonetheless the guiding principle. Even now the bulk of the music is arranged in three consecutive series, Nos. 1–4, 7–9, and 10–14, which present the settings of the Gloria, Sanctus, and Agnus in liturgical order. The twofold sequence of a Gloria and Sanctus (Nos. 4–5 and 6–7) in direct succession on the same folio indicates that the Credo did not constitute a separate group, as it does in OH. The exceptional position of the Credo closely corresponds to the order of liturgical books in which the various plainsongs of the Gloria group are succeeded directly by those of the Sanctus group, with the Credo appearing at another place. It should not be overlooked that in the two instances where Gloria and Sanctus overlap in the manuscript *cantus collateralis* and score notation are used side by side. The scribe obviously tried to utilize every inch of space, and it is very likely that the two groups ran parallel in this manner for a number of folios. The six Glorias—there are actually only five different compositions, since No. 4 is the same as No. 16—are all composed in a style that calls for notation in choir-book form. The same is true of the Credo, while all compositions of the Sanctus (four settings) and Agnus (five settings) are composed in conductus style and written in score in keeping with the English tradition. The old layer of OH consists only of conductus-like settings in score which always precede the settings in *cantus collateralis*. We do not know whether or not LoF ever included Glorias in conductus style; if it did, they must have come at the very beginning of the manuscript, which has not been preserved. The Sanctus and Agnus groups in OH are nearly all conductus Masses; only a few compositions in separate parts are added at the end of each series—in the case of the Agnus no more than two. In LoF the Sanctus group and probably the Agnus

[82] See the table of rests in Wolf, *Notationskunde*, I, 336.

group also consisted originally of conductus settings exclusively, as we can infer from fol. 11 v, which fortunately preserves the end of the one group and the beginning of the other. It is significant that the repertory of LoF corresponds to the old layer of OH and the retrospective Masses in separate parts, but not to the more progressive settings at the end of the OH series. This concentration on early types of composition adds emphasis to what has been surmised about the date of the fragment.

The only leaves without a recognizable plan are fols. 13–14, the original position of which is not known. In them a Credo, contrary to liturgical order, directly precedes a Gloria; the latter is in turn followed by two motets, of which the first is based on the *Deo gratias* of the Mass. The haphazard nature of the order is confirmed by the fact that Gloria No. 4 is inadvertently recorded here a second time. In OH no such duplication occurs. The double entry may be due to an oversight of a second scribe; there are some minute deviations in handwriting between the two copies of the composition, but it is difficult to decide whether or not they fall within the margin of individual variation. It is, incidentally, a curious coincidence that No. 4 records precisely the two voices that are wanting in OH. Even if we did not have the complete piece we should still be able to reconstruct it from the two sources in the same manner as the Credo.

2. ANALYSIS OF THE MUSIC

The music of the Fountains fragment may be conveniently discussed under five headings. The first four relate to Masses composed (1) in conductus style, (2) in the free treble style of the secular song, (3) in Italian duet style, and (4) in isorhythmic motet style. The fifth category comprises isorhythmic motets proper.

The first and largest group of compositions includes the Sanctus and Agnus series in score notation, which are based without exception on liturgical cantus firmi. Written in a style of utmost simplicity, they correspond to the simplest and presumably earliest settings of the old layer in OH. The pronounced stylistic conservatism serves as additional argument for the suggested date of the manuscript. The plainsongs are very plainly "harmonized" in breves and semibreves, with some minims appearing here and there in the free voices, especially at the cadence, to relieve the rhythmic monotony.

Certain compositions, e.g. Sanctus No. 8, proceed in breves and semi-breves and adhere so closely to the liturgical melody that their liga-tures are literally transferred to the cantus firmus, which usually moves in steady breves throughout. For a very typical example of this type the reader may refer to Agnus No. 12 (= OH 122), which is readily available in print (OH III, 108 [33]). Here the outermost voices move against a rigidly progressing plainsong and provide a very sonorous yet strikingly archaic "counterpoint" with numerous paral-lel fifths and even parallel triads. The latter are not errors of the scribe; they appear in identical fashion in both sources.

For the sake of sonority one of the voices is at times divided in two by additional black notes which must be sung simultaneously and thus call for at least two performers to one part. However, the addi-tions often merely double notes already present in another voice, as in Sanctus No. 7, or Gloria No. 3, where the division occurs at the very end. In OH and LoM similar practices can be found occa-sionally.

Compositions appearing in OH as well as LoF do not always agree in their accidentals, rhythmic details, part writing, or even length. A general rule with regard to the use of accidentals cannot be stated; at times they are more numerous in LoF, as can be seen if OH 97 is compared with LoF 9 (Vol. III, 20 and [76]). Conversely, the striking g♯ in the opening measures of OH 122 (III, 108) is not prescribed in LoF 12, and there are, moreover, a few rhythmic variants which demonstrate the customary laxity of medieval scribes in matters of copying. The greatest differences exist between the two variants of Agnus No. 14. In OH only two invocations are written out fully, and the third Agnus is sung after the music of the first one. In LoF all three are fully given, the first of which agrees, save for some rhyth-mic variants, with that of OH; the two others are both related to the second of OH but show considerable variations in detail. Strangely enough, it is the third Agnus in LoF that agrees best with the second in OH. The respective settings are both written in perfect time and have for several measures the same music, though there are deviations from time to time.

The stylistic conservatism of the Masses in conductus style extends also to the treatment of the cantus firmus. In OH the plainsong ap-

[33] The transcription substitutes straight duple meter with occasional triplets for major prolation called for by the notation (two dotted quarter notes per measure).

pears most often in the middle voice, but sometimes already in the upper voice, paraphrased in the style of a secular song.[34] The latter procedure found increasing favor in England, so that by the middle of the century, or shortly thereafter, the situation is practically reversed. This is shown by the Meaux Abbey MS, in which the cantus firmus is placed most often in the treble. It seems significant that in LoF the cantus firmus never appears in the upper voice, but is presented either in the middle throughout in gymel fashion or as migrant cantus firmus alternately in the middle and tenor voice. Thus LoF again conforms to the English tradition with regard to cantus-firmus treatment. The appearance of migrant cantus firmus indicates how widely the technique was adopted in English music. In the following table the nine Masses in conductus style are analyzed as to treatment and source of their plainsongs.

LoF		POSITION OF CANTUS FIRMUS	Source: Sarum	Roman
No. 5	Sanctus	migrant (middle and tenor)	3	IV
No. 7	Sanctus	middle	1	II
No. 8	Sanctus	middle	9	XII
No. 9	Sanctus	migrant (middle and tenor)	5	XVII
No. 10	Agnus	middle	1	XII
No. 11	Agnus	"	2	IV
No. 12	Agnus	"	6	II
No. 13	Agnus	"	3	XIV
No. 14	Agnus	"	9	XV

The numbers of the Vatican edition have been added here solely for the sake of orientation. The plainsongs in LoF always follow the Sarum use and are numbered here after the *Graduale Sarisburiense*. Other Sarum books do not give the same order or the same number of plainsongs. Of course, not all the chants were set in polyphony; manuscripts of polyphonic music usually present settings of selected plainsongs and arrange them according to liturgical occasions. The Agnus series in LoF which definitely represents the original order of the manuscript begins with Sarum 1 and then continues with 2 6 3, etc. It may not be a coincidence that the corresponding series in OH runs 1 2 3 6. However, the liturgical designation of the chants was by no means invariable. In LoF, Sanctus No. 7, based on Sarum 1, is marked [*feria*] *tertia* in the manuscript and Agnus

[34] The use of cantus firmus in the repertory of OH has been analyzed on pp. 47 f.

No. 11 (Sarum 2) *Martyr.* The *Graduale Sarisburiense* classifies the same plainsongs as *in festis majoribus duplicibus* and *in festis minoribus duplicibus* respectively.

Our analytical table discloses that in seven compositions the chant lies in the middle; migrant cantus firmus occurs twice, and even here it starts as middle voice before it migrates to the tenor. Settings with the cantus firmus fixed in one voice frequently have crossing of the voices, which makes the chant at times the lowest-sounding part. Such crossings are mentioned in several treatises on improvised discant, but in these the chant is always assumed to be the fundamental voice. The conductus Masses in LoF and OH are perhaps a little too complex for being actual improvisations; the position of the cantus firmus in the middle and, especially, migrant cantus firmus make notation a necessity, yet the closeness to improvisation transpires unmistakably in their stark rhythmic simplicity.

Sanctus No. 5, the first part of which is printed in Ex. 1, gives us

Ex. 1. Anonymous: Sanctus with migrant cantus firmus.

a singularly clear idea of migrant cantus firmus because the chant is presented, as in most other compositions of the series, without any melodic embellishments. The final cadence of the excerpt on a passing six-four chord deserves some comment. In OH as well as LoF such endings are quite common in those settings in which the cantus firmus lies in the middle voice and ends with a repeated note. Here the stepwise descent to the final in the tenor practically rules out any other form of cadence.[35]

As to the treatment of the migrant cantus firmus, a small but significant detail should be noticed which easily escapes attention. The composer has distributed the notes of the chant (marked by asterisks) with special care: whenever the cantus firmus crosses over from one voice to the other (see the arrows in the example) the two parts involved come to a unison which guarantees a smooth and at the same time clearly audible transition. Except for the passage at *Dominus*, all crossings are effected in this manner, also in the unpublished remainder of the piece. The consistent use of unison at points that can literally be called "crucial" bespeaks a singularly deliberate and conscious approach to migrant cantus firmus to which no exact parallel has been discovered so far. It goes without saying that the voices presenting the chant must have been composed conjunctly, as they no longer submit to the additive methods of the time.[36] Other compositions with migrant cantus firmus make only sporadic use of "unison-crossings," as can be seen in LoF 9, or OH 96 (III, 18). The latter composition—which, incidentally, should have been transcribed in major prolation—lends itself to an illuminating comparison with LoF 5. Although both compositions treat the same plainsong in migrant fashion, the result is different enough to make us realize how wide the range of possibilities was within the limits of the same style.

The harmony of the conductus Masses is characterized by frequent use of full triads which may be combined in unorthodox progressions. The strangely chromatic beginning of LoF 10 should be compared with OH 128 (III, 125) and LoF 9 (III, 20). These passages illustrate the highly developed sense for sonority and color effects which, at that time, were among the main components of harmonic thinking. It should be observed how the original mode of the plain-

[35] This special type of cadential six-four chord brought about by cantus firmus is not discussed in Haydon's *Evolution of the Six-Four Chord*, Berkeley, 1933.

[36] The stylistic premises of migrant cantus firmus are discussed more fully on p. 46.

chant stands often in direct opposition to the harmonic progressions used; the discrepancy between "mode" and "harmony" is, in fact, the most absorbing musical feature of the conductus settings.

Before we leave the first group of compositions the question of plainsong variants must be raised. It has already been stated that the cantus firmi of LoF agree with the Sarum variants. This comes as a surprise, because Fountains Abbey observed the Cistercian, that is to say a monastic, use, which differs from the Diocesan uses of Salisbury and York. The musical differences between the latter have not yet been systematically explored, and what can be added here to the question is of necessity limited to the material at hand. The chant *ad usum Eboracensem* can be gleaned from a York Gradual of the early fifteenth century, now in the Bodleian Library (MS lat. lit. b 8), which is, according to Frere, the only comprehensive musical source of its kind.[37] The manuscript discloses that the York variant takes an intermediate position between the Sarum and Roman versions, sometimes agreeing with the former, sometimes with the latter, and sometimes going its own way. Certain peculiarities of the Sarum use are not to be found in York.[38] In order to see whether the York chant had any effect on the music of LoF, the plainsongs in LoF have been compared with the versions of the York Gradual (fols. 88–90). The result is always the same: whenever there is disagreement between Sarum and York it is the Sarum version that prevails in the polyphonic setting. In the case of LoF 7 the evidence is unmistakable. The Roman and York versions of this Sanctus are virtually the same, but the cantus firmus adopts the distinct Sarum variant. How far, on the other hand, the Cistercian and Sarum uses disagree or agree I cannot say, as I have not been able to locate a Cistercian Gradual of English origin. However, the point is immaterial for our discussion because a Cistercian missal of English origin, now in Stonyhurst College,[39] informs us that the Cistercians admitted the Sarum use at least optionally. The manuscript records several Prefaces,

[37] See the preliminary description in Frere, *Journal of Theological Studies* II (1901), 578.

[38] For example, the ending of the sequence *Johannes Jesu Christo* (see p. 61) and the *Exultet* finale, discussed in Kantorowicz, *Laudes Regiae*, University of California Publications in History, Vol. 33, Berkeley, 1946, 231 and 211. In either case the York Gradual agrees with the Vatican version. Frere, *loc. cit.*, has made some selected comparisons between Sarum and York which show in part agreement and in part disagreement.

[39] MS II; see the list in Frere's *Biblioteca Musico-Liturgica*.

the last of which bears the inscription *secundum usum Sarum*.[40] This is an interesting indication of how the Cistercians made allowance for the English tradition of plainsong. The Fountains fragment confirms the point also with regard to the chants of the Mass. If we did not have this information one could easily jump to the conclusion that the presence of Sarum chants in the manuscript proves that the compositions could not possibly have originated at Fountains Abbey. We see now that this assumption does not hold; but neither can the opposite be asserted. The place of origin is uncertain, but it may be the same as that of OH in view of the numerous correspondences. At any rate, the fact that the Mass settings elaborate Sarum chants apparently did not disturb the singers at Fountains Abbey.

The second type of composition, Masses in free treble style, is represented only by Gloria No. 2, which OH ascribes to Rowland, a composer about whom nothing is known. True to type, the composition entrusts the words to the treble, which is led against the two supporting parts with frequent melodic clashes and lively and rather angular rhythms. They suggest that the author belonged to the older generation of composers in OH. The piece is remarkable for a syncopated hocket section which abounds with dissonances and for the fact that the section at *agimus tibi* returns at the end as some sort of *da capo* with different text—a rather exceptional occurrence in Masses of this type.

The four-voice Gloria No. 16 (= No. 4) belongs to the third group. In this type two upper voices form a vocal duet, usually in rapid declamation and often with imitation, set off against a more sustained accompaniment of two or more instrumental parts. The style was cultivated especially in the Italian motet and Mass of the turn of the century, to a lesser degree also in France, and was taken over by English musicians, as the repertory of OH attests. The duet of Gloria No. 16 is hardly imitative at all but for a few snatches of rhythmic imitation and contains, like the four-part pieces in OH, numerous dissonant appoggiaturas. The voices run on with practically no rests, and no attempt is made at alternate pairing of voices, which is characteristic of Italian compositions of the type. The fragmentary Gloria LoF 6 also falls, apparently, into the third group, if we can judge by

40 Fol. 149v–151v. I am indebted for this information to the Reverend H. C. Chadwick, Librarian of Stonyhurst College, Lancashire, who was kind enough to check the MS for me.

the rapid declamation of the extant voice and by its mode of preservation. It stands on a recto, with the rest of the folio being taken up by
the following Sanctus. The other voices were recorded on the opposite verso, now lost, and since the verso usually begins with the highest
voice, we may infer that the lost superius and the extant voice formed
a vocal duet which was supported by one or two parts.

The isorhythmic Masses constitute, next to the first category, the
largest group, comprising Nos. 1, 3, and 15. Again we notice a close
parallelism to the repertory of OH, in which isorhythmic technique
is much more common than has generally been thought. The austere
four-voice Credo LoF 15, with its introductory canon and a verbal
"canon" prescribing cancrizans motion in the tenor, has already been
discussed in connection with the compositions in OH [41] and need not
concern us here. The two other Masses, both fairly extended compositions, are noteworthy for their sophisticated modification of isorhythmic principles. Gloria No. 1 (see Plate 2) is built on a tenor
and contratenor which carry no text and which are both isorhythmic.
The melodic design of the tenor suggests Gregorian origin, but in
the absence of any textual designation the identification of the melody
would be a hopeless task if there were no other evidence on which
to proceed. Fortunately, a few hints can be discovered in this case,
as will be seen presently.

The isorhythmic structure can be analyzed as follows. The pair
of lower voices comprises three *taleae* of fourteen measures each,
which, though notated only once, must be stated twice; after that the
taleae are stated twice in halved values (comprising now seven measures each), though they are written again only once. The entire Mass
setting contains four *colores* (of three *taleae* each), of which the first
two stand to the next two in the relation 2:1. The diminution divides
the composition into two major parts of uneven length. The upper
voices have a structure of their own which partly conforms to and
partly overlaps that of the lower voices. Superius and alto form a
curious duet in which sections with and without text consistently
alternate. In the first part of the composition the textless (melismatic
or instrumental?) sections observe an isorhythmic pattern that agrees
with the *talea*, while the ones equipped with text are freely composed. Hence, each voice is isorhythmic only in alternating sections
but in combination they present a strictly isorhythmic strand. Begin-

[41] P. 66.

ning with the diminution in the tenor, all voices are isorhythmic throughout, with the additional complication that three isorhythmic periods in the upper pair of voices overlap two *colores* of the lower pair.

The strange idea of distributing an isorhythmic pattern alternately over two voices has, as far as I know, only one parallel, namely the four-voice Credo by Pennard in OH (II, 241).[42] This composition is also divided into two major parts. In view of the highly individual treatment of isorhythmic technique, it is tempting to assume that the two compositions were written by the same author even though they have no thematic or melodic features in common. It is true that the ascription to Pennard would rest on very slender evidence, yet the idea is intriguing enough to be pursued a little further. If the anonymous Gloria were really by Pennard, there should be some relationship other than the similarity of isorhythmic technique. Inasmuch as direct musical similarities do not exist, there may be at least a liturgical connection. Pennard's Credo is based on the Trinity antiphon *Te iure laudant* (*Ant. Sar.*, 293), and the thought struck me that the Gloria might have been composed for the same feast. Turning to the place in the Antiphonal where the antiphon of the Credo is recorded, I was much gratified to discover that the tenor melody of the anonymous Gloria appears, indeed, on the very same folio. This chant, the versus of the antiphon *O beata et benedicta*, carries the words *Tibi laus, tibi gloria, tibi gratiarum actio* and is quoted in the Gloria from beginning to end. It is significant that Pennard's Credo, too, states the underlying antiphon in its entirety, not merely a fragment thereof, as was the custom in isorhythmic compositions. Moreover, the agreement between the chant as recorded in the Antiphonal and the cantus firmus is so exact,[43] including even the repeated notes, that the chance that another plainsong of the same mode was used is practically ruled out. The surprising outcome of what was at first a very tentative idea gives unexpected support to the ascription to Pennard. We may assume, therefore, that the two compositions were written for the same occasion (*in festo Trinitatis*) by the same composer.

Gloria No. 3 likewise presents a rather peculiar modification of

---

[42] See No. 13 of the list of isorhythmic compositions in OH (p. 66), where a detailed analysis of its structure is presented.

[43] There is only one small variant: the ligature *b-a* on *glo*[*ria*] reads a second higher in the Mass tenor.

isorhythmic technique. It is based on a short tenor consisting of only six notes, *a g f g a g*, which are stated nine times in the manner of an ostinato or *pes*, so typical of English motets in the fourteenth century. The six notes form two *taleae* of three notes and six measures each, so that the whole runs up to eighteen *taleae* and nine *colores*. The underlying structure may be described as a unique assimilation of a *pes* to isorhythmic procedure. This interesting combination is one of the many hybrid forms of medieval music that resulted from the adaptation of a specifically English technique to Continental practices.

The contratenor is not expressed in notation but merely implied by the "canon": *hic tenor est arsis and contra sit tibi thesis*. The meaning of this somewhat ambiguous direction can be clarified through the transcription of the piece. The contratenor is a strict melodic inversion of the tenor at the fifth below. Hence "arsis" becomes "thesis," and vice versa. It may be added that the lower right-hand corner of the folio originally contained a few notes which were subsequently erased, but imperfectly, so that some of them are still faintly visible. They can be identified as the resolution of the contratenor. As is usual with illegible passages, the reading becomes certain only when one already knows how the melody should go. The unorthodox placement of the resolution on the side of the folio indicates that somebody must have written out the puzzle and that he or a later user must have thought better of it and erased it again so as to make the other singers use not only their throats but also their heads.

Aside from the implied contratenor the Gloria calls for another one, marked *de se* in the manuscript. This contratenor is indeed "independent of the tenor," as its designation asserts. It comprises only twenty-four measures and ends with a *custos* or "direct" indicating repetition. The part carries no text and must be stated five times, the last repeat being cut short by the end. Each *color* falls in turn into four *taleae* of six measures each which are grouped in contrasting pairs such as a a' b b' :||, a unique disposition. The treble, finally, the only voice provided with text, is through-composed and falls into three isorhythmic periods of thirty-six measures each (the last one is three measures short). The result is a very complex overlap on three different levels: one period of the treble corresponds to six *taleae* and one and a half *colores* of the independent contratenor, and to six *taleae* and three *colores* of the lower voices. This arrangement is made even more complex by the paired *taleae* of the independent contratenor, which straddle the divisions of the isorhythmic periods.

Since in all compositions with a *pes* the harmonic range is necessarily restricted, the Gloria vacillates between three chords; but the composer has nevertheless achieved considerable variety within the narrow limits. The treble contains several isomelic or very nearly isomelic passages which coincide with the isorhythmic returns. They have obviously been prompted by the unchanging harmonies of the lower pair of voices.

The fragmentary Gloria of Brit. Mus. Cotton MS Tiberius A VII, fol. 38 v may round off the discussion of isorhythmic Masses because it belongs stylistically to the same repertory. In the hope that a complete version may perhaps turn up in the future, the incipit, which is unfortunately in part illegible, is given here (Ex. 2). Neither voice is complete in the manuscript.

Ex. 2. Anonymous: Fragmentary Gloria.

Its fragmentary state notwithstanding, some conclusions can be drawn from the music. The two extant parts are upper voices which divide between them the complete liturgical text, and since duets of this kind are usually accompanied by two instrumental parts it is safe to assume that we have here the remnants of a four-voice composition. It falls into three contrasted isorhythmic periods which are stated three times. The lower voices consisted in all probability of three *taleae* which were repeated with different time signatures, the last being in diminution. The last major period ends with a section in hocket, quite common in isorhythmic works, which appears, of course, three times. The first isorhythmic period deserves special comment for a striking feature: the upper voice presents a distinct rhythmic pattern of nine measures which recurs in exactly the same rhythm but different melodic garb eight measures later in the lower voice. The identity of rhythm at different places in different voices does not coincide with the general isorhythmic scheme; rather, it represents a strange correlation and integration of the parts by means of rhythm. In view of the length of the section, this "isorhythmic imitation," as the phenomenon may be called, must be deliberate. Short melodic or rhythmic imitations or even canon may occasionally be found in isorhythmic compositions, but isorhythmic imitation is a unique procedure and no example analogous to it is known to exist.[44]

With the fifth and last group of compositions we leave the Masses and turn to the isorhythmic motets proper. LoF Nos. 17 and 18 both fall into this category. In *Humane lingua*, a fairly short polytextual motet, a lively duet in the high register contrasts with a pair of textless instrumental parts in slower tempo. There is some hocket writing in the upper voices, and the harmony shows, like many English compositions of the time, a predilection for sonorous full triads in which the third is often placed conspicuously on top. The tenor quotes without melodic elaboration the entire melody of a Sarum *Deo gratias*,[45] and it is significant in this connection that the two texts of the motet close likewise on the word *gratias*. The old tradition of the trope which runs like a red thread through English medieval music is still clearly in evidence here. Strangely enough, the tenor lacks in the manuscript its rightful designation. Only the alternative voice is inscribed *solus tenor et cantetur de* [?] *Deo gratias*. Now, of the two tenors the *solus tenor* is precisely the one that does not reproduce the plainsong, because it combines the essential notes of tenor and contratenor in a new line which makes possible a performance reduced to three voices. The erroneous designation betrays a lack of familiarity with the function of fundamental and substitute parts.

A similar lack of familiarity is betrayed in the notation of the isorhythmic repeats. The two isorhythmic periods of the motet are stated twice each and coincide with the two *taleae* of tenor and contratenor which are repeated in diminution by three. Quite unnecessarily the scribe has written out the repeat in reduced note values, as he has done also in Gloria No. 1. In both instances it would have been far simpler to indicate it briefly and clearly by a changed-mensuration sign, as OH and many other manuscripts of the time do.

[44] Other remarkable deviations from the common isorhythmic technique practiced in France may be seen in Italo-Flemish music of c. 1400; cf. the description of the isorhythmic motets by Ciconia in Korte's *Studie zur Geschichte der Musik in Italien*, 1933, 33.

[45] *Grad. Sar.*, Pl. 19ˣ. The chant has been used repeatedly in polyphonic compositions; for a little-known example see the *modulus* published by Handschin in *Acta Musicologica* X (1938), 28.

To the experienced singer of isorhythmic motets it was a matter of simple routine to resume the various diminutions of the tenor from the original notation. The scribe of LoF proves himself again overly cautious, as in the case of the special sign for alteration. His attitude suggests that LoF originated in a provincial atmosphere where thorough acquaintance with isorhythmic procedure was not taken for granted.

Of the second motet, *Alme pater,* only superius and tenor have come down to us. Its structure is simple: three isorhythmic periods of the upper voice correspond to three *taleae* of the tenor. There is no *color;* the tenor melody runs through to the end, and its melodic behavior, frequent skips, sevenths, etc., preclude a plainsong origin. Moreover, the tenor carries only the first words of the motet text, and this manner of designation usually suggests a specially composed melody. Although no rests are given in the manuscript, the tenor enters only at the twelfth measure. The introduction stands outside of the isorhythmic scheme. Such introductory duets were not uncommon and were often canonic, as it is in Credo No. 15 (OH III [68]). It lies close at hand to try canon here too and to see whether or not the lost upper voice can be partially reconstructed. Indeed, the extant voice lends itself to smooth canonic writing up to the beginning of the isorhythmic section. The entry of the canonic voice has been marked in the thematic catalogue by a *signum congruentiae,* although it is not present in the manuscript. The existence of a second upper voice implied in the canonic introduction and the rhythmic design of the tenor leave no room for doubt that the motet is a four-part composition.

The above comments, scattered though they are, will have shown how it is possible to extract a surprisingly large amount of both supplementary and new information from a small fragment. The method of investigation has been to examine first mode of preservation, order, and repertory of the manuscript, and then style, type, and structure of the compositions contained therein. These findings must be seen in the perspective of a larger repertory, and only through integration in it do they become meaningful. That LoF complements OH was already known, but a closer inspection has revealed a far-reaching agreement as to types of composition, cantus-firmus treatment, and isorhythmic procedure. Not only does LoF complete certain fragmentary compositions, but it enlarges the series of conductus Masses which give OH one of its outstanding characteristics. OH in turn discloses the authorship of one composition and suggests by implication that of another. In OH we have proof of a strong Continental influence and even of a direct share in the Italian repertory (Zacharia's Gloria, OH 30); in LoF the same influence is patent in the isorhythmic compositions and those in Italian style, but their harmonies and general "sound dialect" suggest that they are probably all of English origin. This inference is supported by hints of provincialism which make it very likely that the Fountains fragment was compiled in York even if the settings with Sarum plainsongs were not necessarily composed there.

In order to arrive at these conclusions it has sometimes been necessary to push the analysis to small and apparently pointless details, but what has the appearance of overly fine needlework and pedantic enumeration of minutiae may assume heightened significance in a larger context and reflect in turn on the larger context itself.

IV

Holy-Week Music and Carols at
Meaux Abbey

1. THE MEAUX ABBEY MANUSCRIPT

OUR KNOWLEDGE of English music of the fifteenth century has been enriched recently by the discovery of two manuscripts, one of Italo-German and the other of English origin. They constitute the most important and substantial addition to the known sources of English music since the discovery of the Old Hall MS. The first, the Aosta MS (Ao),[1] offers a collection of Continental music from the first half of the century as well as a separate series of almost exclusively English compositions. The circumstance that the English pieces are separately recorded is a striking and noteworthy feature which the Aosta MS has in common with another Continental source, MS lat. 471 of the Biblioteca Estense in Modena. In the arrangement of their contents the two manuscripts recognize the existence of a national English school in the fifteenth century.

The second collection, the subject of this study, is Egerton MS 3307 of the British Museum.[2] It is the largest and most interesting manu-

[1] De Van, "A Recently Discovered Source of Early Fifteenth-Century Polyphonic Music, the Aosta MS," in *Musica Disciplina* II (1948), 5.

[2] Schofield (Part I) and Bukofzer (Part II), "A Newly Discovered 15th-Century MS of the English Chapel Royal," in MQ XXXII (1946), 509 and XXXIII (1947), 38. Part I contains a general description and a thematic catalogue, Part II transcriptions of the *Missa Brevis* and the St. Luke Passion. The works will be cited here according to the thematic list, though the numbering, as will be seen below, is not always accurate.

script of English origin found in recent years, and its discovery is a musicological event of the first order. There is no unanimity about its place of origin. Schofield regards the collection as the product of St. George's Chapel in Windsor because it presents the hymn *Salve festa dies* with a special stanza in honor of St. George.[3] However, while this proves that St. George was honored at the place where the manuscript originated, this need not necessarily be the Windsor Chapel.[4] Recent research by Richard L. Greene has established that the dialect of the English carols points in the direction of York. He has furthermore discovered that the Ivy carol (No. 31) refers to the village Hye (Hyth) which formerly belonged to Meaux Abbey in Yorkshire.[5] This Cistercian house, known especially for its patronage of letters and arts, is in all likelihood the place where the manuscript was written. The collection may therefore be called the Meaux Abbey MS (LoM).

In contrast to the disparate layers of Ao, our collection consists of only two parts. The first presents a unified liturgical repertory, certainly of English origin but unfortunately anonymous throughout. While Ao concentrates on the Ordinary of the Mass, the liturgical part of LoM singles out the services of Holy Week. The second, quite distinct, part contains sacred and secular carols and cantilenas. With regard to contents and musical style, LoM is the more unified but also the more provincial source; because of the local restrictions of its repertory it possesses a special interest even though it does not always reach the artistic level of the music of Ao.

The manuscript was probably written during the reign of Henry VI, about 1450, and dates from approximately the same time as the Selden MS (OS),[6] though the contents of the latter may be a little older. The two sources have several points of contact with regard to mode of notation, individual pieces, and general repertory. Both use full-black notation with scattered full-red and void-red notes; both contain liturgical compositions of the Sarum Processional alongside

[3] Schofield, *loc. cit.*, 514.

[4] The stanza in honor of St. George appears also in a Sarum Processional (Bodleian MS lat. lit. e 7), written for a London church during the time of Henry V, who, incidentally, is mentioned in a subsequent stanza of the London variant.

[5] Dr. Greene, who very unselfishly placed his findings at my disposal, will give particulars in a forthcoming study. It may be added here that the motto *Mieulx en de cy*, which is inscribed at the head of the St. Luke Passion, has not yet been identified. This clue may eventually clear up the exact provenance of the manuscript.

[6] Oxford, Bodl. Libr., MS Selden B 26; facsimile reproduction in *Early Bodleian Music* (ed. by Sir John Stainer, 1901), I, Pls. XXXVII–XCVII.

of carols and cantilenas, and they agree even in certain pieces of the latter group. They differ, however, in the selection and arrangement of the music. While the liturgical compositions of OS consist chiefly of Marian antiphons which are indiscriminately mixed with carols, those of LoM belong essentially to Holy Week and are clearly kept apart from their non-liturgical companions. The Meaux Abbey MS is the more carefully planned and orderly collection, as it is unified internally by the liturgical purpose (first part) and the carol form (second part), and externally by the use of score notation. This notation is to be found also in OS but is employed there less consistently.

There are three compositions in LoM that by their use of *cantus collateralis* or choir-book notation fall outside of the general pattern. The very first piece of the collection, *Gloria laus et honor* (Nos. 1–2),[7] is written in such manner. It is preserved in a gathering consisting originally of eight leaves, of which only the last three now remain. The musical characters differ slightly from those employed in the remainder of the first part, especially the clefs, the key signatures, and the final longs, and thus support Schofield's suspicion that the piece was probably not written by the chief scribe. Moreover, it does not conform to the liturgical order. In all likelihood this composition does not belong to the original repertory, so that the discrepancy in notation is easily explainable. The two other compositions notated in separate parts are *O potores* (No. 51) and *Cantemus Domino* (Nos. 52–53), which form what was originally the end of the collection. The two cantilenas (Nos. 54 and 55) which now conclude the manuscript are clearly additions by a different scribe, hastily written with the initials left unfilled. *O potores* and *Cantemus* are the only genuine exceptions to the use of score notation in the original collection. The reason for the change of notation lies in their musical style: they are the only motets proper and therefore call for choir-book notation. By virtue of their exceptional form and notation they were placed by the scribe at the end.

A few particulars of the description and the thematic catalogue should be corrected. In fascicle VIII, which marks the beginning of the second part (fol. 49), two leaves are canceled. These are leaves 4 and 8 (not 3 and 6) corresponding to fols. 52 and 56 of the modern foliation. Fortunately, however, this does not mean that the music

---

[7] Nos. 1–2 form one composition. No. 1 is a fragment (only tenor and contratenor have been preserved); the continuation (No. 2) is complete.

of two folios is lost. Only that of fol. 52 is gone because the leaf was torn out after the manuscript had been completed. Fol. 56 existed as a stub only from the very beginning. This can be seen in the fact that the carol *Ave rex angelorum,* which appears on two opposite folios (now numbered 55v and 57 respectively), runs continuously from left to right without a gap. The two cantilenas added at the end by a later hand are partly erased. The textless beginning of No. 54 is incomplete as well as faulty in the manuscript. A transcription of the piece discloses that the burden should begin like the chorus section and read as given in Ex. 1. It should be added to the thematic

Ex. 1. Corrected beginning of a textless carol or cantilena.

catalogue that No. 55 contains a three-voice stanza beginning with the words [*Puer*] *natus hodie.* Most of the words and much of the music has been scratched out, but luckily the music can be restored without loss from the shape of the erasures. The composition is incomplete, as the stanza breaks off at the end of the page. The continuation which is indicated by custos or "directs" was never entered in the manuscript.

It can be gathered from the small number of correspondences that LoM stands, on the whole, fairly isolated among other known English sources. This is probably due to the fact that no other collection of music for a special service has come down to us. Most of the concordances are carols, several of which recur in OS, the most closely related source. In the following list of similarities Schofield's references have been somewhat expanded, even in the liturgical part, but the entire list comprises at present no more than eight compositions:

Meaux Abbey MS	Other MSS
PART I	
No. 10 *Inventor rutili*	Cambridge, Magdalen Coll., Pepys MS 1236, f. 62v–63 (first stanza only, a few variants)

No. 17 *Alleluia V. Salve Virgo*   Oxford, Magdalen Coll., B II 3.16,
                                          Fragm. C, f. 89

PART II

No. 22 *David ex progenie*   OS, f. 24v–25
No. 24 *Novus sol de virgine*   OS, f. 25v
No. 39 *Ecce quod natura*   OS, f. 27; see also Bodl. Ashmole
                                          1393, f. 69[8] (transposed to the fourth
                                          below, considerable variants)

No. 41 *I pray yow all* (Greene,
          No. 337a)   OS, f. 5.
No. 45 *Omnes una gaudeamus*   OS, f. 11 (variants)
No. 46 *Alleluia pro virgine*   OS, f. 16

It will be seen that the correspondences of the second part point
exclusively to OS, with the exception of No. 39, which occurs also in
a third source, but here with noteworthy variants. It is so far the only
piece of LoM known to exist in three versions. The unexpected
correspondence between LoM and the Pepys MS commands special
attention because it relates the liturgical repertory of Meaux Abbey
with a much more provincial one, probably from the North of England,[9] which dates from c. 1475 and shows in general a rather primitive style. It is interesting to note that many of the liturgical texts
from the Sarum Processional that are contained in LoM appear also,
but with different music, in the Pepys MS.[10] In the latter source they
appear as unpretentious functional music for the service and are
recorded without any clear liturgical order. The other liturgical
correspondence occurs in an undescribed fragment of English origin,
first noticed by Dom Anselm Hughes. The leaf is one of the many
surprises that old bindings hold in store for us.[11]

Even if the manuscript were less obviously English in external

[8] Facsimile in *Early Bodleian Music*, I, Pl. XXVII.

[9] A northern origin of the MS has been suggested by Daphne M. Bird in her thesis
"A Review of Fifteenth-Century Church Music in England, with Special Reference to
the Pepys MS 1236," *Abstracts of Dissertations . . . in the University of Cambridge*
(1942–43), 32.

[10] The texts that the two MSS have in common are LoM Nos. 1–2 (and 4), 5, 10, 11, 12,
13, 15, 16, 17, 18, and 19.

[11] It belongs to a collection of detached leaves some of which contain fragmentary
motets, Mass sections, and other liturgical pieces from the fourteenth and fifteenth centuries. The folio preserving *All. Salve Virgo* was originally a verso, though it is now
listed as a recto. The other side of the leaf gives the end of a *Nunc dimittis* (beginning
with *oculi mei*) in three-voice score. The style of the piece corresponds to that of the old
layer of OH, the cantus firmus lies unadorned in the middle voice.

appearance (handwriting, illuminations, etc.) and did not in part use the English language, its insular character and origin could be proved conclusively by the numerous political and topical references. The stanza on St. George in *Salve festa dies* apostrophizes this favorite English saint as *pugil Anglorum*. Another carol in his honor, *Enfors we us*,[12] mentions the battle of Agincourt as a matter of past history. The carol *Saint Thomas honour we* is dedicated to the English martyr Thomas à Becket, and the cantilena *Exultavit cor* to the memory of Henry V, the composer-king. The inner strife in England —Schofield plausibly suggests the Wars of the Roses—is the topic of *Anglia tibi turbidas,* and England is mentioned again, this time together with France, in the cantilena *Benedicite Deo,* which reads in the fourth stanza: *Anglia et Francia, cunctaque imperia.* The carol *Ivy is good and glad,* finally, is based on the Ivy cult, a favorite topic of the English carol.

2. HOLY-WEEK MUSIC AND OTHER SACRED COMPOSITIONS

LITURGICAL ASPECTS

The liturgical part of our collection includes mainly compositions for Holy Week, followed by a few other sacred pieces for various occasions (Nos. 17–19). To these must be added the motet *Cantemus Domino* (No. 52–53), which, though it does not externally belong to the first part, should be included here because of its liturgical tenor.

The most significant external characteristic of the first part is the planned sequence of compositions. Aside from No. 1, which, as we have seen, does not belong to the original repertory, the entire Holy Week series (Nos. 2–16) appears in the liturgical order of the Sarum Processional.[18] Such close observance of liturgical function is a unique feature, not even distantly approximated in any other English collection of polyphonic music of the fifteenth century.[14] We would have to go back to the *clausula* and motet collections of the thirteenth century to find sources of comparable strictness, with the difference that the *clausulae* belong to the Proper of the Mass, while our com-

---

[12] Text edited by Schofield, *loc. cit.,* 5.

[18] Text edition by W. G. Henderson, Leeds, 1882.

[14] In Continental sources of the time we find at least groups of pieces within larger collections arranged in liturgical order—for example, groups of the Proper in the Trent Codices (*Monumenta Polyphoniae Liturgicae,* Series II, Vol. 1) and the Office for St. James by Dufay in BL, fol. 121.

positions belong to a special rite. The liturgical cycle begins on Palm Sunday with *En rex venit* and then runs through Holy Week, ending on Easter Monday with *Dicant nunc Judei*.

Aside from its order the series is interesting also because it reveals which chants were performed in polyphony. Plainsong performance was apparently still the rule, and only a few selected items of the liturgy were set solemnly in part music. Closer scrutiny discloses that the items so honored are those chants or sections thereof that are assigned not to the full chorus but to one or several soloists. In its solo polyphony the Meaux Abbey collection clearly continues the old liturgical tradition which associated part music essentially with solo performance and choral singing with unison performance. Infractions of this rule occur as early as the thirteenth century, but only with the rise of choral polyphony in the first half of the fifteenth century do they become so numerous as to cease to be exceptional.[15] The most prominent Gregorian form honored in Meaux Abbey by part music is the processional hymn or *versus*, which appears in our collection no less than six times.[16] It shares the strophic form with the ordinary hymn but distinguishes in text and music between variable stanzas and an invariable burden or what may be called, in analogy to liturgical practice, the *repetenda*. In performance these two units consistently alternate as solo and chorus. According to the rubrics of the Sarum Processional, the *repetenda* is stated first as solo (in our case in the polyphonic version provided in LoM) and is then immediately repeated by the chorus (probably as plainsong in unison); after that the stanzas follow in solo polyphony in alternation with the choral *repetenda*. Like most other sources of this sort, LoM records only the polyphonic portions of the music. The monophonic portions were supplied from the Gradual or Processional.

The Meaux MS records polyphonic settings of all processional hymns of Holy Week required by the Sarum Processional, save *Crux fidelis*, which belongs to the Good Friday service (Adoration of the Cross). This omission is startling, as we know from a composition by Dunstable [17] that this hymn, too, was sung in polyphony. Our collection contains not a single item from the Good Friday liturgy; it turns from Maundy Thursday (No. 9) directly to Easter

---

15 See the outline in the essay "The Beginnings of Choral Polyphony" in this book.
16 Nos. 3, 4 (and 1–2), 9, 10, 11, and 13.
17 DTOe, Vols. 14–15, 183.

Saturday (Nos. 10–12). The fact that there is no break in the manuscript at this place implies that in Meaux Abbey polyphony was excluded from the Good Friday service. The series of LoM is interrupted only in the third gathering, recording the beginning of the St. Matthew Passion (Palm Sunday). The missing leaves contained the end of the Passion and the beginning of the Kyrie, but probably no other piece, as the Passion is a rather extended composition. The Mass belongs, as its plainsong discloses, to the *feriae* or weekdays and stands at the right place in the series. We may infer, therefore, that in spite of the gap the manuscript presents the complete series of chants that were polyphonically performed during Holy Week.

In his description of LoM Schofield has already collated the texts with the Sarum Processional. His findings are supplemented here by the corresponding plainsongs, which can all be identified from the various liturgical books of the Sarum use.[18] In the following the contents of the first part are listed in groups according to the days of Holy Week, with additional references to the directions of performance, as found in the rubrics, and to the source of the plainsong, whether published or not. In each instance it has been noted how the chant has been used, as this point is vital for the stylistic discussion.

Palm Sunday

En rex venit (No. 3), three-voice *versus* or "antiphon" sung by "tres clerici" in alternation with the chorus: This chant shows some affinity to the processional hymn, as several of its stanzas are musically related. Yet the form is exceptional: the text is continuous and the music essentially through-composed; the three choral stanzas which are written in prose begin with a similar motive, while the three solo verses, which are rhymed, begin differently. As is to be expected, the manuscript records only the solo verses *En rex venit, Hic est qui,* and *Hic est ille.* We may infer from the omission of the choral sections that these were sung in plainsong. Source of the chant: *Grad. Sar.,* 81. The melody is lightly paraphrased in the upper voice throughout except at the words *in stola,* where it momentarily migrates, because of the high pitch, to the middle voice.

Gloria laus et honor (Nos. 1–2, and 4), two different settings of the famous processional hymn to be sung by "septem pueri," but

---

[18] For the complete titles of the Sarum publications see the List of Abbreviations. Unpublished sources will be fully cited in the text.

set here for three parts in the usual combination of men's and boy's
voices: Source of the chant: *Grad. Sar.*, 83. The first setting, so far
as it is completely preserved, presents the plainsong in migrant fashion. Since, however, the two extant voices of the fragmentary beginning show no trace of the chant, it was probably carried in the treble
in this section. We can put this assumption to the test by supplying
the missing voice on the basis of the plainsong. If slightly ornamented
in the style of the other compositions, it fits so well to the lower voices
that the setting can indeed be restored without running the risk of
recomposing it (Ex. 2).

Ex. 2. *Gloria laus* with upper voice restored.

It will be seen from the excerpt that the composition is written
in simple conductus style, which would not ordinarily call for notation in *cantus collateralis*. The fact that this notation is used deliberately if unnecessarily confirms by internal evidence the exceptional position of the piece.

The second setting of the text (No. 4) agrees with the first one in
general style but differs in its cantus-firmus treatment. The beginning of the chant is quoted quite clearly in the lowest voice, but
after the words *rex Christe* the music continues freely. The subsequent stanzas, especially *Cetus in excelsis,* occasionally allude to the

plainsong, now in one voice and now in another, but some of these resemblances may well be fortuitous, as they would arise unavoidably in any composition using the same mode as the chant. At any rate, we cannot speak here of any consistent presentation of the borrowed melody. It is significant, too, that numerous cadences do not agree with those of the plainsong.

Unus autem ex ipsis Caiphas (No. 5), verse of the antiphon or respond [19] *Collegerunt pontifices*, sung by "tres clerici": The polyphonic setting comprises only the solo section. The chant (*Grad. Sar.*, 84) lies in the treble with little ornamentation.

Passio . . . secundum Matheum (No. 6), incomplete at the end: Only the *turbae* and the words assigned to persons other than Christ and the Evangelist have been set (in three parts). The usual recitation tone for the Passion (*Grad Sar.* print of 1507, fol. 89) [20] has not been employed in the setting.

Weekdays of Holy Week

Mass (Nos. 7a–7d) [21] including the Kyrie (incomplete beginning), Sanctus (and Benedictus), and Agnus Dei: The omission of the Gloria and Credo, customary on weekdays, makes the Mass a *Missa brevis*. That the work was to be sung on weekdays transpires also from the cantus firmi which are designed *in feriis* (*Grad. Sar.* 9*, 17*, and 18* respectively). The chant is elaborated in all movements in the treble.

Wednesday of Holy Week

Passio . . . secundum Lucam (No. 8): [22] As in the St. Matthew Passion, only the *turbae* and similar sections of the text are composed without reference to the customary Passion tone. The numerous declamatory passages on a monotone in both Passions suggest that the composer either adopted another *tonus lectionis* or freely imitated the style of liturgical recitation.

[19] The designation varies in the Sarum books.

[20] Pollard 15862, accessible in the microfilm series *Books Printed before 1600*, Carton 135, University Microfilms, Ann Arbor. A section of the chant has been published in Peter Wagner, *Einführung in die Gregorianischen Melodien*, III (*Gregorianische Formenlehre*), 248, after a MS of the Vatican Library. I have consulted also a 15th-century version in Cambridge, Trinity College MS B 11 13. This beautifully illuminated source notes the chant of all four Passions in significant excerpts. The recitation tone agrees essentially with that of the Sarum Gradual.

[21] Transcription in MQ XXXIII (1947), 39.

[22] Transcription, *ibid.*, 43.

Maundy Thursday

O redemptor sume carnem (No. 9), processional hymn sung by "tres pueri" in alternation with the chorus: The *repetenda* and several stanzas are set for three parts, other stanzas for two or four parts. Only the *repetenda* is based on the chant (not in *Grad. Sar.;* but see print of 1507, fol. xcv; *Proc. Sar.* 1530, fol. lxiv v; [23] and Worcester Antiphonal, *Pal. mus.* XII, 212). The verses are composed freely (see Ex. 5 below).

Good Friday

[No polyphonic composition included]

Holy Saturday

Inventor rutili (No. 10), processional hymn sung by "duo clerici," set here for three voices throughout: The paraphrased plainsong (*Grad. Sar.,* 104) lies in the treble. Although all verses have the same melody, the chant is not simply repeated with different words but is elaborated differently each time. The resulting set of five "variations" or harmonizations shows considerable ingenuity in the diversified treatment of the cadence. The opening measures of the first and third verses (Ex. 3) clearly demonstrate how diversely the same melody could be articulated.[24]

Rex sanctorum (No. 11), processional hymn or "litany" (*Proc. Sar.*) sung by "tres clerici": In the *repetenda* as well as the subsequent six stanzas the treble elaborates the chant (*Grad. Sar.,* 114). We have here a set of six "variations," but there is less contrasting treatment than in the preceding set.

Alleluia, V. Confitemini Domino (No. 12), sung by "duo clerici": The two-voice setting comprises only the solo sections; the plainsong (*Grad. Sar.,* 115) appears in the treble.

Easter Sunday

Salve festa dies (Nos. 13 and 13a), processional hymn sung by "tres clerici," provided here with five sets of words for Easter, Ascension Day, and other feasts: It is again the treble that carries the

[23] Pollard 16240, University Microfilms, Carton 95.

[24] The *repetenda* of this hymn is published in Bukofzer, "English Church Music of the XVth Century" in *The New Oxford History of Music*. It paraphrases the same melody and should be compared with Ex. 3.

Ex. 3. First and third verses from *Inventor rutili.*

1.Quam - vis   in - nu - me - ro   si - de - [re]

3.Splen - dent   er - go   tu - is   mu - ne - ri   bus

chant (*Grad. Sar.,* 116). The verses are followed by a second three-voice setting of *Salve festa dies* (No. 13a, not mentioned in the thematic catalogue) which presents the plainsong in the treble also, but with hardly any embellishments. It is interesting to compare the ornate with the simple version of the melody (see Ex. 9). The purpose of the second *repetenda,* which is much shorter than the first one because of the lack of ornamentation, is not quite clear. It may have been sung between the stanzas for the sake of brevity; if so, the repeats would have been done by way of exception in polyphony by the chorus. It may, on the other hand, be an alternative or independent composition.

Crucifixum in carne (No. 14), verse of the antiphon *Sedit angelus* for "tres clerici": The plainsong (*Ant. Sar.,* 243) lies in the upper voice of the three-part setting.

Alleluia, V. Laudate pueri (No. 15) sung by "tres pueri" but set here for two voices: As in No. 12, only the solo sections are recorded. The music is freely composed; at any rate, it makes no use of the two known versions of the Alleluia (*Ant. Sar.,* 239; one of the versions appears also in *Grad. Sar.,* 123).

Easter Monday

Dicant nunc Judei (No. 16), verse of the antiphon *Christus re-surgens* for "duo clerici" and written here for three parts: It may be sung also on Easter Sunday before *Salve festa dies.* The liturgical melody (*Ant. Sar.,* 242; *Proc. Mon.,* 66) lies in the treble.

Other Liturgical Occasions

Alleluia, V. Salve virgo mater (No. 17) for the feast of the Puri-fication of B.V.M.: [25] The chant, not available in any published edition, is to be found in the Sarum Gradual of 1507 (fol. xliii of the *Comm. Sanctorum*) and in MS lat. 24 (fol. 214v) of John Rylands Library in Manchester. The melody, which proves to be identical with the *Alleluia, V. Dulce lignum* (*Grad. Sar.,* 185), is freely paraphrased in the treble.

Audivi [vocem], V. Media nocte (Nos. 18 and 19), two different settings of the respond for the Nativity of several Virgins (*Ant. Sar.,* 567 and 576; *Proc. Mon.,* 236, where it is assigned optionally also to the Easter season): The first setting (see Ex. 7 below) elaborates the liturgical melody consistently in the tenor. It is the only example of this treatment in the conductus of the collection.[26] The second composition (see Ex. 4) does not employ the chant. It should be

Ex. 4. Two-part version of *Audivi.*

noted that again only the sections assigned to the soloist are set in polyphony.

[25] See Legg, *The Sarum Missal,* 390. In the thematic catalogue the piece is erroneously classified as antiphon. For the oldest known setting of the *Alleluia* in organum style see W₁, fol. 197v.

[26] The cantus firmus of *Cantemus Domino* represents a different case, inasmuch as it is a motet tenor, not a conductus tenor.

Cantemus Domino socie (No. 52–53), four-part motet: [27] At first glance it is not at all certain that this composition, the last one of the original repertory, should be included in the liturgical part, since its text is sacred but non-liturgical. The beginning of the tenor is, as is stated in the thematic catalogue, illegible because of erasure, but no mention is made of the fact that it carries an erased incipit, of which *G . . . in celis etc. (sic* in MS) is still faintly discernible. This can be identified as the antiphon *G[audent] in celis,* which is sung on the Nativity of several Martyrs (*Ant. Sar.,* 641; the Roman version varies somewhat).

Only the first half of the chant is presented in the first setting of *Cantemus Domino.* The tenor of the second setting carries no designation and gives no hint that it is the continuation of the same chant which should be supplied with the cue *Et quia pro eius amore.* It follows from the distribution of the cantus firmus that what has been listed in the thematic catalogue as two independent settings of the same text is actually one composition. It consists, as was common in the motets of the time, of two parts, the first being in triple meter, the second in duple meter. In the erased portion of the tenor a few stems have remained visible and the space of the ligatures can be fairly well estimated from the erasures. These clues, in conjunction with the known plainsong version of the melody, permit the accurate restoration of the erased beginning without any loss of music (see Ex. 13 below).

The motet is based on a very unusual, so far unidentified, text. The upper voices recite the first eight lines of an elegy [28] by the hymnographer Sedulius (4th–5th c.) whose *Carmen Paschale* set the model for the famous introit *Salve sancta parens.* The poem *Cantemus Domino* is written in elegiac meter in artfully interlocked distichs and is the earliest poetical and non-biblical text of the collection. As in the case of the Goliardic drinking song, discussed below, the manuscript transmits the first known musical setting of the words. It is rather strange that the second part of the motet repeats the text of the first part over a continuous tenor, especially since the elegy is long enough to provide text for a great many compositions. The

[27] Not for five parts, as is suggested in the thematic catalogue.
[28] Chevalier, *Repertorium,* No. 2596, printed in Migne, *Patrologia Latina,* XIX, 753, and *Analecta Hymnica,* 50, 53.

fact that the poem of Sedulius was still familiar enough in the fifteenth century to be set to music is in itself noteworthy and implies that the composition emanated from a learned and clerical center.

The foregoing annotated list of liturgical compositions makes it clear that the music of LoM is in full harmony with the liturgical requirements. Those sections of the text for which the rubrics of the Sarum Processional prescribe performance by a chorus are consistently excluded from polyphony; of the responds only the solo sections, the first word, and the verse are composed. It follows, furthermore, that the performance of the solo sections by more than one singer—the rubrics prescribe from two to as many as seven—was not regarded as choral singing but merely as a "reinforced solo" or soloistic group performance. In the observance of liturgy the Meaux Abbey MS proves to be much stricter than the Pepys MS. Not only does the latter ignore the liturgical order in the sequence of compositions, but it juxtaposes solo sections, normally set in polyphony, with polyphonic choral sections of the chant, not normally so composed. The indiscriminate application of choral polyphony to all parts of the service bespeaks the gradual weakening of the strictly liturgical tradition in the course of the fifteenth century.

From the musico-liturgical point of view *Cantemus Domino,* the *Missa brevis,* and the two Passions are of special interest. The polytextual motet which combines an antiphon with the elegy by Sedulius stands quite by itself outside of the liturgical series, and its liturgical function, if indeed it had a definite one, was in all likelihood not restricted to that of the antiphon.

The Mass holds a significant place in the development of the cyclic Mass. It is to date the first polyphonic *Missa brevis* known from a manuscript of English origin. The individual movements are bound together not by a motto motive or a recurrent cantus firmus but only by the liturgical function of the plainsongs they paraphrase. The *Missa brevis* is a plainsong Mass each movement of which is based on a different chant. The cycle is therefore unified by liturgical rather than musical means, although the use of the same technique of melodic elaboration gives it a certain degree of stylistic unity. The idea of musical unification, the decisive step in the evolution of the cyclic

Mass, applies to the plainsong Mass only indirectly. It signifies the turn from liturgical to aesthetic considerations, characteristic of the Renaissance attitude.

The two Passions are of great historical interest because they are to date the earliest polyphonic compositions of this type on record. As happens frequently in musicology, the distinction of being the "first" example was bestowed on and subsequently withdrawn from several other compositions in the course of historical discoveries, and the time may come when it will be wrested again from the two Passions in LoM. Originally the motet Passion by Longueval, sometimes ascribed also to Obrecht, passed as the first one; [29] a St. Matthew Passion dating from about 1480, preserved in Modena, Est. MS lat. 455, was the next in line to take its place.[30] As in LoM, only the *turbae* are set in polyphony. The fragment of another (unpublished) St. Matthew Passion from about the same time is to be found in Paris, Bibl. Nat. MS nouv. acqu. 4379 (fol. 1). Only the tenor part is extant, and the number of voices (probably three) cannot be ascertained. We do not know at what time the polyphonic performance of the Passion originated. Recitations in part music of the *Liber Generationis* occur as early as the fourteenth century. The two Passions from LoM show in their declamatory conductus style that they are as yet not far removed from chant recitation.

STYLISTIC ASPECTS

The musical style of the liturgical part offers but little variety. The stylistic unity, which is paralleled by the uniformity of notation, suggests that the repertory was composed within a short span of time. A striking feature of the notation of *Inventor rutili* (No. 10) deserves some comment. Notated in LoM as usual in score, the hymn appears in the variant of the Pepys MS in choir-book form, even though the manuscript records many other pieces in score. As the Pepys MS is the later source and score notation fell gradually into disuse, the change of notation would not be in itself remarkable. Yet the arrangement of voices and the distribution of the text are very peculiar: the tenor is written down first, and only this voice carries the full text, while the upper and middle voices have only cues. We must infer

[29] See the references in Schofield, *loc. cit.*, which should be supplemented by those given here.

[30] For further references see the essay "The Beginnings of Choral Polyphony" in this book.

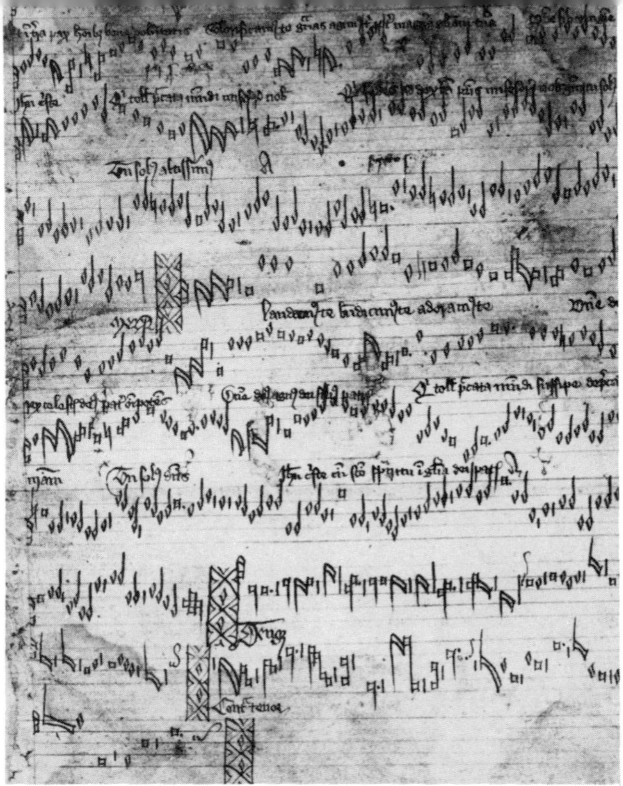

PLATE 1. The Fountains Fragment (Brit. Mus. Add. MS 40011 B, fol. 9)

PLATE 2. Toulouze, *L'Art et Instruction de bien dancer* (1496?)

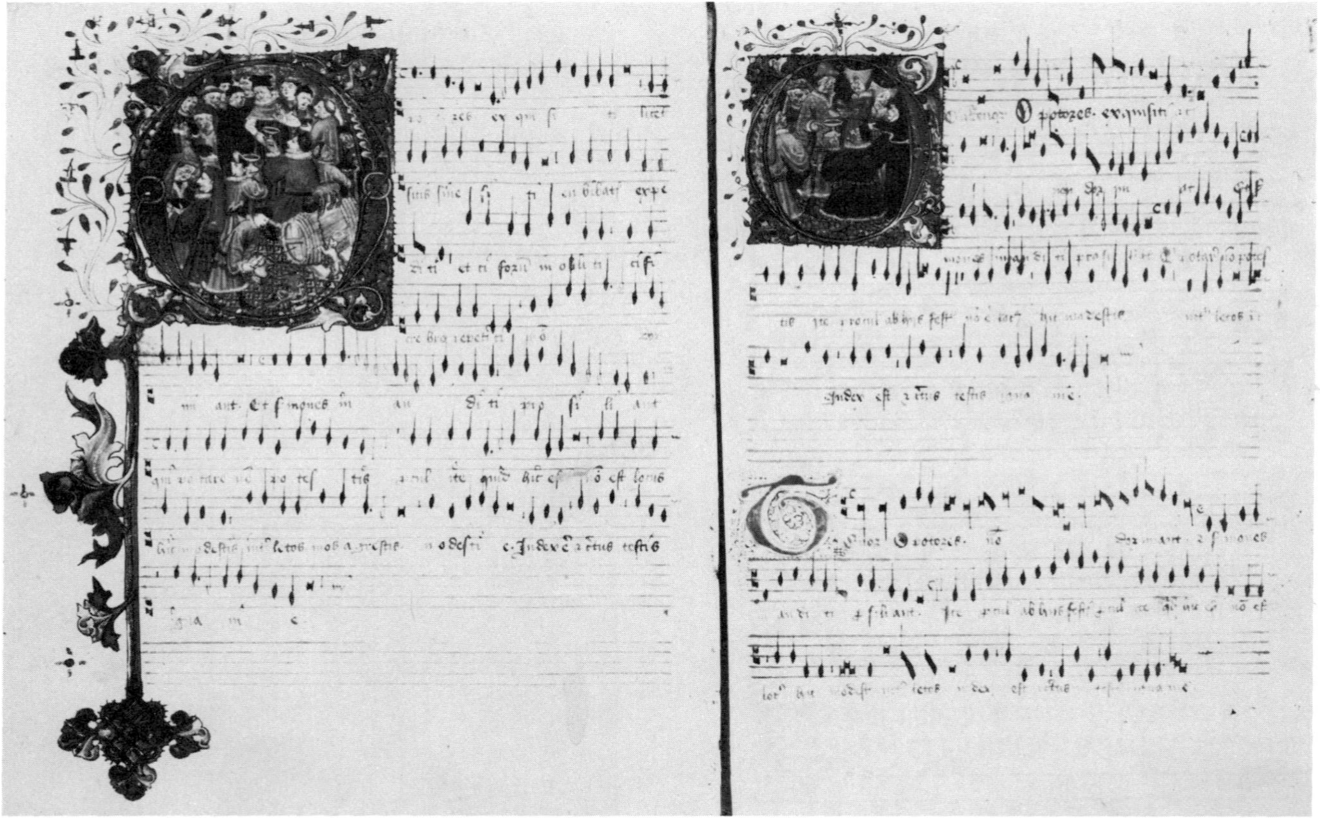

from this highly unusual arrangement that the scribe of the Pepys MS copied the piece from another source in which it appeared in score notation. Transcribing mechanically from a score, he started with the voice that carried the text—the tenor—and when he came to the other voices he found them without text, and merely added cues. The notation in separate parts implies wrongly that the tenor is the leading voice.

The only composition of the liturgical group for which score notation would have been quite inadequate is the motet *Cantemus Domino*. It would have been a considerable waste of precious space to set aside one staff of the score for the tenor and to stretch out its few sustained notes over the space required by the notation of the other voices.

One of the prominent factors lending unity to the music is the moderately florid and ornamental melodic line which proceeds mostly in triple meter in delicate curves and occasional syncopated passages. This free treble style is derived ultimately from the secular song, in which the treble was the leading voice. It is of little consequence to the character of the melody whether or not the composition borrows a plainsong. If it does, the chant participates in the melodic sweep and acquires the quality of a song through ornamentation and cadential formulas, the stereotyped nature of which comes to light after a perusal of even a few compositions. The ornamental sixth cadence, which appears not only at the end of most phrases but at times even as an integral part of the melody, reigns supreme. If no plainsong is used, the same formulas are nevertheless in evidence. Free and bound compositions differ, therefore, not so much in their melodic (or harmonic) style as in the fact that the cadences of the latter group coincide with those of the chant. It follows that the presence of a borrowed melody can be detected only if the chant is known independently.[31]

The rhythmic uniformity of the music results from the predominance of triple meter. Duple meter never occurs at the beginning but appears only as an interlude in intermediary stanzas, after which the triple meter is resumed, or else in the second part of a larger work, e.g. *Cantemus Domino*. The gently flowing rhythm which governs the music of the first half of the century may be occasionally intensified and even upset by a clash between 3/4 and 6/8 time. This characteristic hemiola effect of mensural music occurs either in direct juxtaposi-

---

[31] Cf. on this point "The Music of the Old Hall MS," p. 52.

tion or simultaneously in treble and tenor, with the middle voice
following the one or the other part or even having an independent
syncopation. The heightening of the cadence by means of hemiolas
is to be found in nearly every composition.[32] Only the *Missa brevis*
and the two Passions make considerably less use of the device. This
can be easily explained by the declamatory character of the Passion.
In the Mass the cadences are approached by lively subdivisions of
the regular meter or by gradual retardations of the movement and
holds on sonorous chords. Another favored rhythmic formula in the
cadence is the simultaneous use of ♩ ♩. ♪ and ♩. ♩ ♪ in the two upper
voices outlining the ornamental sixth cadence in parallel fourths.
This figure, which has been adopted also in the restoration of Ex. 2,
may be seen in countless examples, e.g. the Passion according to
St. Luke.[33] The strangely shifted parallels of this cadence should not
be mistaken for an error of the scribe; they are a deliberate device
of achieving not only rhythmic interest but also harmonic variety, as
the delay in the one voice produces a passing six-four chord.

Perhaps the most noticeable stylistic factor of the repertory is the
uniformity of harmony, a harmony that bears clearly the imprint of
the sixth-chord style. Chordal sonorities with frequent sixths and
thirds alternating in parallel and contrary motion had been the main-
stay of the English conductus style ever since the late thirteenth century. This style with its characteristic score notation still forms the
background to the music of LoM. During the first half of the fifteenth
century it had become sufficiently flexible in texture and rhythm to
be combined with the free treble style of the chanson. In this modernized form it coincides in effect with certain Continental compositions
that can be described as elaborate fauxbourdon settings. In pieces of
this type the mechanical accompaniment of a melody in parallel
sixth chords is stylized and raised to a higher level. It is unlikely that
this stylistic parallelism should be just a chance development; more
probably it represents the first reaction of English music to the fauxbourdon fashion that swept the Continent around 1430. While fauxbourdon never became a fashion in England comparable to that on the
Continent—its main appeal, sonority, was nothing novel in English
music—it gave a new aspect to the traditional sixth-chord style. The
Meaux Abbey MS appears to be the first English source to reflect the

[32] Compare Examples 2, 4, 7, 9, 10, etc.
[33] See MQ XXXIII, 43, end of section A.

influence of the fauxbourdon style, which appears here, however, characteristically transformed to stylized part writing.

It should be clearly understood that fauxbourdon in its strict form [34] does not occur in LoM. Not in a single piece is the improvisation of the middle voice called for by the direction *a fauxbourdon,* so frequently found in contemporary sources on the other side of the Channel. Only in the chain of parallels before the cadence can vestiges of primitive fauxbourdon writing be discovered. The repertories of the Old Hall MS and the Fountains fragment do not yet show any trace of fauxbourdon and by this feature alone bespeak an earlier phase of English music. It goes without saying that sixth chords are used extensively in OH and LoF also, but they alternate quickly with perfect consonances. Moreover, the leading position of the treble is not yet clearly established, as the cantus firmus is carried mainly by the middle voice. In LoM the chant appears more often than not in the treble.

The transformation of fauxbourdon to stylized part writing, which is an accomplished fact in LoM, can be traced in its various stages in Continental music. In the works of Burgundian composers the strict fauxbourdon for two written-out voices and a third improvised part occurs sometimes side by side with an optional, more elaborate version for three fully notated voices. These alternative settings consist of a treble, tenor, and two mutually exclusive contratenors, one specified only by the directive *a fauxbourdon* (= to be improvised at the fourth below the treble), the other written out in full with the remark *absque fauxbourdon.* The elaborate contratenor is freed from its slavish adherence to the treble and moves above and below the tenor. The two versions of the hymn *Lucis creator* by Benoit [35] give a good example of this practice. Dufay has gone even a step further in the assimilation of fauxbourdon to art music. In his hymn *Exultet celum laudibus* [36] he presents two alternative versions of essentially the "same" composition. Only the treble which elaborates the chant remains unchanged. The fauxbourdon setting adds a simple tenor and leaves the contratenor to improvisation. The more elevated

[34] For a general definition see Bukofzer, *Geschichte des englischen Diskants und des Fauxbourdons,* 1936, 10; and Besseler, "Dufay, Schöpfer des Fauxbourdons," in *Acta Musicologica* XX (1948), 26.

[35] Facsimile and transcription in Bukofzer, "Popular Polyphony in the Middle Ages," in MQ XXVI (1940), 46–47.

[36] Edited in *Das Chorwerk* 49, 20–22.

version supplies a different tenor and a written-out contratenor. While the tenor of the fauxbourdon setting must needs sound sixths (and octaves) with the treble in order to permit the improvisation of the middle voice, that of the elaborate version is no longer bound to this restriction. It moves freely in imperfect intervals with the treble while the contra serves the double function of filler and support of the harmony. The expanded form of three-part writing which naturally favors the open position or spacing of triads takes its point of departure from fauxbourdon, though there is little left of strict parallels except at the cadences. The fauxbourdon has been expanded into a piece of art music.

It is this stylization and expansion of part writing that appears most prominently in the Meaux Abbey MS. Texture and part writing show imaginative flexibility, parallel motion in two parts is counterpoised by contrary motion in the third voice, and the outermost voices branch out in tenths or come together in thirds so that the contratenor may gain independence. That the connection with fauxbourdon technique is even less apparent than in the Continental parallels is not surprising, because the English sixth-chord style tended toward a similar stylization of three-voice writing. Even the two-part pieces of LoM are self-contained settings that do not call for an improvised third voice. Any additional part would have to be carefully composed, as the lack of consistent parallel motion would rule out the duplication of the treble at the fourth below.

In view of the fauxbourdon stylization it is to be expected that the harmonic aspects of the cadence are extremely simple. Except for the *Missa brevis,* which is a special case with regard to harmony also, the conventional sixth-chord cadence (VII$_6$–I) rules almost absolute, even in the few four-part pieces. Although the contratenor is free to cross below the tenor at any time, it does not do so at cadence points. Continental composers avail themselves of precisely this opportunity of producing V–I progressions and thus betray a more progressive attitude toward harmony than their English colleagues. A further sign of harmonic conservatism is the fact that the cadential sixth chords in LoM frequently take the form of the double leading-note cadences which are diatonic only in the Lydian mode.[37] In the other modes one or sometimes both leading notes are often expressly prescribed by *musica ficta,* as was the practice in the music of the

[37] Cf. Ex. 5, m. 5–6.

late fourteenth and early fifteenth centuries.[38] The treatment of accidentals in LoM would be a study in itself. It must suffice here to draw attention to a few examples that specifically call for the double leading-note cadence. They are to be found most often in open spacing with the two upper voices inverted: what would normally be the middle voice lies an octave higher than usual, so that the voices move in parallel fifths instead of the customary parallel fourths.[39] This is, in spite of the parallels, a perfectly correct form of the sixth-chord cadence. Of special interest are those closes in which the chord of the double leading note is sustained at the end of a phrase.[40] Marked by a fermata and clearly functioning as a half-cadence, it is resolved directly afterward to a perfect consonance at the beginning of the next phrase. The striking interruption of the expected harmonic progression bears some resemblance to certain remarkable chord sequences in the works of Dufay.[41] They show a growing awareness and sensitivity toward the coloristic values of harmony. The four-part compositions (*Cantemus Domino* and the stanzas from *O redemptor*) do not add anything new because the fourth voice merely doubles one of the tones of the sixth-chord cadence. The parallel octaves that inevitably result may be written openly or may be slightly covered up by florid turns.

Certain four-part cadences of the *Missa brevis* distinctly differ from the type just described. The Mass is composed essentially for three voices, but the bass line is at times divided into two parts, of which one is written in red notes.[42] The color has in this particular case no mensural significance but serves merely as an expedient to distin-

[38] See, for example, the Sanctus by Tapissier in the Apt MS (ed. by Gastoué, *Publications de la Société française de Musicologie*, 10, 41) and the Credo by Chierisy (*Polyphonia Sacra*, ed. by van den Borren, 1932; No. 10, m. 200–210.) Compare also Lowinsky, "The Functions of Conflicting Signatures in Early Polyphonic Music," in MQ XXXI (1945), 227.

[39] Compare *Missa brevis*, Sanctus, m. 40–42; Agnus, m. 21–23; St. Luke Passion, section DD, etc.

[40] Sanctus, m. 5; St. Luke Passion, section V. Similar passages occur also in the St. Matthew Passion.

[41] Compare the antiphon *Alma redemptoris mater*, easily accessible in Davison-Apel's *Historical Anthology of Music*, No. 65, or in *Das Chorwerk* 19, 5, and DTOe, Vol. 53, 19; and also the chanson *Resveilles vous*, printed in Pirro, *Histoire de la musique de la fin du XIVe siècle* . . . , Paris, 1940, 60.

[42] Such splits occur also in other voices, especially in sustained chords; see Sanctus, m. 11, and Agnus, m. 31 and 54. Measure 54 is incorrectly reproduced in the transcription: the notes f' and c' of the middle voice should sound together as whole notes and carry a fermata like the other voices. Similar divisions of parts are to be found also in OH and LoF.

guish the voices which are notated on the same staff. The part written in red notes comes in and drops out unpredictably and is obviously supplementary. On the other hand, it cannot be a later addition, as Schofield is inclined to believe, because the red notes are
often essential to the harmony. Without them certain cadences would
become sustained six-four chords, which would obviously be faulty.[43]
Since there are no erasures in the middle voice indicating that the
six-four chords were originally sixth chords, the music must have
been conceived from the outset as a mixture of three- and four-part
harmony. The four-part sections are remarkable not so much for the
number of voices as for the use of the modern cadence in which the
downward step to the final in the tenor is supplemented by a bass
that brings about the progression V–I. This type occurs sometimes
before 1450 in intermediary cadences, but only after the halfway
mark of the century was it established as the main form of final
cadence. In the *Missa brevis* it appears as the final cadence only
in the Sanctus and Benedictus; in other parts of the Mass it occurs
at less prominent places.[44] In respect to harmony the Mass displays
a slightly more advanced harmonic style than the rest of the repertory, though this does not necessarily mean that it was composed at a
later date.

   Another important aspect of the harmonic idiom is the treatment
of consonance and dissonance. In conformity with the common practice of the first half of the century, thirds and sixths may be freely
written in any combination and alternation, with the provision that
they should not occur in the final chord. The degree of consonance
is consequently very high in this music; dissonances are as a rule prepared. Those on the strong beat occur as single or double suspensions [45]
against the tenor. In triple meter they may appear at the beginning
of the perfection or on beat two as a hemiola cadence. The latter,
quite characteristic device has the effect of a written-out retard (one
measure of 3/2 seems to take the place of two in 3/4). Unprepared
dissonances on or between beats such as appoggiaturas, accented passing notes, and the various forms of the cambiata and échappée are
very common and often appear in syncopated patterns. They are resolved immediately in downward direction. Purely melodic in na-

---

[43] The passing six-four chords at the cadence, such as we meet in the music of OH and
LoF (cf. pp. 51 and 103) are, of course, correct.

[44] Kyrie, m. 17–18; Sanctus, m. 9–11, 49–51; Benedictus, m. 23–26, etc.

[45] *Inventor rutili, V. Splendent* (Ex. 3), m. 3, or *Salve festa* (Ex. 9), m. 5.

ture, they do not require any preparation, because of their short duration. A sharp dissonance arises invariably whenever the middle voice performs the ornamental sixth cadence at the fourth below the treble. Here it must needs sound a second against the tenor. The clash originates from the melodic ornament and serves to enhance by contrast the essentially consonant progression of the outermost voices.

By and large, the music of the Meaux Abbey MS agrees stylistically with that of the Burgundian school, especially with that of Binchois and the early Dufay, which probably served as model for the English composers. The antiphons and hymns of Binchois and Dufay, which either are freely composed or elaborate the chant, reflect in their style their modest liturgical function. The liturgical part of LoM is likewise *Gebrauchsmusik* for the service and is written in simple conductus fashion. This style does not favor imitation. Significantly, no use is made of the device in the liturgical compositions, although it is well known in English music. Imitation is common and indeed essential in many pieces of the Old Hall MS.

CANTUS-FIRMUS TREATMENT

With only a few exceptions, the compositions of the liturgical part are based on plainsongs which in the polyphonic context appear as imaginatively rhythmicized mensural melodies. It may be stated once more that as far as the melodic style is concerned no clear distinction can be made between freely composed pieces and paraphrases. The discussion of the relation between chant and polyphonic settings may therefore begin with a brief review of pieces not dependent on plainsong. There are only two items that fall completely into this category, *All. Laudate pueri* (No. 15) and the second setting of *Audivi* (No. 19), both written as gymels in a very smooth manner. The excerpt from *Audivi* (Ex. 4) has been selected not only because it illustrates this style but also because it enables us to compare a free and a paraphrasing composition of the same text (cf. Ex. 7 below).

Two other settings in this category are freely composed only in part. The second version of *Gloria laus* (No. 4) probably abandons the chant after the quotation at the beginning. The vague references to plainsong will be discussed under migrant cantus firmus. The other partially free composition is the hymn *O redemptor* (No. 9). None of its verses, of which there are eight, have any relation to the known liturgical melody. The fact that the stanzas differ melodically makes it very unlikely that they are based on an unidentified plainchant. In setting the eight stanzas for three, two, and four parts in alternation the composer has endeavored to employ as much variety of texture as was possible within the limits of conductus style. There are only two stanzas in four parts: *Stans ad aram* (Ex. 5) and *Laus per-*

Ex. 5. Verse from *O redemptor.*

Stans   ad   aram   im-mo sup - lex   in - fu - la - tus   pon -

ti - fex,   de - bi - tum   per - sol - vat

hennis, the last one. They are of very special interest, as they represent the only two conductus settings for four independent parts that are written in score notation on four separate staves. It will be seen from Ex. 5 that the four-part writing is fairly clumsy. It must have presented considerable difficulty, because a real bass line (evolved by Dufay in his late works) did not yet exist. The tenor moves in true conductus fashion at almost the same pace as the other voices, but the rhythmic independence of parts makes the setting as a whole unwieldy and somewhat clogged. The voices cross incessantly, get in each other's way, and at times clash harshly. It is indicative of this situation that the numerous short rests in the upper voices have really no rhythmic justification but are merely expedients to solve an impasse in the part writing. In the absence of a bass register the range is severely restricted. In both settings the total range of the four voices does not exceed a twelfth, and the frequent crossings make the texture even more opaque. The harmonic clashes are obviously produced by the number of parts, as each one taken by itself forms a correct progression with the tenor (e.g., m. 5 and 8). The accumulation of parts creates a stodgy effect but also sonority and richness, which was apparently the goal of the composer. The setting clearly betrays the limitations of four-part writing in conductus style and in a harmonic idiom that had not yet evolved the modern cadence. Characteristically the two settings end with very similar sixth-chord cadences in which one of the voices is simply doubled.

As the two Passions are not based on the customary tone of recitation, they either use an unknown one or are freely composed. Even if the latter alternative should be true, the declamatory style strongly suggests a *tonus currens,* which places the music halfway between the categories of bound and free composition. Stylistically, the two Passions resemble each other very closely, especially in their harmonic turns and sustained chords. This may be shown in an excerpt from the St. Matthew Passion (Ex. 6), which should be compared with section C of the St. Luke Passion.[46]

Ex. 6. Turba from St. Matthew Passion.

46 MQ XXXIII, 44.

While the Passions usually cadence in the Mixolydian mode, mostly on *g* and *d*, they close for dramatic reasons (question, exclamation, and the like) on less conclusive notes, such as *a* or *f* (sharp). The latter cadence occurs on the question *hec?* in Ex. 6. The diverse inflections of the cadence are, of course, directly borrowed from the liturgical recitation. Because of the extreme use of declamation it is not surprising that the fauxbourdon style suggests itself in the Passions more openly than in any other composition of the collection. It appears in certain sections even in its most elementary form, re-iterated sixth chords.[47] The primitive style of the Passions corresponds very well to their historical role as the oldest known compositions of the type. How quickly, however, the polyphonic Passion developed may be seen in the St. Matthew Passion of the Modena MS. The latter work is accessible in an excerpt [48] containing the same words as Ex. 6 above. The Modena Passion is written for no less than six voices and carries the cantus firmus in the tenor in motet fashion. Both works declaim the words in reiterated chords, but the sharply rhythmicized recitation in triple meter which characterizes the English work is smoothed out in the Italian Passion to an evenly proceeding declamation in duple meter. The latter composition makes generous use of the modern cadence and is noteworthy for its unusually full sonority.

The remaining compositions of the liturgical part treat the plain-song in various ways. All of them, except for the motet *Cantemus Domino,* elaborate the liturgical melody; they do not present the notes in strict cantus-firmus fashion nor simply clothe it in a poly-phonic garb, but interpret it by means of coloration in an individual spirit. They attest to the significant turn from the objective statement or "presentation" of the melody to a more subjective "interpretation" which made itself increasingly felt as the century ran its course. The "personal note" of the artist comes to light as much in the transformation of the borrowed melody as in the way he sets it in part music. In the LoM this personal trend is seen only in its incipient stage, as the melody is still clearly recognizable. Through assimilation to the free treble style the melody loses its original austerity and acquires a new human, even intimate quality.

[47] This simple form of fauxbourdon was favored by Burgundian composers in the compositions of canticles; see the settings of the Magnificat by Binchois in Marix, *Les Musiciens de la Cour de Bourgogne,* 1937, 131 and especially 148.

[48] Cf. "The Beginnings of Choral Polyphony," Ex. 2.

The Pepys MS gives perhaps the clearest examples of this transformation in monophonic, yet specially composed versions of the chant. Here the *cantus planus* has become a *cantus fractus* by means of melodic embellishment and incisive mensuration. The hymn *Inventor rutili*, for example, appears in the Pepys MS first in this curious one-voice form (fol. 62) and then directly afterward in the three-part setting that LoM also records.

There are no *cantus fracti* in LoM, but nearly all other forms of cantus-firmus treatment may be found. These may be classified in three groups: the chant is carried (1) in the tenor, (2) in more than one voice as migrant cantus firmus, or (3) in the treble. The first two alternatives are quite rare in the collection. The fact that the treble is the preferred voice for the elaboration of the plainsong underlines what has been said about fauxbourdon, in which this very feature is essential. It is striking that one possibility, namely the presentation of the chant as the middle voice throughout, is completely lacking in our collection. This circumstance, more than any other single factor, reveals the difference between the Meaux Abbey and Old Hall MSS with regard to style in general and cantus-firmus treatment in particular. It is precisely the plainsong in the middle voice that occurs most often in the old layer of OH and similar settings in LoF. Significantly, these give hardly more than modest and archaic polyphonizations of the Gregorian melody and stand clearly apart from the Masses in free treble style. However similar the contents of OH and LoM may be in other respects, the different cantus-firmus treatment demonstrates how rapidly musical practice changed in fifteenth-century England.

The respond *Audivi* (No. 18) is the only case in which the chant appears as the lowest voice (Ex. 7). It is of interest primarily as the sole example displaying the influence of English discant. This form of improvisation appears here in written-out and stylized form. In English discant the chant cannot be as freely elaborated as in fauxbourdon because its position precludes use of the free treble style. It will be noted that there is little coloration in our example; the notes are often sustained for one or two measures. Even so, the desire for melodic elaboration can be detected in free insertions which are set off by animated rhythms.[49] Although the music centers round the lowest voice, the treble is a distinct and fairly florid melody in its own

[49] See m. 4–5 and the end of the excerpt.

Ex. 7. Three-part version of *Audivi* with plainsong.

right. The part writing of the piece transcends, of course, the limits of improvised English discant, but nevertheless there are sometimes pure sixth-chord progressions (see m. 4–12).

The small group of compositions with migrant cantus firmus comprises only the first (and possibly also the second) setting of *Gloria laus* (Nos. 1–2, and 4). Since the paraphrasing technique of migrant cantus firmus is usually freer than that of treble cantus firmus, certain cases remain doubtful, as for example No. 4. After the unmistakable quotation of the chant at the beginning there are several fleeting references which turn up erratically now in one voice and now in another. In migrant cantus firmus the danger of reading the chant into the music, as either deliberate or "unconscious" reference,[50] increases with the number of voices, as the chant may appear in any one. Some cadences of the verse coincide with those of the plainsong, even on the correct word, but many others do not. If this is migrant cantus firmus it would be one of the freest examples of the kind.

The first setting of *Gloria laus,* on the other hand, unquestionably elaborates the chant. Although it is very freely treated, the cadences are always observed, as may be seen from the beginning of the third verse *Plebs Hebrea* (Ex. 8). Set as gymel, the numerous thirds and

---

[50] The idea of "unconscious references" is actually a contradiction in terms. If they are not intentional they are purely external similarities such as would naturally occur between any two compositions in the same mode.

Ex. 8. Third verse from *Gloria laus*.

sixths alternate so freely that it would be impossible to improvise a third voice in fauxbourdon fashion. The cantus firmus is not migrant throughout. The fragmentary *repetenda* carries it, as the reconstruction (Ex. 2) shows, in the treble. The first section of the first verse, a gymel of which only the lower voice has been preserved, can be restored in similar fashion. In the second section of the same verse the cantus firmus appears in the lower voice with hardly any embellishments, and a free counterpoint must be added in the restoration. In the subsequent verses, completely preserved in the manuscript, the cantus firmus wanders back and forth chiefly between the two upper voices [51] in rather free coloration.

Treble elaboration, the most common and prominent cantus-firmus technique in our collection, applies to all compositions not previously mentioned. In certain compositions of this group (e.g., Nos. 5 and 11) the chant may appear temporarily in the middle voice if the treble pauses. These duet sections do not make the cantus firmus migrant because its relative position in the setting remains unchanged. The elaborations range from almost literally exact statements of the liturgi-

[51] In certain two-voice settings it is not always clear which voice elaborates the chant because they cadence at the octave and thus both follow the plainsong. The last phrase of Ex. 8 is a case in point.

cal melody to fairly ornate versions, but even in the latter the chant does not lose its identity. The two settings of *Salve festa dies* (Nos. 13 and 13a) very neatly illustrate the two alternatives as they refer to the same cantus firmus (Ex. 9). The primitive fauxbourdon pro-

Ex. 9. Two settings of *Salve festa dies*.

No.13: Sal - ve fes - ta di -

es. No. 13a: Sal - ve fe - ta di - es qua de - us

gressions of the second setting (duple meter) should especially be noted.

The movements of the *Missa brevis* belong to the elaborate group. Because of their syllabic brevity the Gregorian melodies call for extensive coloration in order to give proper length to the movements. Stylistically the *Missa brevis* is patterned after the Masses of the Burgundian school. It is revealing to compare it with a two-voice Sanctus [52] and a three-voice Agnus Dei [53] by Binchois which elaborate the same chants, though Binchois' variants do not exactly agree with either the English or the Vatican version (LU, No. XVIII). The stylistic similarity is apparent not only in the frequent use of fermatas but especially in certain harmonic progressions which are at times almost literally the same.

[52] Marix, *op. cit.*, 182.
[53] DTOe, Vol. 61, 50, and Einstein, *A Short History of Music*, Examples, 271.

The recasting of the chant into a figural melody is usually effected in such a way that one note of the cantus firmus is valid for one perfection of the mensural version. These notes often coincide with the first beat of each measure and thus stand out clearly as the essential ones, as may be seen in the opening measures of *O redemptor* (Ex. 10). This type of paraphrase comes close to the very mechanical meth-

Ex. 10. *Repetenda* from *O redemptor.*

ods of cantus-firmus elaboration expounded in the writings of Guilielmus Monachus.[54] We find in LoM another type of setting, in which the borrowed melody appears in mensural rhythm but with only a few ornamental notes because the chant itself is melismatic. Such a type of setting is found in the beginning of *Unus autem* (Ex. 11), in which almost every single note of the treble is borrowed.

Ex. 11. Beginning of *Unus autem.*

It will be seen from the quoted examples that whether freely or literally adopted the chant is transformed in any case into a flowing line to which the collection owes much of its stylistic unity. Similar procedures, though perhaps on a less artistic level, may be found in the Pepys MS, which, in addition to a setting of *Inventor rutili*, con-

---

[54] See the reference in the essay in this book, "A Polyphonic Basse Dance of the Renaissance," p. 206.

tains several settings of texts that occur, with different music, also in LoM. It is instructive to compare the setting of *Rex sanctorum* from LoM (Ex. 12a) with that of the Pepys MS (Ex. 12b).[55] The latter is

Ex. 12. Two settings of *Rex sanctorum* (from LoM and Pepys MS.).

notated in separate parts, all with full texts, but shows the characteristics of conductus style as clearly as the parallel setting from LoM. The chant is treated in very similar fashion, but it should be observed that in the Pepys version the caesura after *sanctorum* is lacking and the cadence does not correspond to the known version of the chant. Although the Pepys MS is the later source, its version is in no way more advanced stylistically than that of the Meaux Abbey MS. This is not surprising in view of the generally retrospective and provincial style of the Pepys MS.

55 Fol. 63v; as in the case of *Inventor rutili*, only the *repetenda* is set to music here.

PLATE 4. The Washing of the Feet (Paris, Nat. lat. 17325, fol. 27 v)

PLATE 5. The Washing of the Feet (Albrecht Dürer, *Kleine Passion*)

PLATE 6. *Venit ad Petrum*, Antiphon (Manchester, John Rylands Library, lat. 24, fol. 90)

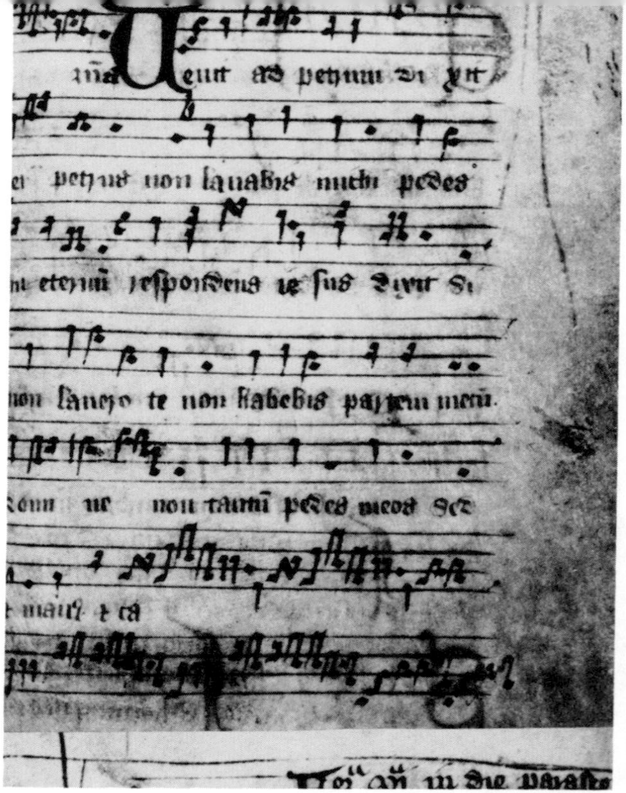

PLATE 7. *Venit ad Petrum*, Antiphon (Brit. Mus. Harley 2942, fol. 48–48 v)

The six subsequent verses of *Rex sanctorum* constitute the longest set of "variations" in our collection. In each stanza the coloration of the plainsong respects the essential notes, but it is at the same time free enough to avoid repetitiousness and monotony and to attain variety within the restrictions of style.

The *Alleluia V. Confitemini* and *All. V. Salve virgo*, the only two two-voice compositions with cantus firmus, do not differ in their treatment of the chant from the three-voice settings, though the part writing is perhaps a little smoother, owing to the small number of voices.

Cantemus Domino, finally, the only sacred motet of the collection, stands in every respect apart from the other liturgical compositions (Ex. 13).[56] The tenor presents the chant, in true motet fashion, as

Ex. 13. Motet: *Cantemus Domino.*

[56] In our transcription the bracketed passage has been restored with the aid of the plainsong and the remnants of ligatures and stems that have escaped the erasing knife. A subsequent study of the manuscript in ultraviolet light, which makes the erasures clearly visible, has confirmed the accuracy of the restoration.

cantus firmus proper in fairly prolonged note values. The slow pace differentiates the structural voice from the florid duet of the upper parts, which carry texts, and the textless contratenor. The latter serves occasionally as lowest voice when the tenor pauses, but mostly as true contratenor or *vagans* moving above and sometimes also below the tenor. The two main parts of the piece begin very similarly with extended duets. These gymels are notated in a very peculiar fashion: the beginning is scored for two trebles directly juxtaposed on the same folio. For the first nineteen measures the treble part is split into two voices with the other parts pausing. The next section of the duet continues for one treble and alto and is set down in the usual manner; the supplementary treble part drops out. This section is musically similar to the first one (compare m. 13 ff. and 22 ff.). The entry of the two lower voices marks the end of the gymel, and from here on the motet proceeds essentially in four voices. The texture is occasionally thinned out to brief duets or trios. The second part of the motet then repeats the same general plan over the continued cantus firmus. The striking symmetry between the two parts must be recognized as one of the last vestiges of isorhythmic organization. The change from triple to duple meter was of course a standard procedure in the isorhythmic motet which the later motet retained long after the principles of isorhythm had been abandoned. What is even more suggestive is the manner in which the rests divide up the tenor into roughly corresponding sections. The first one comprises seven measures, then they vary in length. The symmetry is further emphasized by a textural feature. The beginning of the four-voice section of the second part corresponds very closely to the analogous place of the first part. After the introductory gymel has reached the cadence on *c* the alto leads off both times, with the treble following suit.

With regard to technical command of composition the motet is unquestionably the most advanced and finished piece of the collection. This is revealed especially in the unconstrained flow of the four voices. Unlike the stodgy four-part pieces in conductus style, the motet shows skill and planning in the general design and ease in the management of four voices. The rests are no longer excuses for difficult situations in the part writing, and their spirited alternation gives the voices literally breathing space and airy texture. It is a mark of superiority that the voices are no longer crowded together; the total range is much wider than that of the conductus settings and exceeds two octaves. The slow-moving tenor induces a slow harmonic rhythm that puts an end to the erratic alternation of harmonic progressions. The frequent occurrence of full triads should especially be noted; and their sonorous effect is reinforced by the judicious placement of the third in the treble. All these factors indicate the progressive style of the piece. The fact that there is not a single modern cadence in the entire composition bespeaks, on the other hand, a relatively early date. The fairly numerous parallels and dissonant frictions between the upper voices point likewise to the initial stage of four-part writing.

Imitation, which is absent in all pieces in conductus style, plays also a very negligible role in the motet. It applies only to the upper voices and manifests itself in brief hints, mostly of rhythmic imitation. The contrast between conductus and motet with regard to procedure and style throws light in retrospect on the music of the first part of the collection. Apparently the conductus settings were composed as deliberately modest functional music for the service. Their simplicity seems to be the result of self-imposed restrictions rather than of objective limits of musical technique. The motet shows what an English composer could do when a more elevated style was in order. On the whole, however, the music of the Meaux Abbey MS does not yet display the ease of writing characteristic of the English contributions to such later sources as the Trent and Aosta MSS, not to mention Bodleian MS Add. C 87.[57] It holds an intermediary position between the repertory of OH and LoF and that of the later manuscripts and thus forms a link of great musical, historical, and liturgical prominence.

3. CAROLS AND CANTILENAS

The liturgical collection is easily equaled if not surpassed in importance by the carols and cantilenas of the second part of LoM. If we disregard smaller fragments, there were until now only three sources known to communicate the music of the fifteenth-century carol: the Trinity Roll,[58] the Selden MS (OS), and the old layer of Add. MS 5665 in the British Museum, the first two belonging to the middle of the century, the last one to the late fifteenth and early sixteenth centuries. The Meaux Abbey MS is the fourth musical source of note, valuable especially for the number of hitherto unknown compositions. The small number of musical manuscripts stands in striking contrast to the large number of literary sources.

While carols and cantilenas do not belong to the liturgy proper, their presence in an otherwise liturgical manuscript implies that they may have been performed as optional insertions in the liturgy. This assumption is confirmed by the rubrics of Add. MS 5665, which assign them to various days of the liturgical year. The liturgical use of popular forms in the vernacular has no exact parallel in the sources of Continental Europe. Widely popular in England, the carol did not spread to the Continent, although Masses and motets by English composers were taken over with alacrity. It is true that the English words may have prevented wider dissemination, but the difficulty did not exist in the case of the Latin cantilena, and moreover it was overcome in the case of secular English part songs by substitutions of texts in other languages and by *contrafacta*. Nevertheless, it is a remarkable fact that so far not a single Continental source has been discovered

[57] See the reference on p. 221.
[58] Trinity College, Cambridge, MS O 3 58 [1230]; ed. by Fuller-Maitland, *English Carols of the Fifteenth Century*, 1891.

that contains the music of English carols or cantilenas—a silent testimony to the rootedness of the genre in the English tradition.[59]

The carol and its Latin counterpart, the cantilena, do not differ in form. As a rule, an invariable burden leads off and then consistently alternates with an undetermined number of uniform stanzas or strophes. Since burden and stanza have different music, two strains alternate in performance. In his fundamental treatise on the English carol, Greene [60] has shown that the burden is the essential principle of carol structure. He has given an illuminating account of the various French and Latin prototypes of the carol form, the secular dance song, and such liturgical forms as hymn, sequence, and antiphon. His list of liturgical antecedents should perhaps be supplemented by the processional hymn with *repetenda,* which is more closely akin to the carol, and especially the cantilena, than any of the Latin forms cited by him. The general structure is the same in both forms: they both fall into burden and stanzas, which may differ in metrical structure and music, they both have the regular repeat of the burden after each stanza and the uniform pattern of the stanza itself, and they are

[59] It should, however, be mentioned that certain Continental compositions of the early fifteenth century are very similar in both form and style to the cantilena—for example, *In tua memoria* by Arnold de Lantins (*Polyphonia Sacra,* No. 42) and *Verbum caro factum est* (ibid., No. 49 *ter*). Both compositions are related to the Italian *lauda*. *Verbum caro* with the stanza *In hoc anni circulo* carries the melody in the tenor and is built like a *virelai*. In accordance with that form *ripresa* and *volta* are musically identical, although the counterpoint varies. Another setting of *Verbum caro* appears in Venice, Bibl. Marc. MS it. IX 145, fol. 1 (see Jeppesen, "Ein venezianisches Laudenmanuskript," in *Theodor Kroyer-Festschrift*, Regensburg, 1933, 69, and Besseler, AMW VII [1925], 237). The tenor melody is essentially the same as in the first setting, but the counterpoint is different and *ripresa* and *volta* are not differentiated. The MS contains two further settings of the text (fols. 104–104v and 116–117), based likewise on the same tenor melody. The melody of *Verbum caro* is characterized by a popular tone and is written, like the carols and cantilenas, in triple meter. An entirely different and rather complex composition of the same text by Lymburgia is to be found in BL, fol. 278v–279. Still other settings (which I have not seen) include Florence, Bibl. Naz. Magliab. MS XIX 112 *bis*, fol. 47v–49, 59v, and 60 (three compositions) and Trent 1374 (Fauxbourdon); in the latter the melody lies in the treble. The beginning of the melody is quoted also in another setting (*Polyphonia sacra* No. 49), in which only the burden is set to music. The entire text appears with a different melody as late as 1582 in *Piae Cantiones*, No. II (ed. by Woodward, London, 1910).

The lines *Verbum caro factum est/de Virgine Maria* occur as the burden of a cantilena in the important Anglo-Irish text collection *The Red Book of Ossory* (for the entire cantilena see Robbins, "The Earliest Carols and the Franciscans" in *Modern Language Notes* LIII [1938], 241). It is interesting to note that the Venetian MS quoted above is essentially a source of Italian *laude* and is obviously related to the musical activities of the Franciscans.

[60] Greene, *The Early English Carols*, 1935.

both performed antiphonally or, strictly speaking, responsorially, in alternation between chorus and solo. The cantilena would indeed be identical with the processional hymn were it not for the difference in liturgical function, subject matter, metrical simplicity, and spirit which proves the important role of secular antecedents to the form. A further point of disagreement comes to light in certain internal repeats and subtle musical relationships between burden and stanza, highly characteristic of the musical structure of the carol, which will be extensively discussed below. Yet even these relations are not entirely unknown (though they are less conspicuous) in the processional hymn. A glance at the plainsong version of *Rex sanctorum* (No. 11) tells us that the opening notes of the *repetenda* and the stanza are the same. It is probably no more than an accident, and may be noted for whatever it may be worth, that the two favorite forms of LoM are precisely the processional hymn and the carol.

The forthright and direct literary style of the carol and cantilena finds a perfect counterpart in the musical style. However, the simplicity of text and music is to some degree deceptive. On the literary side the numberless quotations of liturgical texts amply attest to a learned, clerical atmosphere. The carol writers apparently took special pride and pleasure in weaving stock phrases in Latin into the lyric. In exceptional cases they larded it with as many liturgical allusions as possible, sometimes even at the expense of continuity and sense.[61] Certain verses are little more than a cento of "familiar quotations" held together by rhyme but hardly by reason. In our present collection such quotations are quite numerous. It is worthy of note that they refer mainly to hymns and antiphons, not to responds of the Nocturns or the Proper. Obviously, the carol could more easily substitute for the simple chants of the Office than for the more solemn ones of other services.

One of the most interesting macaronic carols with extremely rich textual associations is *Novo profusi gaudio* (No. 23), which is written in three languages (French, English, and Latin) or, if one counts the Greek bit "alpha et ω," in four. The text is essentially a *Benedicamus Domino* trope; burden and stanza end with these words, and, in addition, the lines *A solis ortu cardine, Enixa est puerpera,* and *Gloria tibi trinitas,* all borrowed from the first-named hymn, are woven in. The burden of *Tibi laus, tibi gloria, tibi gratiarum actio* (No. 20)

[61] Greene, *op. cit.;* see the tables in Ch. III, "The Latin Background of the Carol."

is identical with a Trinity antiphon,[62] and the beginnings of the strophes are taken from the hymns *A solis ortu* and *Jam lucis orto*. From the numerous other references the following may be cited: burden and stanza of *Qui natus est* (No. 27) quote the antiphon *Salvum me fac Domine;* the first stanza of *Verbum patris* (No. 43) begins with the first line of the processional hymn *Salve festa dies* (No. 13 of the liturgical part); *Exultavit cor in Domino* (No. 37) paraphrases the antiphon *Exultavit cor meum in Domino,* and its last stanza is another trope of the *Benedicamus Domino; Illuminare Jerusalem* (No. 30) takes up a section from *Surge et illuminare,* the *versus* of the gradual *Omnes de Saba; Almyghty Jesu* (No. 40) quotes in the second stanza the antiphon *Ecce ancilla Domini;* the stanza *Sicut sponsus de thalamo processit* (No. 50) is patterned after the antiphon *Sponsus ut e thalamo processit;* and the last cantilena of the collection, *Lauda salvatorem, ducem et pastorem* (No. 55), obviously leans on the sequence *Lauda Sion salvatorem, lauda ducem et pastorem.*

The liturgical quotations mentioned thus far are exclusively textual—that is to say, no recognizable attempt is made at matching them with musical quotations from the proper plainsongs. This seems to be the general rule in the carol. The only exception I have found in LoM is the cantilena *Johannes Jesu care* (No. 34). Its elusive liturgical source has already been touched upon in the discussion of the Old Hall MS.[63] The first line of the burden, which serves also as the refrain of the stanza, quotes the end of the sequence *Johannes Jesu Christo multum dilecte* in the Sarum version.[64] The music of the cantilena is "rounded"; the opening measures of the burden and the closing measures of the stanza (Ex. 14) present the same music

Ex. 14. Refrain from *Johannes Jesu care.*

with but slight variation. In the refrain *Johannes Jesu care* the first five notes of the treble correspond exactly to those of the plainsong.

62 See the discussion of that antiphon in connection with LoF on p. 107.

63 Compare p. 61.

64 Greene, *op. cit.,* quotes the full text of the Continental version, which ends with *Johannes Christi care.* This ending, too, has been borrowed in a carol (Greene, No. 105).

The music of the burden differs from that of the refrain only in the pickup note *c* in both voices (the chant would call for a *d* at this place). It cannot be categorically decided whether the plainsong reference in the refrain is intentional or accidental; the fact that text and music coincide with the plainsong would favor the former alternative, but, on the other hand, it ought not to be overlooked that the first note of the burden varies and that the remainder of the treble is a commonplace opening in English compositions.

Nearly all compositions conform, as far as literary form is concerned, to the customary scheme of burden and stanza, the former being always written down first in the manuscript. Only in two pieces, *Omnes una gaudeamus* (No. 45), and *Ecce quod natura* (No. 39), do we find a deviation from the pattern. No. 45 is a very short composition which occurs with considerable musical variants also in OS. It is exceptional in that it begins directly with the varying stanzas, each of which ends with the refrain line *Qui natus est de virgine.*[65] The cantilena has an immutable refrain but no independent burden.[66] *Ecce quod natura* presents a different formal problem. It is modeled exceptionally after the *ballata* or *virelai,* in which the music of the *ripresa* or burden is repeated with different words as part of the stanza. This fact is obscured in the manuscript because burden and stanza are not separated by a double bar, as they usually are. Moreover, the *volta,* or second part, of the stanza *Quem non novit mirum* appears only as a cue with *etc.* at the end of the stanza as though it were the burden.[67] But the text is written out in full under the burden, and quite correctly so, as the *volta* has the same music. It could be doubtful that there is a burden at all were it not for the version of the Selden MS in which the section *Ecce quod natura* is clearly set off as the burden. The variant of Ashmole 1393 makes this even more obvious because the music is varied when it recurs as *volta,* and is consequently written out in full.

[65] The refrain differs in text and music from the burden of No. 27 although the latter begins with the same words.

[66] Here Greene's careful distinction between burden and refrain (*op. cit.,* 1) proves indispensable. The refrain is an integral part of the stanza, the burden a self-contained formal and metrical unit. The distinction is valuable also with regard to music, as burden and refrain of the rounded carol have the same music, yet serve different structural functions.

[67] Owing to this fact, Schofield classified this line erroneously as a burden in the thematic catalogue.

MUSICAL AND LITERARY STRUCTURE OF THE CAROL FORM

With regard to musical form the compositions are far more varied and complex than can be suspected from the uniform structure of the lyrics. This diversity is due to two factors, which will be taken up in turn. The first of these relates to the more palpable external features of the musical form. It is common knowledge that the burden (and certain parts of the stanza also) is frequently composed twice in the same piece. The second settings are sometimes specially marked as *chorus*—a designation that occurs in *Qui natus est* (No. 27) of our collection, and in numerous compositions of the other carol manuscripts, especially OS. It should be noted that the chorus sections are often written for more voices than the remainder of the composition. All choruses of our collection are for three parts, although the carols, with the exception of Nos. 28 and 55, which have three voices throughout, call for only two voices. It should not be thought that the increased number of voices is an essential characteristic of the chorus section; we know from OS that there are also two-part choruses.

The differentiation between burden and chorus raises some vital questions as to the performance of the carol. It has generally been held by analogy with the French *carole* and other dance-song parallels that burden and stanza stand for choral and solo performance respectively. While this view is correct in respect to the monophonic dance song, a difficulty arises in polyphonic settings, which were traditionally reserved for soloists.[68] Indeed, the special direction *chorus*, which always follows and never substitutes for the burden in the manuscripts, makes sense only if the first statement of the burden was performed by a group of soloists, and the repeat by a choral group, that is to say by more than one singer to a part. We see here that the number of parts required by the music must be distinguished from the number of singers assigned to each part. Even if burden and chorus called for three voices and were identical musically, they would still differ in performance as a solo ensemble does from a full chorus. This is equally true of the chorus sections of the stanza, which indubitably represent choral interludes in the solo ensemble of the stanza. The alternation of chorus and solo, typical of the monophonic dance song, is clearly in evidence here. The carol thus offers con-

[68] Cf. Reese, *Music in the Middle Ages*, 1940, 234; Bukofzer, MQ XXVI (1940), 40, and p. 185 of this volume.

clusive proof of the existence of choral polyphony in English music, which was still an innovation at the time when LoM was written. The parallel between the polyphonic carol and the processional hymn, which has been drawn above with regard to form, holds there-fore also with regard to performance: the rubrics leave no doubt about the fact that the *repetenda* was stated first by a group of solo-ists and then again by the chorus, exactly like the burden and chorus of the carol.[69] In certain exceptional cases the contrast between solo and choral polyphony affects even the musical style. For example, the end of the two-voice burden of *Qui natus est* (No. 27) is written in a distinctly florid style, while that of the three-voice chorus section states the same melody in simplified form.[70]

That burden and chorus were sung antiphonally in direct succes-sion is clear from the manner of notation in the Selden MS.[71] In our collection the chorus sections are written separately after the two-part sections in order to save space. The arrangement of OS demonstrates that the direct alternation of two- and three-part scores is a more accurate though less economical form of notation. The entries of the chorus are clearly indicated in LoM by repeat marks (:||:). It should be noted, however, that these marks sometimes have a different mean-ing, because they occur also in carols that do not have a chorus.[72] In the latter case we must assume that the sections thus marked were simply repeated, or else that the scribe omitted the chorus, thus im-plying a simpler method of performance. About half of the composi-tions in LoM have separate chorus sections [73] for the burden, and no less than ten of these have choruses also in the body of the stanza.[74]

The appearance of chorus sections in the stanza on variable texts proves conclusively that the customary usage of treating burden and

[69] There is no definite proof that in the performance of the carol both burden and chorus were repeated after each stanza; either repeat would satisfy the demands of the form. Since, however, the chorus sections within the stanza were certainly sung each time, the same is probably true of burden and chorus. The great, if not excessive, amount of repetition resulting from this practice would be quite in keeping with the style of the popular refrain forms such as the *lauda* and *frottola*.

[70] See Ex. 3 of "The Beginnings of Choral Polyphony" in this book.

[71] Schofield, *loc. cit.*, 523. The view that they are alternative settings, held by R. H. Robbins (*Modern Language Notes* LVII [1942], 16), is not supported by the musical sources.

[72] These are Nos. 20, 34, 38, 42, 44, and 49.

[73] It should be noted that the sections are not necessarily called chorus in the MS, but that they must be thus designated is evident from the context as well as the concord-ances with OS.

[74] Nos. 21, 22, 25, 29, 32, 35, 40, 43, 48, and 54.

chorus as synonymous literary and musical terms is patently inadequate. The chorus never adds a new line of text; it always repeats what has been stated before. Since it invariably adds musical but never textual variety it must be motivated by music rather than text. This is borne out by the fact that it sometimes destroys the symmetry of the lyric, for example when it repeats not a whole line but just a few words. The chorus has therefore little bearing on the verse structure, its musical significance outweighing its literary significance.

The music of the chorus is treated by the composers with great imagination. In the musical relations between burden (or stanza) and chorus three types may be distinguished: (1) repeat, (2) variant, and (3) complete independence. In the first case the two-voice burden of the soloists is restated as chorus with no change other than the addition of a middle voice. This expanded repeat may be illustrated by *Seynt Thomas honour we*, which contains three chorus sections, one for the entire burden and two in the stanza. The first chorus of the stanza (Ex. 15) [75] shows that the composer did no more

Ex. 15. Chorus section from *Al holy chyrch.*

than add a third voice, and even this simple task he performed but clumsily. The two-voice setting is beyond doubt the original composition. There are awkward skips in the added voice, and the consecutive octaves at the cadence are avoided only on paper by the insertion of a rest. It did not occur to the composer to use the modern cadence, which would have fitted in neatly had he made the penultimate note of the middle voice an *a*. We see that the conservative harmonic style of the piece does not differ from that of the liturgical part.

Not in all carols of this category has the middle voice been added in so perfunctory a fashion. The chorus of *Illuminare Jerusalem*

[75] Only the chorus is given in Exs. 15 and 16 because the burden reads the same if the middle voice is omitted.

(No. 30) definitely enriches the original duet, and in *Verbum patris hodie* (Ex. 16) the new part has been woven in skillfully in spite of its angular line.

Ex. 16. Chorus section from *Verbum patris*.

While the expanded repeat represents the simplest case of relationship between burden and chorus, it is not the most common one. The larger group of carols belongs to the second category, in which the desire for variety is unmistakable. Here the chorus is a more or less closely related variant of the burden, which may extend or condense the original music, reharmonize the melody, or vary one or more of the elements. In the chorus to *Qui natus est,* which has already been mentioned above, the first phrase of the melody is kept intact, but it is provided with different harmonies; the second phrase is also essentially the same, though it is shortened by one measure and displays a less florid style, quite in keeping with the choral idiom. *Ave rex angelorum* (No. 28) presents a somewhat different case, as both burden and chorus call for three voices. There are significant harmonic and melodic changes, but the connection between the settings nevertheless remains quite clear. The same is true of the textless burden and chorus of No. 54.

In other carols the relations are less pronounced and sometimes even tenuous. They range from similar beginnings or endings, over short intermediate passages, to hardly recognizable snatches in the treble or tenor. In dealing with the more obscure relations caution must be exercised because the mode, the stereotyped cadences, and the style of the carols inevitably create chance similarities which may be mistakenly assumed to be intentional. Context and internal evidence usually serve as guides in doubtful cases. The carol *Almyghty*

Jesu (No. 40) exemplifies a rather subtle type of relationship (Ex. 17).[76] The only link between burden and chorus is the tenor. This

Ex. 17. Burden and chorus from *Almyghty Jhesu.*

voice, which seems to be the leading one, appears the second time slightly shortened in a distinct variant,[77] but the characteristic angular beginning is retained. It is not a very obvious correspondence, because the tenor does not impress itself as strongly as the treble. It should not be overlooked that the supplementary function of the middle voice comes out again in the awkward part writing; note the skip of the ninth!

The idea of connecting burden and chorus by means of the tenor only comes to light also, though less clearly, in *Cum virtus magnifica* (No. 29). Here the first phrase of the chorus is a condensed and varied version of the burden in all voices, while the second phrase repeats the tenor exactly but with changed counterpoint.

[76] Ex. 17 gives only the opening measures, after which the correspondence disappears completely. The chorus of the stanza, on the other hand, is a plain repeat of the preceding music and belongs, therefore, to the first category.

[77] A discrepancy in the adaptation of the words should be noted: the cadence of the burden falls on *assumpsit,* that of the chorus on *blysse.* As only the latter version agrees with the musical and literary structure of the piece, it is likely that the scribe fitted the words hastily in the burden. They should probably read as I have suggested in brackets.

It will not be necessary to run the entire gamut from compositions in which the correspondence becomes increasingly vague to those in which none whatsoever can be discovered. The line between the second and third category is naturally somewhat fluid, and there may be a difference of opinion about the classification of a particular piece. Such a borderline case is *Ivy is good and glad* (No. 31), which adds one more item to the Holly-and-Ivy group of carols (Ex. 18). There

Ex. 18. Burden and chorus from *Ivy*.

is a vague similarity between the soprano of the burden and the tenor of the chorus, as though the latter had been modeled after the former. Those who are ever ready to invoke "organic unity" as the supreme arbiter may perhaps be inclined to regard this as an intentional connection, but we shall probably never be able to prove, or for that matter to disprove, that it actually is. However this may be, it will be agreed that the relation is an extremely tenuous one. Only the Phrygian cadence at the end of the phrase definitely ties burden and chorus together.

Carols with completely independent burden and chorus constitute the smallest group of the collection. The chorus of *Sol occasum* (No. 25) stands apparently in clear contrast to the beginning of the burden and thus seems to illustrate this category. However, upon closer scrutiny it will be discovered that the music of the chorus is freely patterned after the *second* part of the burden (with the necessary change in the distribution of words); the cantilena represents, therefore, only a special case of the second category. A true example of the third type is found in *Omnis caterva fidelium* (Ex. 19), in which the chorus presents musical ideas that occur in neither burden nor stanza. This cantilena demonstrates that the repetition of the same text did not rule out the use of musical contrast.

Ex. 19. Chorus section from *Omnis caterva*.

Om - nis ca - ter - va   fi , de - li - um

The above examples are representative enough to warrant the conclusion that the function of the chorus is not always the same, and that musical and literary principles do not necessarily coincide in the carol. In the first category the musical repeat by the chorus parallels and reinforces its literary function, the repeat of a line. It serves the same function, but less strictly so, in the second category, the chorus variant, which in view of its frequent occurrence must be regarded as the norm. In this category musical considerations come to the fore and make themselves felt in the same measure as the variant differs from the burden. In the rare cases of the third category they reign supreme: the literary repeat appears as musical contrast.

It has been necessary to explore the burden-chorus relations at some length not only because they represent an aspect of carol structure that has been neglected so far, but also because they bear on the musical relations between burden and stanza. Here again literary and musical form are not necessarily in exact congruity; the possible modes of deviation are, indeed, even more numerous and varied than those just considered. The principle of carol composition is simple enough: burden and stanza receive different settings, both self-contained and clearly separated in the manuscript. The music fully supports Greene's contention that a structurally independent burden is the decisive element of the carol form. In spite of this independence, however, burden and stanza are quite often connected by means of structural "cross relations." In respect to literary structure they take the form of quotations from the burden, of tail-rhyme or cauda, or, if invariable, of refrain. The refrain of the stanza may rhyme with the last line of the burden, or may even be the same. In respect to music the parallelisms take the form of musical rhyme, so called by analogy to the literary form. It would be stretching a point to apply this term also in cases where the musical correspondences appear at the *beginning* of phrases, as they frequently do. However, they are all methods of rounding off the carol form; the rounded carol is indeed by far the most common type.

The carol form allows of a bewildering number of possibilities on account of the criss-crossing of literary and musical factors. For example, a carol without any textual relations between burden and stanza may nevertheless have musical rhyme, and vice versa. Although the number of permutations is high, a rough classification of the four major possibilities may prove helpful. These are (1) rounded text and music, (2) rounded music not paralleled in the text, (3) the reverse case, rounded text not paralleled in the music, and (4) no rounding in either text or music.

Carols of the first type are quite numerous in our collection. The most spectacular roundings are to be found in those, comparatively few, cases in which the entire burden serves a double duty, first as burden and then as refrain of the stanza. In *Sol occasum* (No. 25) the burden is written out in full at the beginning and is indicated again at the end of the stanza by a cue of three measures. It is unlikely that the cue should refer only to the burden, because its repeat is always understood and because the music of the stanza runs continuously into the cue in the manner of a refrain. Besides, the directions of the manuscript are unequivocal in an analogous case. In the cantilena *Princeps serenissime* (No. 38), reproduced *in toto* in Ex. 20, the burden serves a double duty and is fully notated twice, the second time as an integral part of the stanza. The double function of a section seems especially fitting in a short composition like this one. The attentive reader will not fail to notice that the initial phrase of the tenor is identical with the celebrated *L'homme armé* melody—a fact that bespeaks the similarity of tone in the carol and certain Burgundian chansons.

In other rounded carols it is not uncommon for a section of the burden to be employed again. *Qui natus est* (No. 27) offers an example of this kind. All its stanzas end with the refrain *Salvum me fac Domine,* which is musically and textually identical with the last line of the burden, while the variable section of the stanza has no relation to the burden. The political cantilena *Anglia tibi turbidas* (No. 32) is rounded in a strictly analogous fashion.

Ex. 20. Cantilena: *Princeps serenissime.*

Princeps se-re - nis-si - me   Te lau-da - mus   car-mi - ne.1. An - ni do-num
2.Quod lu-men de

do - mi - ne   pro   bo-ne re - gi - mi - ne me-re - ris
lu - mi - ne   do - nec ti - bi ho - di - e qui na-tus

mi - ri-fi - ce
est de virgi - ne } Prin-ceps se-re - nis-si - me   Te lau-da - mus   car-mi - ne.

A different and perhaps more interesting realization of the same principle is found in *Illuminare Jerusalem* (No. 30). In contrast to Nos. 27 and 32, it is the *first* line of the burden that functions later as refrain, that is to say as *last* line of the stanza. The music of the refrain is again fully written out in the manuscript. The stanza of *Johannes Jesu care* represents exactly the same type. This particular method of rounding presents the composer with the difficulty of inventing a strain that serves in the burden as antecedent phrase and in the refrain as consequent phrase. The problem is met more successfully in *Johannes Jesu care* than in No. 30.

In spite of their differences the pieces dealt with so far have in common the characteristic that music and text are in strict correspondence; in other words, the return of a line is paralleled by a musical repeat. Such clear-cut cases of internal repetition are easily discovered, but there are other carols, still falling into the first general category, in which musical and textual repeats do not exactly coincide. This type may be illustrated by *Parit virgo filium* (No. 50), of which only burden [78] and stanza are given in Ex. 21. It will be

[78] The burden is followed by a chorus that belongs to the second type (free variant).

Ex. 21. Burden and stanza from *Parit virgo.*

[Burden]

℥ Pa-rit vir-go fi - li - um re-ga - li stir -

℥ -pe Da - - vid.

[Stanza]

℥ 1. Si - cut spon - sus de tha-la - mo pro-ces-sit matris u - te -
2. Pu-er na - tus in Bed-le - cem un-de gaudet Je-ru - sa -

℥ ro } re - ga - li
lem

seen that music and text of the burden line *regali stirpe David* are taken up again in the stanza in such a way that the musical repeat (m. 5) begins sooner than the textual repeat (m. 9). It might be argued that this is merely another instance of careless fitting of the words to music,[79] but there is no valid reason to distrust the scribe in this case. Burden and chorus agree in their distribution of words, and if the same pattern were adopted in the stanza also there would not be notes enough to accommodate the syllables of the text. We must conclude, therefore, that the lag between textual and musical repeat was intended. A similar discrepancy in the rounding of text and music exists in *Gaudeamus pariter* (No. 49), in which the repeat is further complicated by musical variation. Still more intricate is the stanza of the macaronic carol *Ave rex angelorum* (No. 28).[80] Here

[79] See note 77.
[80] Printed in *The New Oxford History of Music.*

again the *first* line of the burden, *Ave rex angelorum*, reappears as the *last* line of the stanza, but the music associated with the textual repeat in the stanza is that of the *last* line of the burden *Ave princepsque polorum*, and, to make things even more confusing, in the variant of the chorus. Ignoring the inverted position of lines in the poem, the composer has used the consequent phrase of both burden and stanza as musical rhyme. Literary and musical repeat, though both present, are diametrically opposed. Similarly, in *I pray yow all* (No. 41) the refrain line of the stanza *Amendith me and pair me noght* is borrowed textually from the last line of the burden, but musically from its first line.

The second type of burden-stanza relations proves by its very existence the need for musical rounding even if this is not suggested by the lyric. In this type burden and stanza are generally connected by musical rhyme, which is, of course, always supplied with different words. The correspondences range from a minimum of two measures [81] to repeats of a whole section. The first alternative is to be found in *Illuxit leticia* (No. 44) and *Seynt Thomas honour we* (No. 35), the second in *Ivy is good and glad* (No. 31) and *Omnis caterva* (No. 47). It will be remembered that in the last cantilena burden and chorus are unrelated; the piece belongs to the third category of burden-chorus relations and to the second type of burden-stanza relations. The interrelations between all three units, burden, chorus, and stanza, will not be discussed here, as they do not add anything fundamentally new, but the permutations arising from the two groups of categories should at least be mentioned. Needless to say, a carol may belong to more than one pair of categories.

In all cases where only one of the elements is rounded, music and lyric cannot be at cross purposes as they may be in the first category. *Enfors we us* (No. 36) and *Novo profusi* (No. 23) belong to the second category, but show some affinity with the first in that at least one of the stanzas ends with the same words as the burden. They have what may be called "incipient refrain." Mention must be made also of *The holy martyr Steven* (No. 26) in which, by way of exception, burden and stanza are rounded not by musical end-rhyme but by the same musical beginning.

Carols of the third type, much less common than those of the second, disregard the rounded text in their music. The comparative

---

[81] Shorter correspondences will not be considered here.

rarity of this type is in itself indicative of the predilection for rounded musical form. Carols that borrow a refrain line from the burden but set it to new music are *Tibi laus* (No. 20), *Princeps Patris* (No. 21), and *Ave plena gratia* (No. 42).

The fourth category, which shows no trace of rounding in either text or music, is also rather infrequent. *Exultavit cor* (No. 37), *Verbum patris* (No. 43), and *Alleluia pro virgine* (No. 46) exemplify this type. As No. 43 is very short, and No. 46 fairly long, it follows that the length of the composition has nothing to do with the absence or presence of musical or textual relations.

The foregoing remarks and observations will have demonstrated that a clear understanding of the carol form can be arrived at only if the musical and literary aspects are considered in their interrelations. This conclusion ought to be a commonplace, but it is precisely this point that has been frequently ignored in previous discussions.

STYLISTIC FEATURES OF THE CAROL

The music of the carol discloses a consistency of tone that sets it distinctly apart from other music of the time. We find a peculiar forcefulness and an unmistakable lilt in almost the entire group of carols that match the strong rhythm, concise verse, and accentual meter of the lyric. How stereotyped the musical means are can be seen especially in the cadences, but even the melodies of different carols are sometimes very similar, as though one were "derived" from another. However, this impression is deceptive and is merely the outcome of the high stylistic uniformity. The most prominent unifying factor of the musical style is the reliance on a forthright and lilting rhythm. It is a curious fact—strangely enough, it has not yet received the attention it deserves—that carols in duple time do not seem to exist in the fifteenth century. They are written either in compound time (*prolatio major*) or triple time (*tempus perfectum*),[82] both of which permit a springy rhythm still closely associated with the dance. It is, however, very improbable that the stylized polyphonic settings were actual dance music. They are "plainly songs to

---

[82] Transcribed here in 6/8 and 3/4 time respectively. The former meter suggests today a rather fast tempo because of the short note values. However, it must be remembered that in major prolation the unit of the beat shifted from the semibreve to the minim. If one wanted to keep the unit the same in both meters, major prolation would have to be transcribed in 6/4 time; this is, in fact, the better alternative in cases where the florid upper line would otherwise call for thirty-second notes. All examples in this study are transcribed in reduction by four.

be sung in company, but not to be danced to." [83] Whether in compound or triple time, the carols invariably introduce the hemiola ($\musEighth\ \musEighth\ \musEighth = \musSixteenth\ \musSixteenth\ \musSixteenth\ \musSixteenth$) either simultaneously in two voices or in successive measures. The device is, indeed, so typical that the carol might well be called hemiola music pure and simple. There is literally not a single carol in the collection that does not have it. For a representative example the reader may refer to Ex. 20. The hemiola occurs here incessantly in all conceivable combinations. It manifests itself in m. 10 in an especially intricate pattern of the upper voice which is characteristic only of melodies in major prolation. This seemingly irrational rhythm can be unraveled as $\musEighth.\ \musEighth.\ \musEighth\ \musEighth$; that is to say, one measure of 6/8 is subdivided into equal halves (6/16 + 3/8), and this fractional hemiola is superimposed on another one that covers an entire measure ($\musEighth\ \musEighth\ \musEighth$). Thus we have a clash of hemiolas on the lower and higher rhythmic level.

The law of the *senaria*, the constant hovering between 6/8 and 3/4, governs all carols regardless of the meter they adopt. However, it should not be thought that the selection of meter is immaterial. It is, on the contrary, a factor of historical significance which throws some light on the development of carol music. At the beginning of the century major prolation was clearly the favorite meter, as may be gathered from the Burgundian chansons by Fontaine and Vide,[84] and to a lesser degree from those by Binchois and the early Dufay. As the century progresses, *tempus perfectum*, more straightforward and stable than the ambiguous 6/8, is in the ascendant and gradually supplants the older rhythm.[85] The question whether the carol conforms to this evolution has never been raised but is definitely worth investigating. The four major carol manuscripts give, indeed, an unequivocal answer. In the Trinity Roll major prolation obtains in nearly all compositions; in the Selden MS it still governs two-thirds of the repertory, and it is probably no accident that pieces in the more recent *tempus perfectum* are more numerous toward the end of the collection. In the Meaux Abbey MS major prolation has dwindled to one-third of the pieces, and in Add. MS 5665 it has practically disappeared. The stylistic changes of the carol thus parallel those of the Bur-

83 Greene, *op. cit.*, lviii. He has shown that carol meant originally "a dance with song" and that this meaning changed at the beginning of the fifteenth century to "a song in a special form not accompanied by dancing" (xix and lix).

84 Marix, *op. cit.*, 9 and 17.

85 Besseler, AMW VII, 240.

gundian chanson, a fact that is all the more surprising as there is no direct contact between the forms.

Although the four manuscripts necessarily give a more or less haphazard cross section of a much larger repertory the dimensions of which are not known, they disclose a definite trend from 6/8 to 3/4, which has, moreover, some bearing on the relative age of the sources. LoM takes an intermediate place between the Trinity and Selden MSS, which represent the oldest known collections, and the late London MS. Even if we have no definite information about the exact dates of the first three manuscripts, the meters used suggest a chronology by internal evidence. This is borne out also by the concordances and stylistic findings. The Trinity Roll overlaps with the Selden MS, and the latter in turn with the Meaux Abbey MS, but there are no correspondences between the first and the third source.

The same historical order is suggested stylistically by those remarkably primitive burdens that are either partially or entirely monophonic. These must be recognized as survivals of the early stage of the carol when choral polyphony had not yet been evolved and the music was still danced to, or at least was quite close to the dance. In these pieces the choral unison of the burden (which should not be confused with a solo [86]) alternates with the solo polyphony of the stanza. Characteristically, choral unison passages are still rather common in the Trinity Roll, much less frequent in the Selden MS, and completely ousted by part music in LoM. Whatever its date may be, the Trinity Roll certainly imparts the polyphonic carol in the earliest known stage of development.[87] The other two manuscripts testify to the fairly rapid stylistic changes about the middle of the century.

The carols of LoM are written in an emphatically consonant style with stress on quickly alternating thirds, sixths, and tenths. Extended parallel motion in any one of these intervals is infrequent. Aside from suspensions, dissonances occur only in passing or as ornamental notes. The Trinity Roll betrays in the use of fourths as harmonic intervals a slightly less finished dissonance treatment and a somewhat archaic style. The texture is essentially that of a gymel with frequent crossing of parts, smoothly written with ease and grace, al-

[86] Greene, *op. cit.*, lvii, falls into this error.

[87] Although written in white notation, the MS was compiled probably a decade or so before 1450; for the question of when white notation was introduced see our discussion on p. 94. Greene, *op. cit.*, 343, also dates the MS in the first half of the century.

though, as has been shown above, the added middle voice of the three-part sections is often clumsy enough. It seems that the carol composers of the fifteenth century were really at home only in the two-voice medium. In keeping with the simple style, imitation and learned integration of voices are practically nonexistent.[88] The three-part passages never go beyond a very simple sixth-chord style. This chord appears invariably in the cadence. Obviously the carols were composed before the time the modern V–I cadence was generally accepted. It is true that there are a few V–I progressions—for example, in *Ave rex angelorum* or in the chorus of *Illuminare*—but these occur as intermediate, never as final, cadences.

In respect to melodic structure, the cadence appears either as an ornamental sixth with its typical leap to the final from the third below, or as leading-note cadence in which the final is reached directly by half-step. The difference between the two is minute and does not affect the contrapuntal relations at all. Yet if cautiously considered in context it has some historical significance, because the ornamental sixth gave way to the leading note in the course of the latter half of the century. This process can be traced in the manuscript transmission of the same composition. For example, certain chansons of the Burgundian school, originally composed with the ornamental sixth and thus recorded in the oldest sources, often appear in later versions with the more recent form of cadence. This modernization is due to scribes who felt free to bring the music up to date.[89] In the carol manuscripts the situation is somewhat more complex, inasmuch as both forms occur side by side. Comparing the relative frequency of the two forms, we find that in the Meaux Abbey MS the leading-note cadence is more common than the older one, while the opposite is true of the Trinity Roll. This does not mean anything in itself, but in conjunction with the other points raised it strengthens what has been said about the stylistic position and chronology of the carol manuscripts.

While the harmony of the carol conforms to the general practice of the time, its melodic style is singularly distinctive. Taken by them-

---

[88] I have found so far only three snatches of imitation in the thirty-three carols, namely in the two-voice sections of Nos. 31, 32, and 50. The first one is clearly set in relief by a preceding rest, but is not exact as to pitch, while the reverse is true of the second.

[89] A most interesting, and probably the last, example of this practice in the sixteenth (!) century is reported by Einstein, *The Italian Madrigal*, 1949, I, 278. Corteccia revised his own madrigals by eliminating all the ornamental sixth cadences, which by that time had become an anachronism.

selves the melodic lines are characterized by vigor, exuberance, and pristine simplicity, though their contrapuntal combination leads to intricate rhythmic overlaps. They have a decidedly popular flavor and tone, resembling in this respect certain intentionally popular melodies of Burgundian chansons, such as *L'homme armé.* In these compositions the emphasis rests unmistakably on melody pure and simple. In contrast to the lines themselves, their phrase structure is rather complex. Far from being evenly distributed in two-by-two or four-by-four measures, the phrases are extremely variable in length. They always coincide with the lines of the text and thus attest to the close relations between music and lyric. However, these relations go no further than that. The natural accent of individual words is as loosely observed as in other music of the time, and before cadences, and sometimes at other places, the melody may often become florid and melismatic. There is a tendency to begin syllabically and to place melismas toward the end of the phrase. The Ivy carol (No. 31) proves the rule by a short melisma at the beginning.

Since the carols are composed essentially as gymels, the single voices are of very nearly equal importance and move at approximately the same brisk pace. If the parts are rhythmically differentiated, the treble is written in shorter note values [90] than the other voices and is plainly conceived as a florid counterpoint to the tenor, which stands out as a melody of independence and "character." Carols with "tenor lead" sometimes have, indeed, some affinity with the German "tenor lied," as found in the Schedel [91] and Glogau [92] songbooks.

The two voices of the gymel frequently exchange cadences; that is to say, the tenor performs the leading-note cadence and the treble the tenor cadence. This free inversion of functions bespeaks the essential equivalence of voices, even if one of them may be more characteristic. The question of which voice carries the "tune" of the carol is therefore, more often than not, moot: the parts were complementary and were composed for each other. The question cannot be answered because the problem it poses is wrong. It has already been shown in the discussion of the burden-chorus relations that any one of the voices could be singled out and repeated in the chorus.

Carried by a vigorous rhythm, the melody is paradoxically both

[90] See Ex. 21, where sixteenth notes appear in the upper voice only.

[91] Selected transcriptions by H. Rosenberg, Kassel, 1933; see also Eitner, *Das deutsche Lied,* 1876 and 1880.

[92] Partial edition in *Reichsdenkmale,* Vols. IV and VIII.

smooth and angular, and definitely not what would be considered today as a finished vocal line or an easily singable tune. The smooth melodic design is derived from the extensive use of repeated notes or patterns that cover up the reiteration of the same note by turns to the lower and upper second and third. The angularity, on the other hand, is due to the insistence on disjunct motion between structurally important notes of the melody. This is immediately apparent in the manner of joining phrases. Carol composers have a penchant for large "dead" intervals such as octaves and even sevenths. Also within the phrase the essential notes are preferably disjunct, although they may be joined by conjunct motion on the weak beat. Progressions outlining the triad, skips of the third, fifths, and sevenths are quite common. The latter interval substantially contributes to the modal flavor of the music.[98] The melodies sound fresh but at the same time very much alike, so that if one knows a dozen the rest sound somehow familiar. The characteristic angularity would be much more noticeable were it not for the driving rhythm that propels the melody and gives it its springy, masculine quality. The interaction between angular design and rhythmic vigor is the secret of the popular style of the carol.

4. POPULAR OR FOLK MUSIC?

The conformity with the general style of the fifteenth century, the skill displayed in the counterpoint, the rigid form and its imaginative variants, the melodic types, and the delight in hemiola patterns characterize the polyphonic carol as the product of trained musicians, as art music composed in the popular vein. In the happy phrase of Greene,[94] the carol is "popular by destination" rather than "popular by origin"—a statement that applies to lyric as well as music. The pleasant fiction that it is a folk product, which certain scholars and musicians maintain, rests on a set of unproven, fanciful, and often self-contradictory assumptions which are derived from the nineteenth-century ideology of folk song and which are incompatible with the evidence of the sources. If the polyphonic carols of the manuscripts under discussion were folk music, they would be transmitted by oral tradition, which would invariably bring about widely differing vari-

[98] For example, the tenors of Nos. 25 and 40 (chorus) circumscribe the seventh.
[94] Greene, *op. cit.*, xciii.

ants in music and text. In his study of the literary variants Greene has shown that about half of the carol texts found in more than one manuscript "derive from written copies without dependence on oral tradition." [95] The recorded versions agree, indeed, so closely as to rule out any other possibility. The evidence of the musical sources leads us to exactly the same conclusion. The musical variants are not greater than those commonly found in the repertory of the Burgundian chanson.

It may be added here that *Omnes una gaudeamus* and *Ecce quod natura,* the only two cantilenas with a somewhat unorthodox form, are exceptional also in that their variants differ more widely than usual. Of the three extant versions of *Ecce quod natura* [96] those of the Meaux Abbey and Selden MSS are practically the same, but that of the Ashmole MS shows considerable deviations, especially in the stanza. The music easily persuades us that the changes are the work of a skilled musician, and besides, nobody would seriously assume that this Latin song was a folk song handed down by oral tradition. Another argument against the folk origin is the fact that the carols were sometimes set to new music in later sources when the old setting was felt to be out of date. A case in point is *I pray yow all* (No. 41), which appears with the same music in OS and LoM and with a different setting in later style in Add. MS 5665.

The mode of transmission contradicts the folk-song theory by external evidence. More significant even is the internal evidence of the stylistic findings. Unfortunately, "stylistic evidence" is a thing unknown to those who, ignorant of history and of scholarly procedure, are unable to evaluate fifteenth-century style in its own terms. They are satisfied with the convenient solution of declaring the carol to be folk music pure and simple. We may take as an example of this attitude the preface to an edition of Sir Richard Terry, in which he justifies his modernizing arrangement of carol melodies.[97] The passage deserves to be quoted in full, as it is probably unique in its succinct and categorical statement of common fallacies and in its sincere belief in wrong premises that lead to unacceptable consequences.

[95] Greene, *op. cit.,* cv–cvi.

[96] It may be added here that the burden of *Ecce quod natura* appears in two macaronic carols (Greene, Nos. 65 and 66). The entire poem occurs with different music also in *Piae Cantiones,* No. VII.

[97] Terry, *A Medieval Carol Book,* Oxford University Press [1931].

As they stand in the MSS. (in the crude and experimental counterpoint of their period) these carols are of the highest antiquarian and historical value, but only the sheerest preciosity would suggest their public performance in that form, or claim for them any aesthetic appeal to musicians of to-day. Their unsuitability for performance in their original form is not due to their antiquity; the folk-tunes on which they are founded are of even earlier date but are nevertheless grateful to modern ears. It is merely that the folk-tunes of the carols are a finished artistic product, while the crude counterpoint which is woven around them is the first fumbling attempt in search of a technique which did not attain perfection until the sixteenth century.

. . . In the MSS. to which I have gone for this present collection we have evidence that the tunes associated with the carols were sufficiently well known for the fifteenth-century contrapuntists to take them as *canti fermi* for their more elaborate settings. That they should have done so is fortunate, as it meant the preservation in MSS. of many noble tunes which might have perished if handed down (like those which have disappeared) by oral tradition.

We shall not quarrel here about the *non sequitur* of the jumbled last sentence, which amusingly reflects the contradictory premises of the folk-tune theory, nor shall we take issue with the merits of Sir Richard's musical arrangements.[98] There may still be some who prefer the Wardour Street flavor in the modal harmonies of a nineteenth-century musician to the freshness of the original counterpoints. However, at the risk of being charged with "sheerest preciosity" I should deny that in proper performance the carols have no aesthetic appeal to musicians of today.[99] It is not without irony that Sir Richard, who worked so devotedly for the proper recognition of English music of the sixteenth century, betrays here with regard to fifteenth-century music the same lack of historical and musical understanding that he combated himself with regard to the music of Byrd's time. It is this lack that prompted him to arrange the carols in order to make them "grateful to modern ears."

Let us examine the premises of Sir Richard's position. The funda-

[98] They are, musically, unquestionably superior to the pitiful arrangements by Rockstro in Fuller-Maitland's edition.

[99] Only after the completion of this study did I have occasion to verify the above statement in a public performance of a group of carols at the Second National Convention of the Music Teachers National Association in San Francisco, August, 1949. The audience, which could not exactly be accused of bookishness or scholarly proclivities, responded with an enthusiasm that exceeded even the highest expectations.

mental assumption that the carols are founded on folk tunes is not borne out by any musical or even circumstantial evidence and is no more than a wishful thought. The second assumption, that the alleged folk tunes are "even of an earlier date" than the settings, is a logical but nevertheless equally fanciful corollary of the first one. If the carols were originally independent folk tunes, it would indeed be logical to assume that they must be older than the polyphonic settings which record them in the earliest known form. However, the proof rests entirely on the validity of the first premise.

There is a curious desire in folklorists to date their material as far back as possible, as though the tunes were antiques which increase in value with age; the statement that a tune is "of ancient origin," with which they liberally sprinkle their writings, is to them the epithet of highest distinction. This is the antiquarian's point of view, not that of the historian. The naive reverence for age for its own sake, for old things merely because they are not new, of which the music historian is sometimes unjustly accused, betrays the total lack of historical thinking; it evaluates the artistic manifestations of the past not in their own terms but as interesting curios that have been salvaged for the present.

It is somewhat surprising that Sir Richard characterizes the alleged folk tunes as "a finished artistic product," which indeed they are, but precisely this fact would refute rather than confirm their popular origin. While he accepts the "finished" melodies at face value, he rejects their contrapuntal settings as "crude and experimental." We have seen, however, that there is no such discrepancy, that melodic inventiveness and contrapuntal skill are on an equally distinguished level. It is not admissible to compare the settings, as Sir Richard does, with the standards of sixteenth-century part writing. But even if the comparison is made, the opposite of his assertion is true: the counterpoint of the polyphonic carol conforms by and large to the classic contrapuntal rules of the "Golden Age," and it is precisely the angular melodic line which does not submit to them. By considering in his comparison only the contrapuntal settings but not the lines themselves —which, after all, constitute the counterpoint—Sir Richard performed a mechanical and unmusical division of elements. Had he taken into account the melodic and rhythmic characteristics of the carol tunes, he would have found that they are incompatible with sixteenth-century melody writing.

He claims, finally, that there is "evidence" in the manuscripts that the folk tunes served as cantus firmi, but he does not divulge the nature of his evidence. His failure to do so is unfortunate but not surprising, because not a shred of such evidence exists. On the contrary, what can be gathered from parallel repertories points to the opposite conclusion. Had the carol melodies or the tenors of Burgundian chansons been pre-existent tunes, we should expect to find them sometimes in monophonic form, that is to say in their original state before they were adjusted and adapted to polyphony. Indeed, we know of several collections of the late fifteenth and early sixteenth centuries that contain monophonic Burgundian chansons,[100] but what do they reveal? They present the tenors in precisely the rhythmic form called for by the polyphonic setting; they even retain long rests which have no function here. The one-voice versions do not represent the "original state" of a hypothetical *Urmelodie,* but single voices detached from their polyphonic settings. The part songs are therefore not the survivals, in art music, of lost folk songs, but the originals themselves from which collectors and amateurs selected tenors for monophonic performance. The manuscripts in which the monophonic versions appear are without exception later than the polyphonic ones. The tenors could subsequently serve as cantus firmi in compositions by later composers, but even they usually retain the original rhythm in deference to the original.[101] Since the polyphonic settings of the carol, Burgundian chanson, and German tenor lied of the fifteenth century are original compositions, it is small wonder that they transmit the earliest known versions of the "tunes"; and by taking them out of their polyphonic context the musical folklorists of our time have unwittingly imitated the musical amateurs of the fifteenth century. The three types of composition were addressed to different audiences and their degree of popularity varied with the social level of the audiences, but the persistent legend that the settings are based on folk songs is at variance with all known facts, the treasured beliefs of musical antiquarians notwithstanding.

The Meaux Abbey MS furnishes, moreover, conclusive proof that

[100] There are three collections of this sort in Paris, Bibl. Nat. MS n.a.fr. 4379 (see the list of contents in Besseler, AMW VII, 233), MS fr. 12744 (ed. by Gaston Paris, *Chansons du XVe siècle,* 1875, new ed. 1935), and MS fr. 9346 (ed. by Gérold, *Le Manuscrit de Bayeux,* 1921).

[101] Bukofzer, "An Unknown Chansonnier of the 15th Century," in MQ XXVIII (1942), 31, n. 75.

popular art music could well be reconciled with the most learned musical devices known at the time. The drinking song *O potores exquisiti* (No. 51), the penultimate piece of the original repertory and the last one to be discussed here, stands quite properly alongside of the popular carols and cantilenas. Its text, a now famous Goliardic song, occurs in the *Carmina Burana* and another thirteenth-century manuscript.[102] With regard to this text the much abused qualification "of great antiquity" may for once be used with full justification. Although the composition is, as its topic discloses, unquestionably "popular by destination," it is written in motet style and consequently notated in separate parts like the companion piece *Cantemus Domino*. It differs from the latter, however, by virtue of its tenor. Not based on a liturgical melody, it shows at several places unwonted rhythmic life, which leaves no doubt about the "spirited" subject matter of the text. This is made doubly clear by the style of the upper voice, which declaims the words in a rapid parlando with some fanciful syncopations. The song is adorned by two charming miniatures representing the less austere side of monastic life (see Plate 3). They are the two most elaborate miniatures of the manuscript, and the only ones that depict everyday human scenes, thus placing special emphasis on this particular piece.

Schofield has correctly stated that the three strophes of the song have been given separate settings. Aside from a brief motto in the first and last one, they are melodically unrelated. Yet there exists an undeniable musical resemblance between them which is difficult to account for at first glance. Closer scrutiny has brought to light what is perhaps the most startling discovery in the non-liturgical part of the collection: the song is isorhythmic in all its voices, and the strophes are treated exactly like the three periods of an isorhythmic motet. The first part of the first strophe has been transcribed in Ex. 22. Certain idiosyncrasies of the isorhythmic motet are clearly preserved; for example, there is a temporary change of meter in the middle of the isorhythmic period and the end is set off by an animated hocket section.

The harmonic style of the music, the circumstance that the tenor no longer employs the artifices of *color* and *talea*, and the melodic style rule out the possibility that we have here a composition of the late fourteenth century that by chance found its way into a mid-

102 Schofield, *loc. cit.*, 524.

Ex. 22. Isorhythmic drinking song: *O potores.*

O po-to - res ex - qui - si - - ti li cet si - tis si-ne si -

ti en bi-ba-tis ex-pe-di - ti et ci- fo-rum in o-bli-ti ci - fi cre-bro re-pe-ti-ti

non dor - mi - ant Et ser-mo-nes in -

Et ser-mo-nes in -

Et ser-mo-nes in-

fifteenth-century manuscript. It must have been written at the same time as the rest of the repertory. The striking use of isorhythm in a drinking song, of all places, smacks of parody and learned ostentation. By the middle of the century isorhythm, if used at all, was set aside for the most austere and dignified composition but was already a thing of the past. Its appearance in a partly liturgical, partly semisecular collection of compositions in unpretentious style adds a touch of irony and marks a reversal of trends, possible only at the end of an era. The drinking song has the double distinction of being not only the earliest known setting of the text but also one of the latest isorhythmic compositions in English music.

V

The Beginnings of Choral Polyphony

AT WHAT time did composers begin to write polyphonic music for chorus? This is a question not only of the traditions or code of performance, but also of the evolution of musical style. Composition for chorus requires a certain idiom; when and how was this idiom developed? To put it differently, one might ask: When did composers become chorus-conscious?

The first great achievements of polyphonic vocal writing, such as the *organa quadrupla* by Perotin and the motets of the thirteenth and fourteenth centuries, are often regarded as choral music to be sung by the church choir.[1] This opinion, however popular it may be, is quite at variance with the facts. We know definitely that medieval polyphonic music was written generally not for large groups, but for soloists. Besides internal evidence that indicates performance by them, thirteenth-century records of the Notre Dame archives show that only four singers were employed for polyphonic singing, who, incidentally, received twice as much salary as the other singers.[2] The only type of choral singing generally practiced in the Middle Ages is that of the choir in unison. Gregorian chant had developed to a high degree of

[1] See, for example, the edition of Perotin's *organum quadruplum, Sederunt principes*, by Rudolf Ficker (Universal Edition, 1930). This practical edition assigns the choral unison sections of the chant to a solo voice and the soloists' polyphony to a chorus. A correct performance would call for the exact opposite. Ficker's arrangement is tantamount to assigning the solo arias of the St. Matthew Passion to a chorus and the chorales and choruses to a solo quartet.

[2] *Cf.* Jacques Handschin, "Zur Geschichte von Notre Dame," in *Acta Musicologica*, IV (1932), 8.

perfection the art of contrasting, in monophony, solo and choir singing. With the introduction of polyphony, only the sections which the
chant had intended for soloists were recast for two or more voices,
while the rest remained choral monophony. This is true of the great
collections of clausulae and motets in the thirteenth century, which
record only the polyphonic sections and occasionally a short cue for
the monophonic continuation. The situation remains essentially unchanged until the beginning of the fifteenth century, as may be seen
in several Mass compositions of the Trent codices which specifically
assign the plainsong to the "chorus" and, by implication, the polyphonic settings to the soloists.[8] The difference between solo and choral
performance, present in purely monophonic renditions of Gregorian
chant, was at first weakened by the polyphonic settings, since the contrast between one solo singer and a choir group was replaced by op-
posing a group of solo singers to the choir. However, the substitution
brought to light the new distinction between polyphony and monophony.

The musical manuscripts are not very generous in their indications
for performance. Usually it was taken for granted that the singers
knew what to do. If we find directions at all, it is always for special
reasons. For instance, in the famous Office of Sens,[4] the manuscript
preserves a careful record of the various kinds of performance desired;
unus, chorus, ad organum, and *cum falseto* are among the indications
that appear. Since this music belongs to the thirteenth century, it
should not surprise us that the term *chorus* refers here to monophonic
choir singing; *unus,* however, indicates organum for the soloists.

We may expect to find directions for performance when, for some
reason, a traditional type of performance is abandoned. Thus, the
manuscripts are likely to afford special indications when polyphonic
choral singing was at its inception. But if we want to approach our
subject without mere speculation, we should present conclusive proof
of the existence of such singing. The first definite evidence occurs in a
group of Italian manuscripts, in which certain sections of the music
are marked *unus* and others *chorus.* Usually the term *unus* is placed

<hr>

[8] A Gloria by Dufay (Trent 1443, facs. in DTOe, Vol. 14, Pl. IX) sets the entire chant
alternately for choral monophony and solo polyphony in fauxbourdon style. A similar
Credo (Trent 179, DTOe, 61, 20) presents the monophonic sections as *cantus fractus* for
the chorus.

[4] See *Office de Pierre Corbeil,* ed. by Villetard, *Bibliothèque musicologique,* IV, 1907;
also Ludwig, *Repertorium,* 229.

before a duet, while the term *chorus* appears before a three-voiced section. Here we find the earliest record of the use, in a polyphonic piece, of the contrast between choir and a duet of soloists. The first manuscript to indicate this contrast in a considerable number of compositions is Codex 37 of the Liceo Musicale in Bologna.[5] In more than twenty works [6] we find remarks referring to performance by choir and soloists, written by the scribe who also notated the music. The indications are therefore authentic. A great number of the compositions refer to political events, while others are actually dated—facts that reveal the manuscript to have been written, most probably, between 1430 and 1440.

Taking the Bologna codex as a starting point, we find additional evidence in other manuscripts of Italian origin, namely the celebrated manuscript Canonici Misc. 213 of the Bodleian Library, the Aosta MS, the fragment Munich 3224, Modena lat. 471, and Cambrai 6 and 11. The Bologna, Munich, Oxford, Aosta, and Modena MSS, of which the first two are in black notation, form the first group of sources referring to polyphonic choral music. In the Oxford codex, the indications say clearly *dui* for the sections for soloists and *chorus* for those for choir. And where the Bologna MS says *unus,* the MSS from Cambrai say *duo*. All these duets are sections for soloists. Of course, the term *duo* would prove nothing in itself. It could, for instance, simply indicate that the respective section is for two parts instead of three. But, when used in conjunction with the contrasting term *chorus,* the meaning is unequivocal.

The term *duo* occurs also in the Trent codices, which are often unreliable both in their notation and in their attributions to composers. But through comparison with variant copies in other manuscripts we can ascertain that the *duo* sections are for soloists and the other sections for chorus. The directions of the Trent codices, however, are neither consistent nor complete; frequently the indications are

[5] Mention should be made also of two flyleaves from MS Rome, Vat. Barb. lat. 171, which formed part of an Italian MS now lost (cf. Bannister, *Monumenti Vaticani*, I, 185; Ludwig, AMW V [1923], 201, fn.; Besseler, *ibid.,* VII [1925], 228; and de Van, *Les Monuments de l'Ars Nova*, No. 8, which contains a Gloria with the trope *Clementie pax*). In one of the fragments on f.223r a two-voice Gloria trope is set off against the regular (three-voice?) Gloria text by the indications D[uo] and C[horus]. Since the MS seems to be somewhat older than Codex 37, we may have here the earliest documentary proof, in a musical source, for polyphonic choral singing.

[6] Only a few of these are available in print. Cf. Johannes Wolf, *Geschichte der Mensural-Notation*, III, 1904; DTOe, Vol. 76; *Polyphonia Sacra* (ed. by van den Borren), 1932; *Les Musiciens de la Cour de Bourgogne* (ed. by J. Marix), 1937.

omitted, even though the same piece may appear with them in more trustworthy manuscripts.

Let us turn now to the stylistic side of the question and see whether we can find a musical criterion that distinguishes music for soloists from that for chorus. Surprisingly enough, a contrast between the two does not appear in these early compositions. The duets are composed in the same manner as the rest of the music. One would expect to find the choral sections simpler in rhythm and melodic design. But if a difference is to be noted at all, it is the opposite that would seem to be true: the sections for soloists sometimes have a smoother rhythm than the choral sections. How are we to explain this puzzle? Our natural assumption would be that the solo passages must be sung by two soloists, the rest by a three-part chorus. However, for a number of compositions this is not the case. Actually, only the upper voice of the choral sections is sung by the chorus in unison, while the other two voices are played by instruments. In the best manuscripts the directions for performance are appended to each voice. Thus both voices of the duet sections have the indication *unus,* and both have the text carefully distributed. In the choral sections, however, *chorus* is indicated only in the cantus and the text is placed only under that part; moreover, the two lower voices are notated with many ligatures, suggesting instrumental performance.

In these exceptional works the familiar contrast between solo polyphony and choral monophony is preserved, while at the same time it is adapted to compositions that are entirely polyphonic. The interest of these pieces lies in the fact that they represent a transitional stage between polyphony for soloists and polyphony for chorus. The earliest compositions of this type, and there are only a few, are by Binchois [7] and Ciconia. The presence of choral unison in one part of a polyphonic setting explains why we do not find a stylistic difference between sections for soloists and those for choir. One voice of a polyphonic setting, however complicated it may be, can easily be sung by a choir. True polyphonic choral music is not yet developed. Why composers should have imposed the contrast between choir and soloists on a polyphonic piece is understandable only if we consider

[7] A Credo by Binchois is printed in *Polyphonia Sacra,* No. 9, 63. For the indications *unus* and *chorus,* see the note on p. xvi. A similar Magnificat by Binchois may be found in Schering, *Geschichte der Musik in Beispielen,* 1931, No. 43, 37. See also the Kyrie by Dufay in Schering, No. 39. The fragmentary Gloria from MS Rome, Vat. Barb. lat. 171, mentioned in note 5, belongs in all likelihood to the same type.

the Gregorian background of their tradition. It is significant also that, when the contrast occurs in Mass compositions, the tropes of the Mass, which belong traditionally to the soloist, are usually treated as solo duets.[8]

There is no way of knowing whether or not the compositions of Ciconia and Binchois were originally intended to be performed in the manner just described. It may well be that the presence of the unusual choral unison within a polyphonic composition is the result of an adaptation, made at a time when the tendency toward choir performance was in the air. Another stage of this development is represented by a Mass composition of Ciconia's,[9] in which we find the contrast between choir and duet of soloists; here the choir sections already comprise two vocal lines, and there is only one instrumental part.

The final step toward polyphonic choir music is taken by Guillaume Legrant in a Gloria and Credo.[10] In the choir sections, indicated by *chorus,* the text is carefully placed under all three voices. The Gloria is composed in a stark chordal style quite suitable for choral performance, and the simplicity of style obtains even in the duet, so that no attempt is made to differentiate between solo and choral style. However, in the Credo, for the first time, a stylistic contrast is discernible between solo and choral polyphony. The sections for soloists are written in more complex rhythms, while those for the chorus display a strongly chordal design. It is fortunate that this composition is dated 1426; we thus have a neat record showing when the first known piece of choral polyphony was written.

The fact that the manuscripts expressly give directions concerning the manner of performance indicates that it was something out of the ordinary at the time. Once established, choral polyphony developed at a rapid pace. The manuscripts so far referred to are still of the usual small size, only big enough to allow three or four people to sing from them. Even a small choir could not use them for performance.

[8] For a confirmation of the rule, see Ciconia's *Et in terra* (*Polyphonia Sacra,* No. 11, 82) in which, by way of exception, the chorus sings just one section of the trope. See also Peter Wagner, *Geschichte der Messe,* 1913, 83. The duos from the troped Gloria of the Vatican fragment pose a different problem. Here the extant upper part is several times split into two voices, one of which is written in red notes. In order to perform both, the part had to be sung by at least two soloists—unless we assume that it was doubled by a string instrument capable of playing double stops.

[9] *Polyphonia Sacra,* No. 11, 82.

[10] *Polyphonia Sacra,* No. 18, 123, and No. 19, 127.

A change takes place in the middle and second half of the fifteenth century. The "modern" type of music manuscript at that period was the giant choir book, which could be read from a distance by a large group.[11]

The earliest manuscripts of this type are the Codices Cambrai 6 and 11, Modena lat. 454, 455, and 456. While the Cambrai manuscripts contain chiefly works by Binchois and Dufay, perhaps not originally intended for choral performance, the Modena manuscripts give us the first examples of choir music in which even the external appearance of the manuscript points to the type of performance. The size of the manuscript as well as the style of the music indicates that what we have here is choral music, designed as such from the outset. Appropriately enough, we no longer find the term *chorus* in these sources, because choral performance is now taken for granted; however, the sections for soloists are still sometimes marked *duo*.

The choir books are of Italian origin, and we must regard Italy as the homeland of polyphonic choral music. It is here that composers of polyphony first became chorus-minded. This does not necessarily mean that they themselves were Italians; they were, on the contrary, mostly of Franco-Flemish descent. In one of the Modena manuscripts (456) we find a late work by Dufay, the *Missa Ave regina,* as well as the anonymous Mass on *O rosa bella.* Both seem to make use of choral polyphony. The rapid development of choral music may be observed in the other two huge choir books at Modena. These two codices are of special interest,[12] as they are the first sources to give evidence of performance by a double chorus. They contain mostly settings of psalms and hymns, but also a polyphonic Passion that calls at one place for no less than eight voices. According to the Gregorian tradition, hymns and psalms were chanted antiphonally. The use of polyphony modified this tradition to the alternate singing of the plainsong in unison by the choir and of the polyphonic setting by the soloists. The Modena manuscripts, however, call for two choirs

11 The size of the staves varies between one and two inches, the size of the whole page between 20 × 14 and 28 × 19 inches. Such a giant choir book is depicted in a charming miniature showing Okeghem and the members of his choir grouped around a big lectern; see Plamenac, "Autour d'Ockeghem," in *Revue Musicale* IX, 1928, and Besseler, *Musik des Mittelalters und der Renaissance,* 234.

12 The MSS Modena Estense lat. 454 and 455 have not yet been adequately described. References in Besseler, *Musik des Mittelalters und der Renaissance,* 217; Moser, *Die mehrstimmige Vertonung des Evangeliums,* I, 1931, and *Heinrich Schütz,* 1936, 561; Bukofzer, *Geschichte des Englischen Diskants,* 1936, 122.

which sing, polyphonically, alternate stanzas of the hymns or alternate lines of the psalms. Each choir has its own manuscript; two books are needed, each containing only one-half of the composition. We have here the beginnings of polychoral composition, almost a hundred years before Willaert, generally regarded as its inventor, wrote his famous psalms for double chorus.

The musical style of most of these compositions is that of fauxbourdon in strict and sometimes in elaborate form. It will be illustrated by excerpts from Psalm 72, set for double chorus of three voices each (Ex. 1). The cantus firmus (psalm tone 8) lies in the discantus

Ex. 1. Psalm: *Quam bonus* for double chorus.

and is slightly ornamented. The piece consists of simple three-part settings and strict fauxbourdon sections for which only the two outer parts are notated; the middle part must be improvised.[13]

It may be gathered from the example that the simple declamatory style it displays was apparently the typical idiom of choral polyphony as it was conceived at the time. This raises the question whether faux-bourdon was choral music from its inception. We have no positive proof that it was. An affirmative view would be a very tempting one, with far-reaching consequences. It is striking that Codex 37 of Bologna, the first to record polyphonic choir performances, is also the first to record the term fauxbourdon—not, however, in the same section of the manuscript. If fauxbourdon really was choir music from the beginning, it would be plausible to suppose that this is true also of English discant and certain compositions of the Old Hall MS in con-ductus style. However, evidence supporting this theory is lacking; moreover, there are some positive indications that fauxbourdon was performed by soloists.

It is not to be overlooked that the treatises on English discant and fauxbourdon improvisation [14] speak of the performers of the various "sights" in the singular, implying that the parts were performed by soloists. More convincing and important is the evidence of the musi-cal sources themselves. As we have seen above (see note 3) the Trent

[13] The improvised voice appears in small print. The accidentals for this voice, sug-gested in parentheses, are optional. The version with the optional sharps would be more in the style of the early fifteenth century; the one without them in that of the late fif-teenth century.

[14] See Meech, "Three . . . English Musical Treatises," in *Speculum* X (1935), 242; Bukofzer, *op. cit.*; Georgiades, *Englische Diskanttraktate*, 1937.

codices assign to the chorus the Gregorian intonation, but not the following polyphonic section. Exactly the same practice is observed in the numerous fauxbourdon settings of Modena, Est. MS lat. 471.[15] Fauxbourdon, then, must have been originally music for soloists, but was very soon taken over by the trend toward choir music. In the polychoral manuscripts of Modena we have not only fauxbourdon settings, but also declamatory compositions for six voices with a real bass—a style that later in the century became known as *falso bordone* and retained this name for centuries to come, although it meant no more than a simple declamatory composition in note-against-note style. It has never been questioned that *falsi bordoni* are choral compositions. We know of polyphonic settings of psalmody from as early as the thirteenth century, but not before the second half of the fifteenth century are we able to prove choir performance. We give in Ex. 2, taken from Modena, Est. MS lat. 455 (M I. 12), a six-voice *turba* from the St. Matthew Passion (XXVI, 8–9), composed in *falso bordone* style. This is one of the earliest fully chorus-conscious compositions for six voices. The Gregorian *tonus lectionis* lies in the tenor as cantus firmus. The other parts form a highly sonorous setting which makes full use of the low bass register. The final cadence, incidentally, shows perhaps the earliest known occurrence of a passing dominant-seventh chord resolving to a full major triad.

In addition to the contribution of the composers in Italy to the beginnings of choral polyphony, that of the English school must be considered. There is one type of English music in which the indication *chorus* appears very early, namely the carol and cantilena. The carol, originally, as we have seen, a monophonic dance song performed by chorus and solo in alternation, gradually appropriated polyphony and became an essentially polyphonic form in the course of the fifteenth century. With the increasing stylization the erstwhile dance song changed character and turned into a part song sung at social and religious occasions. The polyphonic carol consists of variable stanzas and an invariable burden which were originally sung by soloists only. However, in both stanzas and burden we find sometimes musical repeats specifically marked in the manuscripts as *chorus*. This can only mean choral polyphony.[16] The English carol tradition has

15 For a published example see Marix, *op. cit.,* 192; a variant reading of the same piece may be found in MQ XXVI (1940), 45.

16 The performance of the carol is discussed at some length in "Holy-Week Music and Carols at Meaux Abbey," where literature and editions are cited.

Ex. 2. Six-voice turba from St. Matthew Passion.

apparently no direct connection with the Italian trend toward choir music, but it makes its appearance at approximately the same time —i.e., about 1430. The four most important carol manuscripts with music are Cambridge, Trinity Coll. 1230; Bodleian, Selden B 26; British Museum Egerton 3307; and the oldest layer of Add. MS 5665.

Of these the Trinity Roll contains the oldest repertory. The solo and choral sections of the early carol do not show any conscious sty-

listic differentiation between the solo and choral idioms. Only occasionally do we meet with compositions in which the chorus repeats
the music of the burden in clearly simplified form. This case may
be illustrated by the cantilena *Qui natus est* (Ex. 3) from the Meaux

Ex. 3. Burden and chorus from *Qui natus est.*

Abbey MS (Egerton 3307, No. 27). Here the burden is set first as
gymel for soloists, and its melody is then taken up by the chorus in
different harmonization and a less florid style.

English composers of Power's and Dunstable's generation show a
strong predilection for solo duets in their sacred compositions, which
alternate with three-part chorus sections. It cannot always be decided
whether the latter should be sung chorally in all their parts or whether

they still belong to the transitional works in which only the upper voice is assigned to the chorus. The solo duets have the peculiarity that they frequently come to a complete standstill, expressly indicated by rests of one or more measures.[17] We find numerous examples of this English type of composition—in which the indications *unus* and *chorus* appear—in Codex 37 of Bologna; but these indications occur in English and Italian compositions indiscriminately. In English compositions preserved in the Trent codices—for example, those of Benet, Leonel, Bloym—we come across this technique so frequently that we could almost recognize them as English by this feature alone. In the giant late fifteenth- and early sixteenth-century choir books of English origin we sometimes find, instead of the term *duo*, the term *gymel*. The original meaning of the word is simply "duet for soloists," in contradistinction to choral performance. The big choir books of Lambeth Palace, Cambridge, Caius College, and Eton College, and also a few German sources, all agree in this point. The tie-up of this term with fauxbourdon and with the style of parallel thirds seems to be of secondary importance, judging from its actual appearance in musical sources. I must confess that I myself, in an earlier study, did not sufficiently discriminate between the historical and the systematic meaning of the term.[18]

It is difficult to make out whether the English predilection for duets was caused by Italian influence, since duets occur in Italian music as early as the fourteenth century. The Old Hall MS gives ample evidence of a positive Italian contact. But as far as the duet style is concerned, the English composers may well have developed this feature by themselves. At any rate, it can be stated that about 1430 choral polyphony was in the air, in Italy as well as in England. There is a certain affinity—either by design or by chance—between the movements toward choral music in the two countries. A very curious English practice is the interruption of polyphonic compositions by unison passages, with the same notes written out in different parts. We find examples in the Agincourt Carol and other pieces of Bodleian Selden

---

[17] For an example see Dunstable's *Alma redemptoris mater* in Reese, *Music in the Middle Ages*, 1940, 419; also Benet's Sanctus in Apel, *The Notation of Polyphonic Music*, 2nd ed., 1944, facs. 24. This custom, which is primarily English, accounts for the problem that Apel (*op. cit.*, 118) was at a loss to explain.

[18] "The Gymel, the Earliest Form of English Polyphony," in *Music and Letters*, XVI (1935), 77.

B 26, as well as in compositions of the retrospective collection, Cambridge, Magdalen College, Pepys 1236.[19]

The size of the choir for polyphonic performances must not be overestimated. The Papal chapel had only nine singers for polyphonic performances in 1436 and gradually increased the number to twelve, sixteen, and finally twenty-four persons in the second half of the century.[20] Usually we have to assume two or three singers for one part, except for the soprano, which was performed by a few more boys. Big choral groups with more than thirty singers were still very unusual at the time of Palestrina and Lasso. We even know of performances of Palestrina's works by soloists with strong voices. Though this music is primarily intended for a chorus, it was frequently treated as music for soloists. This can be proved by the surviving versions that are provided with embellishments; Hermann Finck [21] states on good evidence that such embellishments were sung by soloists.

Thus we have two trends side by side. One is the development of choral music from its beginnings about 1430 to the liturgical and chorus-conscious music of Okeghem, Obrecht, and Josquin, the polychoral extension of the choral idiom with Willaert and the Venetian School, and the synthesis in Palestrina and Lasso. The other is the soloist trend, which is particularly strong in the secular literature of the chanson and madrigal. Polyphonic choral music took its cue from and developed out of the Gregorian unison chorus; this explains why the first polyphonic choral music occurs in the church and why the secular compositions are slow in taking up the new fashion.[22] The medieval church knew principally only the unison choir and the solo ensemble. The polyphonic choir was an idea foreign to the medieval tradition. The beginnings of choral polyphony coincide with the beginnings of the musical Renaissance.

19 It may be added here that the Pepys MS contains the direction *chorus*, but not *gymel*. In his *History of English Music* Davey mentions a gymel in this MS, but he mistook the Hebrew letter *gimel* which belongs to the text of the Lamentations for a musical direction.

20 Haas, *Aufführungspraxis*, p. 108.

21 *Practica Musica*, 1556. For a survey of these and related questions see Bukofzer, "On the Performance of Renaissance Music," in *Proceedings of the Music Teachers National Association* (MTNA), 36 (1941), 225.

22 Peter Wagner, *op. cit.*, 77, points out that the change from solo to choral polyphony necessitated a careful treatment and setting of the words.

VI

A Polyphonic Basse Dance of the Renaissance

1. THE BASSE DANCE MELODIES

THE MUSICAL nature of the basse dance and its manner of performance has been the object of controversy and speculation for many years. The numerous, if contradictory, passages on basse dance in literary documents stand in sharp contrast to the scarcity of musical sources, which alone can give us a concrete notion of what the dance was like. Halfway between literary and musical sources stand the dance manuals and treatises on dance music of the Renaissance, of which more than twelve are extant. Most of them have been listed by Kinkeldey in his excellent study on Guglielmo Ebreo,[1] and several of them have been published in their entirety (see bibliography). The most recent survey on dance manuals can be found in a study by Michel.[2] Unfortunately, the authors of the manuals are rather reticent about the music and very rarely record basse-dance melodies. Kinkeldey has tabulated the twenty-five extant tunes, twenty-two of which are *balli,* and only three basse dances proper. The difference between *ballo* and *bassadanza* has been succinctly set forth by Gombosi[3] and discussed at length by Sachs,[4] whose findings have in turn been modified by Gombosi.

[1] See No. 48 of the bibliography at the end of this essay, which takes Kinkeldey's list as its starting point.

[2] No. 55.

[3] No. 42.

[4] No. 69.

Of all the dance tutors only Cornazano [5] offers any basse-dance melodies proper, and these three are recorded, as was usual, in monophonic form. They are entitled *Cançon de pifari dicto* [5a] *el Ferrarese, Collinetto,* and *Re di Spagna,* respectively. The last one, *La Spagna,* is the "theme song" of this essay. A large repertory of basse-dance melodies has been preserved in the famous, sumptuously ornamented Brussels MS,[6] which contains altogether fifty-nine compositions, consisting mostly of basse dances and a smaller number of *balli.* Until recently this manuscript represented our chief source of information for the basse-dance tunes aside from widely scattered isolated examples. As a rather remote source the Mass cycle by Faugues in the Trent Codices (No. 1151–1155) may be mentioned, the tenor of which is designated as *La Basse Dance.* The same title in Italian, the Mass *De la Bassadanza,* has been found in a manuscript index of the theorist Spartaro,[7] but whether or not this work is identical with the Mass by Faugues is not clear because the music is lost. In view of the repertory of the post-Josquin period it is very probably a different Mass founded on one of the basse-dance melodies. The *Spagna* melody, too, has served as a Mass tenor in a work by Isaac, printed by Petrucci (1506) under the title *Missa La Spagna.*

There are, furthermore, three ostensibly instrumental melodies which Handschin, in a lengthy footnote to one of his book reviews,[8] has connected with the basse-dance question. Although his discovery turns out to be abortive, a few particulars should be given here, even if by so doing we interrupt our line of investigation.

The three monophonic parts are contained in a fifteenth-century manuscript of the Vatican Library (Reg. lat. 1146, fol. 72v–73) which deals primarily with music theory and which Handschin suspects to be of English origin. The parts were first discovered by Bannister,[9] who classified them somewhat vaguely as "motetti"; Ludwig [10] corrected him and called them "tenors," although he was not able to identify them. Ludwig's statement was in turn emended by Handschin, who took them for "instrumental dance melodies" and who

[5] No. 5.

[5a] Torrefranca, *Il segreto del quattrocento,* 1939, 215, proposes the reading *Domenico* instead of *dicto.*

[6] No. 9.

[7] See Jeppesen, *Die italienische Orgelmusik am Anfang des Cinquecento,* 1943, 95.

[8] No. 45, n. 20.

[9] *Monumenti Vaticani di Paleographia Musicale Latina,* 1913, No. 869.

[10] AMW V, 201.

published a transcription of the first melody. All three melodies are tripartite and move in flexible rhythm, mostly in breves and semi-breves, but also occasionally in minims. If these tunes had any relation to dance literature at all, they would be *balli*, because the usual basse dance does not fall into several sections and is not composed in free rhythm. Actually, however, the tenors are neither dances nor instrumental music, but Kyries. They appear also on a flyleaf (fol. 151v) of MS Lansdowne 462 of the British Museum with the full Kyrie text, which explains also their tripartite structure. They form part of a series of nine monophonic Kyries in *cantus fractus,* such as we find in several manuscripts of the fifteenth century. The three melodies in question are assigned to *feria sexta, quarta,* and *Dominica die* respectively.

In the Vatican MS the name *Lambertus* is partially visible at the top of the page, and the third melody, assigned to *Dominica* in the Lansdowne MS, carries here the designation *le roy.* If *Lambertus* can be interpreted as the name of the composer, as it probably should be, the same interpretation may possibly apply also to *le roy.* Could this be Roy Henry [V], who appears with two compositions in the Old Hall MS, or is it only a title? The latter alternative is probably correct, since the *le roy* or *Dominica* Kyrie holds another surprise in store: it is the same melody as the tenor of a three-voice Kyrie by Ludford, a composer of the Fairfax period about whom next to nothing is known.[11] The identification of the Kyries refutes Handschin's suggestion that they belong to dance music, but confirms that the Vatican manuscript is, at least in part, of English origin.

The most significant addition to our knowledge of basse-dance melodies has been the discovery of the incunabulum *L'Art et Instruction de bien dancer,* printed some time before 1496 by Michel Toulouze.[12] Scholderer, the editor of the facsimile edition, was unaware of the very close relations between the print and the Brussels MS. The print, in its short prefatory treatise, not only duplicates the theoretical dance description of the manuscript, but gives in its music almost the same repertory of basse dances. The incunabulum

---

11 The Kyrie belongs to Ludford's *Missa Dominica,* preserved in Brit. Mus. Royal App. MS 45–48. A fragment entitled *le roy* appears in Brit. Mus. Add. MS 30520. Professor Gurlitt has kindly informed me of the existence of another fragmentary Mass by Ludford which for some inexplicable reason has turned up in the Ratsschulbibliothek in Zwickau (see *Zeitschrift für Musikwissenschaft* XIII [1930/31], 562).

12 No. 10.

includes, however, only forty-nine melodies, arranged in an order somewhat different from that of the manuscript. The question whether the one source was copied from the other or whether both go back to a common source has been raised and left open by Kinkeldey.[13] The sequence of certain melodies is identical in the two sources; e.g., Nos. 1–4 and 35–38 of the print correspond respectively to Nos. 16–19 and 12–15 of the Brussels MS.[14] If the latter were a copy of the print, the divergent order could in part be accounted for by a disarrangement of the leaves prior to the binding, as Kinkeldey suggests. Closson [15] and Blume [16] have shown that the manuscript has indeed been bound together incorrectly, but there are still too many stray single numbers the position of which cannot be accounted for by this assumption. On the other hand, it appears unlikely that the print was copied from the manuscript, for there is no good reason why ten melodies should have been omitted. We must conclude, then, and there are several indications confirming this assumption, that the two collections cannot be directly dependent upon one another. Although their repertory is largely the same, the incunabulum contains five melodies that do not recur in the manuscript, a fact that is all the more striking as the latter source is the larger collection. In certain details both the melodies and the dance steps vary, and if the two versions are checked against one another numerous misprints and scribal errors come to light. The *Spagna* melody which we are interested in here is not recorded in the Brussels MS, although its title occurs as *Basse dance du Roy d'Espagne;* however, the melody associated with it is not the *Spagna* and should not be confused with it.[17] At first glance our melody seems to be missing also in the Toulouze print. Closer inspection discloses, however, that it does appear, albeit disguised by the strange title *Casulle la nouele* (see Plate 2). The fact that the famous *Spagna* melody is lacking in the Brussels MS makes it unlikely that the two collections are directly related. They either go back to two different but parallel sources or draw independently from a common source. Either alternative would account for the partial survival of the same order of tunes. The princi-

---

13 No. 49.

14 Although the correspondences have not been investigated here in detail, it is worth noting that the two series quoted above belong to the recto and verso of the same folio.

15 No. 9, p. 3.

16 No. 27, p. 57.

17 Further cause for possible confusion is the fact that both sources carry the *Basse Dance Du Roy,* which is again a different melody.

ple, if any, according to which the order was established is obscure. We have a close parallel to this apparent or real lack of order in numerous chansonniers of the time, whose contents are often collected without any recognizable guiding principle. The Chansonnier Laborde is a case in point.

The extant basse-dance melodies are transmitted invariably in even note values, black breves, which correspond to the row of even semibreves in Cornazano. It is this manner of notation that has aroused the most controversial theories about the performance of the dances. No attempt will be made here to discuss the subject in detail or to review all these theories. Suffice it to point out that in the early stage of the discussion it was tacitly assumed that the melodies were to be played only as monophonies. Given this (erroneous) premise, the inference was unavoidable that the row of even breves could not possibly represent the rhythm of the actual performance. It was believed to be a sort of shorthand notation to be played either in a more or less arbitrarily arranged group of notes in arbitrarily imposed rhythms, or else according to the familiar practices of Renaissance coloration with extensive melodic diminution. Riemann [18] and Blume [19] have advocated the first, Closson [20] and Wolf [21] the second alternative, but all disagree in many important details. Gerson-Kiwi [22] and, following her, Besseler [23] have tried to establish a connection between the basse dance and the practice of the medieval monophonic dances, of which a few do indeed apply melodic coloration to an underlying structure of even notes.

The later stage of the discussion began with the realization that the basse dance of the fifteenth century was performed as a polyphonic composition in two or more voices. This can be gathered not only from certain remarks of the dance manuals, but also from literary documents, from pictures of the time, and, above all, from the few polyphonic arrangements that have so far come to light. It can be stated that at present such specialists as Gombosi, Hertzmann, Kinkeldey, Sachs, and others all accept in principle the view that the basse dance was performed as a rule polyphonically. In fact, only a performance in part music makes it clear, as has been pointed out re-

[18] No. 65.
[19] No. 27.
[20] Nos. 9 and 30.
[21] Nos. 73 and 74.
[22] No. 34.
[23] No. 26.

peatedly, why Cornazano applies the term *tenori* to the basse dance and the term *in canto* to the *balli*. In a polyphonic rendition the tenor serves as the cantus firmus of an improvised setting in which the lower part is played on the trombone, the extemporized counterpoint on shawms or cornetti. Moreover, the derivation of the melodies themselves puts the basse dance into the orbit of polyphony. Several scholars, notably van den Borren,[24] Gurlitt,[25] Hertzmann,[26] and recently also Pirro [27] and Montellier [28] have shown that certain basse dances are derived from the tenor parts of Burgundian chansons dating from the first part of the fifteenth century. In the basse-dance version the mensural intricacies of the original tenor are smoothed out into even note values; although the cases of melodic interdependence are not always equally convincing, there are enough cogent examples to convince even the most skeptical observer. Müller-Blattau [29] has added some further correspondences between basse dance and German part songs, which, however, may have been derived in turn from Burgundian chansons.[30]

The contention, frequently met with, that basse dances and chansons have a common source and go back to "folk songs" cannot be proved, however dear this hypothesis may be to those who refer to folk song as a convenient *deus ex machina*. The claim is all the more improbable because some of the composers of the original chansons are known, e.g. Binchois and Dufay. The basse dance was definitely a courtly dance, and the chansons on which the melodies are based are art music of the highest aspiration. Cornazano is very explicit about this point and affirms that *basse danze* are "fora del vulgo . . . , sol dancati per dignissime madonne, et non plebeie."

2. A POLYPHONIC *SPAGNA*

There is a two-part arrangement of the basse dance *La Spagna*, heretofore unknown, which gives us a very accurate idea of how the dance was actually performed. The composition appears in MS 431 of the Bibl. Comunale in Perugia on fol. 105v–106 of the original

[24] No. 28.
[25] No. 44.
[26] No. 46.
[27] No. 62, p. 148.
[28] No. 56.
[29] No. 59.
[30] See the analogous examples quoted in No. 29, pp. 26 and 48.

foliation, now fol. 95v–96. Wolf [81] and Jeppesen [82] assign the manuscript to the late fifteenth century on the basis of repertory and notation, especially the roundish shape of the semibreves and minims. Among the composers mentioned we find Magister Symon (probably the friend of Dufay, who died one year before the more famous master), Morton (d. 1475), Busnois (d. 1492), and Hayne. All of these belong definitely to the middle and second half of the fifteenth century. On the other hand, the manuscript includes such later composers as Urrede and Isaac. A composition by Pope Leo X,[33] crowned Supreme Pontiff in 1513, is a later addition and has therefore no bearing on the date.

The Perugia manuscript ascribes the composition to one M. [Magister?] Gulielmus. Originally, I suspected that this composer might be Guilielmus Monachus, whose well-known treatise, as I have shown elsewhere,[34] must be dated in the second half of the fifteenth century. However, my identification of the piece as a *Spagna* arrangement makes the original assumption most improbable. In view of the character of the composition it would be very tempting to identify Gulielmus with Guglielmo Ebreo, the famous dancing master of this name, but besides the identity of names there is no evidence to support this hypothesis. The question must therefore be left open.

The tenor of our composition bears the title *Falla con misuras,* which is Spanish rather than Italian. The significance of the first word (*falla* = mistake?) is obscure; it may just possibly be a proper name such as occur in many basse-dance titles. *Misura,* however, is a technical term with two distinct meanings, one referring to dance nomenclature and one to music, both of which have been used by Cornazano and other dance manuals. The title *Falla* does not give any hint of its being a basse-dance melody, and only by a fortunate coincidence did I discover that it is the famous *Spagna* tune. Dr. Gombosi, to whom I communicated Gulielmus' composition, has very kindly informed me that the same piece appears also in Bologna, Liceo Musicale, MS 109 (fol. 59v–60), which has been briefly described by Anglès.[35] In the Bologna MS the composition is anonymous,

[81] No. 74, I, 458.

[82] *Der Kopenhagener Chansonnier,* 1927, lxxii.

[33] See André Pirro, "Leo X and Music," in MQ XXI (1935), 1.

[34] *Geschichte des englischen Diskants und des Fauxbourdons,* 1936, 58.

[35] No. 22, p. 119. See also the complete table of contents in Anglès, *Estudis Universitaris Catalans,* XIV (1929), 254. Neither list is quite exact; for example, the number of voices of our piece is given erroneously as three instead of two.

lacks the beginning of the upper part which has been cut off, and is entitled *La bassa Castiglya*. The title (which recurs in the Cervera MS as *La baixa de Castilla*) marks the piece clearly as a basse dance, but it is interesting that the general and common term "The Spanish Tune" has been replaced here by a more specific one, "The Castilian Basse Dance," which refers only to one province or region of Spain. This may possibly be the original form of the title, which was then changed to *La Spagna* or *Re di Spagna* in Italy. Gombosi has pointed out to me that the enigmatic *Casulle* of the Toulouze print is obviously nothing but a misprint for *Castille*. His interpretation very elegantly solves the mystery of the strange French title. Read as *Castille la nouvelle* the heading makes indeed very good sense; it is the French translation of *Castilla la nueva,* the southern province of Castile.

Before the polyphonic arrangement of *La Castiglia* or *Spagna* is discussed, the melody on which it is based must be considered. Cornazano's version of the melody (Ex. 1) is written in perfect semibreves

Ex. 1. Cornazano: Tenor melody of *Il Re di Spagna*.

(major prolation) throughout, save two lone minims at the beginning.[86] Cornazano's melody, the accidentals of which deserve special attention, should be compared with *Casulle [Castille] la nouele* of the Toulouze print, which is noted in black breves throughout. The print was made in a double process in which the red lines of the staff were printed first and the black notes were added in a second impression. As a result the notes do not always sit very accurately on or between the lines. By and large the level of printing is not very high in this incunabulum, as can be seen in the great number of misprints. In our particular case the following corrections must be made: The first clef has been misprinted as a *c*-clef, whereas it should be an *f*-clef; the small rectangle after the eighth note on the last line is a misplaced flat standing a third too high, as can be gathered from the Cornazano version, which presents the flat correctly at this

[86] For a facsimile of the melody see nos. 5 and 24.

place. Furthermore, the last four notes of the *Spagna* melody *d e d d* are apparently lacking. There was no room for them on the last line, and they were added (without any indication to that effect) at the end of the preceding dance *Le ioyeulx espoyr;* and, even more confusing, they were printed by mistake a second lower.[37] This method of accounting for the complete melody may seem far-fetched, but it is confirmed by the choreographical annotation to the two melodies. According to the print itself, *Casulle la nouele* has forty-six notes and *Le ioyeulx espoyr* eighteen; this proves conclusively that the last four notes of the latter tune are superfluous, while exactly these four are needed to make the necessary forty-six for *La Spagna.*

Comparison between the Toulouze and Cornazano versions shows that the two melodies substantially agree. The only divergencies concern the last two repeated notes of the print, which are contracted into one long in Cornazano, and the group after the fourth note, which is a little more florid in the Cornazano version. At this point a *punctum divisionis* should probably be inserted between the two minims. Otherwise, the melody and the number of units (perfect semibreves and blackened breves respectively) are exactly the same in the manuscript and the printed version.

The appearance of the *Spagna* or *Castille* melody in the Toulouze print has a very special significance because until this time there was no melody common to both the Italian and French basse-dance sources. Although the French basse dance is dependent on Italian models, no Italian melody has so far been traced in the large repertory of the Brussels MS. The *La Spagna* melody is the first, and so far the only, dance tune to bridge the gap between the Italian *bassa danza* and the French *basse dance* [38] and, what is even more significant, the gap between the monophonic and polyphonic repertory.

Let us turn now to the polyphonic *Spagna* of Gulielmus. It is of great interest to see his tenor follow note for note the melody of the Toulouze version, although he adopts, as far as the notation is concerned, the Italian practice of Cornazano. The transcription of the entire composition will make this clear (Ex. 2). The tenor progresses in equally long notes throughout; only when the same notes are repeated in the Toulouze version are they tied together in the poly-

<hr />

[37] I have marked the four notes by pencil in the facsimile.

[38] In order to appreciate the striking contrast between Italian and French choreography the dance steps of *La Spagna* in Guglielmo Ebreo (No. 2, p. 194) and Toulouze should be compared.

Ex. 2. Gulielmus: *Falla con misuras* [*La Bassa Castiglia*].

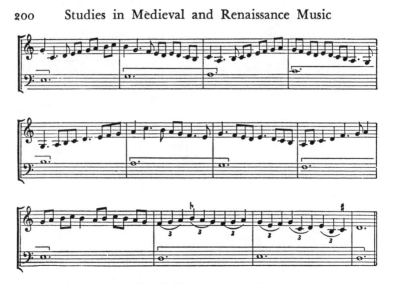

phonic arrangement. This is, however, merely a change in writing.
The upper voice forms a very florid counterpoint in running patterns
and typically instrumental figures. Many of these are stereotyped and
occur in other polyphonic basse dances in exactly the same rhythm.
The rhythmic flow is characterized by the constant wavering in
hemiola rhythm, the old device of the Burgundian chanson; at certain places the contrapuntal voice hovers so much between 3/2 and
6/4 meter that it can be interpreted either way. The manuscript does
not supply any accidentals, although they are distinctly called for.
The ones suggested in the transcription incorporate those of the
Cornazano tenor and can therefore be considered as authentic. There
are very few cadences at which the ceaseless running of the upper
voice is halted, and these occur at irregular intervals, in measures
4, 17, and 29. In its lack of further organization, the setting of Gulielmus stands very close to improvisation, and it can safely be assumed
that it represents the type of improvised dance music that we have
been hoping to find for years and that the sources record so rarely,
precisely because it was improvised.

One of the most interesting features of the composition is the
conflict of mensuration signs in the two voices. The tenor calls for
imperfect time with major prolation ℭ, the counterpoint for diminished imperfect time with minor prolation ₵, our *alla breve* sign.
This sign of mensuration has no rhythmic significance but indicates

merely that the voice is written without any mensural complication. The musical rhythm and the meter of the composition move actually in compound time, as the transcription proves. In order to fit the voices together, the notes of the tenor must all be doubled in value. The augmentation is not especially prescribed in the manuscript, but at this point Cornazano comes to our aid. Both Cornazano and Gulielmus call for the signature ₵, in which each semibreve equals three minims. In explaining the four different types of basse dance, *piva, saltarello, quaternaria,* and *bassa danza* proper (or *misura imperiale*), Cornazano expressly states that in the last one "every note is doubled; three [minims = one semibreve] are worth six, and six are worth twelve." This is literally carried out by Gulielmus, who writes semibreves and leaves the augmentation of note values to the performer. We see that the two-part version cannot possibly be closer to the dance practice of the time.

The dance manuals make it perfectly clear that each note of the tenor corresponds to one step-unit of the dance. In the Brussels and Toulouze collections the number of notes usually coincides with that of the steps, and whenever they do not an error must be assumed. These mistakes, frequent as they are, can often be eliminated through collation of the two collections. Toulouze provides only forty-four steps for the forty-six notes in *Casulle la nouele,* so that two steps are missing. Musically, however, the melody is complete; in fact, it corresponds as exactly to the tenor of the polyphonic setting as if Gulielmus had taken it literally from Toulouze.

This observation brings us to the *point sautant* of our paper. The black breves in the Brussels and Toulouze collections have generally been regarded as a vague sort of plainsong notation or, as Sachs puts it, "choral notes" [89] which fix merely the pitch but not the time value, and it has been supposed that the improvising player ornamented and expanded the tenor and thus brought it into the appropriate rhythm. This view is predicated on the theory that the time value of the single note was more or less haphazardly determined by the improvising musicians. Gombosi has taken the diametrically opposed view, that the melodies are "real cantus firmi, to be read men-

[89] No. 69, p. 316. Only if one knows that the ambiguous term "choral note" is supposed to be the equivalent of the German *Choralnote* does the statement make sense. (See also the article *Plainsong notation* in Apel's *Harvard Dictionary.*) Unfortunately, the section on basse dance in the English edition of Sachs' book is marred by misleading and sometimes even false translations.

surally throughout." [40] He interprets the blackening of the breves as the familiar *color* of mensural notation. When the notes of the basse dance are doubled they become imperfect longs, and the imperfection is indicated by the color.

Far-fetched as this theory may appear at first sight, it is nevertheless borne out by the fully "realized" polyphonic version of Gulielmus' *Spagna*. It confirms the belief that in actual practice the tenor was played in strictly even time values throughout, exactly as called for by the Toulouze print. In other words, the *relative* rhythm of the cantus firmus was faithfully put down in the sources, even if the *absolute* duration of each note varied according to the different types of basse dance. Nevertheless the relation between dance step and tenor note made the equal duration of each a necessity. It follows that the basse-dance melodies are not a shorthand aid to the memory but faithfully mirror in their notation the actual rhythm of the dance. Once the mensural character of the notation is recognized, many "problems" of the basse dance resolve themselves as imaginary. For example, the classification of basse dances in measured and unmeasured pieces, as Blume and others have proposed, must be abandoned because they are all measured, with the important difference that the first group is evenly measured and the second is in mixed time values.

On the basis of Gulielmus' composition, Gombosi's solution can probably be expanded or modified with regard to the black breve. He maintains that the breve was blackened to hint at the fact that, if doubled in value, it becomes an imperfect long. This is certainly true in those polyphonic arrangements in which the tenor notes are augmented to imperfect longs. In the Gulielmus setting, however, they appear as breves (doubled semibreves), and in this case the black breves of the French sources can be understood and read quite literally as they stand. It will be remembered that the dance manuals contradict each other as to the musical rhythm of the basse dance. While the French sources assert that it moves in *maieur parfayt* (perfect time with major prolation), Domenico affirms as emphatically that it moves in *major imperfecto* (imperfect time with major prolation). This dilemma, which has set many pens in motion, can be resolved by a simple consideration of how the rhythm could be presented on paper in actual practice. One way was to write semibreves in imper-

[40] No. 37, p. 26.

fect time and major prolation with the understanding that they must be augmented by two so that breves of six minims each result. This is the Italian method of Cornazano and Gulielmus. The French, on the other hand, give no time signature and write black breves exclusively. Since the *color* means imperfection, a time signature is obviously implied, and this can only be the one for which the theoretical description actually calls, namely perfect time with major prolation ☉. Under this signature the white breve equals nine minims, the black breve only six minims—that is to say, exactly the same value as in Gulielmus' arrangement. It appears, therefore, that the apparently conflicting statements of the theoretical sources are not actually contradictory: they represent only two distinct ways of accounting in theory for what is in actual practice the same rhythm. Had Gulielmus written out his tenor in ☉, he could have notated it only as a row of black breves exactly like those in the Toulouze version; conversely, had we only his upper voice, we could complete the composition simply by incorporating the Toulouze version and reading it strictly mensurally in *maieur parfayt* as it stands, with no change whatsoever. The mensural nature of the basse-dance tenors is fully confirmed by the music itself.

One more word may be added here to the controversy about the rhythm of the basse dance. The polyphonic basse dances of the late fifteenth and early sixteenth centuries move in compound time. Sachs has repeatedly affirmed that the basse dance is "geradtaktig" (two or four units to the measure), but it must not be forgotten that he has qualified his statement to the effect that the subdivision of each unit could be ternary. Unfortunately, the term "geradtaktig" is ambiguous and has been incorrectly translated in his *World History of the Dance* as "even time." Moreover, Sachs has been inconsistent in the application of his own theory, as he has transcribed the basse dance *Beurre frais* in 4/4 instead of 6/4 (or 12/4).[41] In his review of Sachs' book Gombosi has corrected the transcription [42] and emphasized the importance of the hemiola rhythm, or, in terms of mensural theory, the equivalence of *senaria perfecta* and *imperfecta*. Unaware of Gombosi's correction, Apel [43] has countered Sachs' interpretation with another transcription of the same piece which essentially agrees with that of Gombosi. There can be no question that

41 No. 68.
42 No. 37.
43 No. 23, p. 68.

the Gombosi-Apel transcription gives the accurate solution. However, Apel has reduced the values so much that the dance appears to be in 3/4 time, and consequently he has questioned Sachs' statement that the basse dance was "geradtaktig" (which he takes to mean "duple meter"). Yet it ought not to be overlooked that the transcription in 3/4 can be read just as well in compound time (6/8) and that the *mesure ternaire* of which Arbeau speaks refers to the subdivision of the unit, not to the number of units per measure. As far as the musical rhythm of the basse dance is concerned, Apel's "triple meter" is therefore just as misleading as Sachs' "even time" if left unqualified. The controversy could arise only because of the vagueness of nomenclature and the inherent ambiguity of the compound rhythm of the basse dance, which in this case is duple on the higher level, triple on the lower.

Let us now briefly consider some of the other polyphonic settings of *La Spagna*.[44] The arrangement by Francisco de la Torre, preserved in the *Cancionero Musical*,[45] carries the *Spagna* melody in the tenor and is designated as *alta [danza]*. Torre's setting reappears as late as 1552 in the *Libro de musica de vihuela*, by Pisador, who follows the version of the Cancionero so closely in every detail that he must have used it as his source. In his reprint of Pisador's version [46] Pedrell adds the explanatory remark that the terms *alta* and *baxa* refer to High and Low German. This is, of course, sheer fantasy; they are actually the Spanish terms for *saltarello* and *bassa danza* respectively. In Torre's three-part arrangement the treble is written in lively counterpoint, while the contratenor moves freely but at a slower pace above and below the tenor. It is significant that the setting would still be complete if the third voice were omitted; tenor and discant are the two structural voices which form all their cadences at the octave. Only in minor details does the tenor depart from the Toulouze version, especially toward the end, where it becomes somewhat florid. In measures 5 and 6 it almost duplicates the variant of Cornazano.

[44] Ten such arrangements for ensembles, keyboard, or lute have been listed by Gombosi, No. 38, pp. 57–58. His list, which has been reproduced in part by Apel (No. 24), can now be supplemented by several new items, some of which are discussed in this essay. The most recent additions to the list are the *Spagna* settings of the Capirola Lutebook, now at the Newberry Library, which will be published by Gombosi; see the reference to his paper in *Journal* of the AMS I (1948), 58.

[45] No. 25, No. 439; now easily accessible in Davison-Apel's *Historical Anthology of Music*, No. 102a.

[46] No. 60, p. 140.

The melodic coloration notwithstanding, the value of each note of the cantus firmus is one breve of six minims, exactly as in *La Spagna* of Gulielmus. As Torre frequently ignores tone repetitions in the tenor, his setting is apparently not so closely related to the original dance as that of Gulielmus.

Which of the two is the older composition? The sources from which they come are of approximately the same date. Until today the Spanish piece has passed as the oldest known polyphonic *Spagna,* but it now seems that it must cede its priority to Gulielmus' arrangement. Aside from the fact that the latter calls for only the two voices, it is the more primitive stylistically and, moreover, keeps more closely to the dance practice of the time. It is this proximity to dance music that makes the composition historically important.

All other known *Spagna* arrangements are probably of a somewhat later date. The first of these is an anonymous composition contained in Petrucci's *Canti C* (1503). Since Dr. Helen Hewitt is at present

Ex. 3. *Spagna* from Petrucci, *Canti C.*

preparing an integral edition of this collection, only the beginning is given here (Ex. 3).[47] The tenor notes of this version are augmented to imperfect longs (*misura imperiale*) against which two other voices move in very florid and rhythmically rather intricate contrapuntal patterns. The skillful manipulation of imitation between the two free voices (note the snatch of canonic imitation in measures 7–10), the coloration of the cantus firmus itself, and the smooth flow of the music indicate that we have before us a rather stylized dance composition raised above the level of pure *Gebrauchsmusik*. Such imitations cannot be improvised; the composition is the work of a trained composer, though it is straightforward enough to serve as refined dance music. The melodic ornamentation of the cantus firmus is restrained and does not go beyond the degree of coloration normally expected in improvised performance. The manner of coloration is worthy of notice: each unit of the cantus firmus is invariably two measures long; and, however free the "breaking" of the tenor melody may be, it does not affect the strictly equal length of each step unit. The first note of every other measure always coincides with the cantus firmus (marked by asterisks). There is no trace of "free coloration" in the sense that the basic time value of the cantus-firmus note was expanded or contracted at will. The method of making the cantus firmus coincide with the first note of the measure in a figural melody was a favorite device of cantus-firmus treatment in the fifteenth century, as is evident in the treatise of Guilielmus Monachus (c. 1480) who actually teaches this method in very rigid fashion in connection with his discussion of fauxbourdon.[48]

A four-part version of *La Spagna* by Ghiselin found in Florence, Bibl. Naz. Panciatichi MS 27 (fol. 91v–94), is built on a tenor very similar to that of the Petrucci setting; in fact, the coloration at the beginning is practically the same. Ghiselin also augments the cantus-firmus notes to imperfect longs and introduces the free voices in strict imitation. Codex 143 of the Liceo Musicale in Bologna contains two further settings (fol. 48v–49, and 49–50), both in four parts. So far as can be gathered from the incipits, they seem to be less stylized than the Petrucci and Ghiselin compositions. The first *Spagna* of

[47] I am very grateful to Dr. Hewitt for sending me a copy of this piece and the incipits of the other three arrangements.
[48] Coussemaker, *Scriptores*, III, 293 ff.; see also Bukofzer, *Geschichte des englischen Diskants*, 1936, Exs. 14 and 15.

the Bologna MS carries the cantus firmus in semibreves throughout with no coloration whatsoever; it resembles in this respect the Gulielmus arrangement, but the other voices make it a much more elaborate composition. The other *Spagna* of the same manuscript transfers the cantus firmus to the soprano and turns it into a figural melody by means of elaborate ornamentation. Such treatment can be found also in German organ tablatures, e.g. the *Spanyöler Tancz* by Weck.[49]

The *Spagna* tune puts in belated appearances in the *Tratado de glosas* (1553) by Diego Ortiz [50] and the *Libro de cifra* (1557) by Luys Venegas de Henestrosa. The latter is a collection of keyboard music which contains an *alta* [*danza*] by one Antonio, who is in all likelihood Antonio de Cabezon.[51] This arrangement of the *Spagna* is more closely allied with dance music than those by Ortiz, and is therefore discussed first in spite of its later date. Cabezon presents the melody in transposition to the upper fourth and faithfully follows the familiar version except for a few repeated notes, which he omits, and a single change for the sake of cadence in measure 74. The tenor is treated in strict cantus-firmus fashion in equal values, the unit of each note being a dotted breve as in the setting of Gulielmus. The transcription falsely suggests that each cantus-firmus note consist of three measures in ₵, but these three measures must be contracted into one large unit. The ₵ sign here no more indicates the actual rhythm of the music than it does in the *Spagna* of Gulielmus. The two free voices in Cabezon's setting begin in imitation and weave a highly patterned and vigorously rhythmic counterpoint round the cantus firmus, oscillating in wonted hemiola fashion between 3/2 and 6/4 (reduced by half). The flowing quality and skillfully integrated structure of the setting bespeak a superior master and bear out very well the ascription to Cabezon.

In the *Tratado de glosas* by Ortiz we meet with a whole group of

[49] Printed in Merian, No. 53, 48; now also in *Historical Anthology of Music*, No. 102b.
[50] No. 16.
[51] See No. 18, No. V. As has already been pointed out by Apel (*Notes*, Music Library Association, V [1947], 59), the editor has not recognized the piece as a *Spagna* arrangement and has transcribed it with misleading bar lines. It should be noted that Anglès reverses his earlier opinion with regard to the identity of the composer Antonio, mentioned in the collection. He now believes him to be identical with Cabezon and brings new evidence (p. 169) in support of the identification which had already been made by Pedrell. The section relevant to this question in Gilbert Chase, *The Music of Spain*, 1941, 73, should now be corrected.

variations on unnamed *cantus firmi* (*Spagna, passamezzo antico* and
moderno, folia, romanesca, and *ruggiero*) all of which have been
identified by Gombosi.[52] In the second book of his treatise Ortiz gives
a highly illuminating account of various manners of improvisation
for the viola da gamba. He distinguishes three types: improvisation
on (1) tenors, (2) ground basses, and (3) complete compositions (chansons and madrigals). He illustrates the "second manner" of improvisation with six *recercadas* which are all based on the same tenor. This
cantus firmus, or, as he calls it, *canto llano,* is none other than the
Spagna, which is stated here in breves throughout. All repeated notes
of the original melody are omitted, but otherwise the melody is
strictly retained although it is transposed to the lower fifth (compare
Cabezon's setting). The six examples are arranged in three groups,
each of which is differentiated by distinct subdivision of the basic
unit. The first group of *recercadas* (Nos. 1 and 2) moves primarily in
minims and occasional semibreves, the second (3 and 4) in semiminims and fusas; in the third group (5 and 6) the cantus firmus is
diminished to semibreves and the counterpoint runs essentially in
semiminims. In Ex. 4 the beginnings of all six *recercadas* have been
superimposed for comparison.

Ex. 4. Ortiz: Six *recercadas* on the *Spagna* tenor.

52 No. 39.

Ortiz's improvisations are written for harpsichord and viola da gamba, and his instructions prescribe that the harpsichordist play the cantus firmus with improvised chords and the gambist improvise his counterpoint as solos. The *recercadas* are all in duple meter, which could be interpreted as the *quaternaria* of the basse dance. However, the treatise indicates that the *Spagna* had obviously severed its relation with dance music and had become merely a scaffolding for improvisations. The extremely florid nature of their counterpoint characterizes them as highly stylized show pieces for an improvising virtuoso. It seems in this connection significant that Ortiz calls the *Spagna* melody merely a *canto llano* and does not mention its title. Cabezon uses the same name but characterizes his composition at the same time as dance music. The designation *canto llano* (i.e., *cantus planus =* plainsong) has led Einstein [53] and recently again Anglès [54] to the easily understandable, but erroneous, assumption that it was of sacred origin, namely literally a plainsong tenor. Actually, the term *cantus planus* is used here in the more general sense of cantus firmus.

In the treatise of Ortiz the tradition of the basse dance, which is characterized by improvisation on extended cantus firmi, and the improvisation on the more recent and shorter basses of the *passamezzo* family have their point of contact. As Kinkeldey and Gombosi have emphasized, the younger tradition must be understood as an extension of the older one. A similar development in the Italian dance song has been shown by Gerson-Kiwi. The final confluence of the different streams can be seen in the well-known improvisations on the even more concise and tonally more characteristic ostinato basses of

[53] No. 32.

[54] It is strange that Anglès should have made the mistake of looking (vainly, of course) for the tenor in the Gregorian repertory, because he realized that Cabezon's *alta* was a piece of dance music; the identical title of de la Torre's *Spagna* should have given him the right clue. It may be added here that his editorial notes can be corrected and amplified. He has overlooked the fact that several of the interesting *romances* in Venegas' collection are not entirely new musically, but variations on traditional ground basses, such as appear also with Ortiz and many other composers of the time. No. 119, for example, is founded on the *passamezzo antico* and the *Pavana* No. 121 on a variant of the *folia* bass. The bass of the latter piece has been employed by Ortiz in his eighth (and fourth) *recercadas* in almost identical fashion. Anglès correctly remarks that No. 118 is a set of *diferencias* on the *romanesca* bass, traditionally associated in Spain with the song *Guárdame las vacas*. However, I do not understand why he gives credence to and perpetuates Pedrell's far-fetched theory that *Las Vacas* was a formula to memorize the *saeculorum* cadence of the first Gregorian psalm tone. First of all, it is not the melody but the bass (which is far from being Gregorian) that embodies the stable element in these variations, and secondly the countermelody to the bass, which is actually the variable element, is not identical with the formula of the first psalm tone.

the baroque era. The *Spagna* of Gulielmus gives us what is to date
the earliest musical example of the tradition and more nearly reflects the improvisatory performance of the basse dance than any
other of the known arrangements.

3. BASSE DANCE AND CHANSON LITERATURE

A supplementary note may be added here about another basse
dance, the melody of which is not known. In his treatise *Ad suos compagnones studiantes* (1536), Antonius de Arena [55] quotes the dance
Consumo la vita mia a XVI [notes] with the choreography: R c s s
d r c s s d d d s s r d s s r c.[56] Like the authors of many other dance
manuals, Arena does not record the music. However, a polyphonic
chanson of the same title occurs in the Chansonnier Laborde (Library of Congress) [57] on fol. 136v–137. The composition is anonymous
here, but I could identify it as a piece by Johannes Prioris on the basis
of a little-known manuscript (Cambridge, Magdalen College, Pepys
1760) which yields the same chanson with its author's name (fol.
86v). The Pepys MS is an excellent source, especially for the works
of Fevin, and its readings are more accurate than those of the Chansonnier Laborde. In the transcription (Ex. 5) the variants in Laborde
are indicated by downward stems, and obvious mistakes have been
tacitly corrected. The words are supplied in all voices of the Pepys MS,
whereas only the first line is preserved in the Laborde MS. The arrangement of the text has been revised in the transcription because
the scribe has made no attempt at correct co-ordination of words and
music.

It is impossible to say whether or not Prioris' chanson, which dates
from c. 1500, has musically anything in common with the dance
quoted by Arena. It is not even certain that the two identical timbres
of the text refer to the same poem, because beginnings of this sort
were common property and could be applied to different lyrics. In
this particular case at least one example of the kind can be found.
The first two lines of a three-voice *strambotto* by Mantovano [58] agree
with the chanson, except for some slight variants. Musically the two

[55] No. 14.
[56] Wolf, No. 74, II, 457. For an explanation of the dance symbols see Sachs, No. 69.
[57] Cf. Helen Bush, "The Laborde Chansonnier," in *Papers* of the AMS, Cleveland,
1940 [1946], 56; see here also the references to the printed versions of the chanson.
[58] *Smith College Music Archives*, Vol. IV, No. 17, ed. by A. Einstein.

Ex. 5. Prioris: *Consumo la vita mia.*

settings differ completely. All we know about Arena's melody is that it has sixteen notes. Now, it should be noted that Prioris' tenor, while it comprises the equivalent of twenty-four breves, marks off the first sixteen breves by a *signum congruentiae*; the last eight breves could possibly be explained as a varied second ending, inasmuch as breves 17–20 merely repeat breves 11–13 and the continuation is different in order to lead to the final cadence. The separation of the first sixteen breves and the numerical correspondence with Arena's melody may be fortuitous, but if so it is at least a noteworthy coincidence. On the other hand, the chanson in its present four-part form cannot be regarded as dance music.

The most remarkable musical feature of the setting is the gymel structure of soprano and tenor. These voices move almost constantly in similar rhythm in thirds and sixths; they are patently the two essential voices on which the structure of the whole depends. Whether or not the tenor of Prioris' chanson is based on a pre-existing cantus firmus cannot be answered at the present state of our knowledge, and judgment must be suspended in the hope that future findings will shed more light on the subject.

No systematic and comprehensive attempt has as yet been made to correlate all basse dances and chansons of the same or similar title and to compare their music. Aside from the scholars mentioned above who have drawn attention to isolated cases in the fifteenth century, only Blume [59] has taken a step in this direction, but he deals in his lists primarily with material of the sixteenth century. A complete collation such as is suggested here will doubtlessly reveal how close or how loose the relations between dance music and chanson literature actually were in the Renaissance. Here is a promising field, as yet unplowed, for an enterprising musicologist.

BIBLIOGRAPHY

PRIMARY SOURCES

1. Guglielmo Ebreo Pisauriensis: *De Praticha seu Arte Tripudii,* published by F. Zambrini in *Scelta di curiosità letterarie* CXXXI, Bologna, 1873.

2. Guglielmo Ebreo and Domenico Piacentino: *Trattado della danza,* published by C. Mazzi, "Una sconosciuta compilazione di un libro quattrocentistico di balli," in *Bibliofilia* 16 (1915), 185 ff.

3. Guglielmus Hebraeus: *De Pratica seu Arte Tripudii* (see No. 1), unpublished manuscript (Paris, B.N. f.it.973). Description in Kinkeldey No. 48.

4. Johannes Ambrosius Pisauriensis: *De Practica seu Arte Tripudii* (see No. 3), unpublished manuscript (Paris, B.N. f.it.476). Description in Kinkeldey No. 48.

5. Antonio Cornazano: *Libro dell'Arte del Dànzare,* published by C. Mazzi in *Bibliofilia* 17 (1916), 1 ff.

6. Domenico Piacentino: *De Arte Saltandi et Choreas Ducendi,* unpublished manuscript (Paris, B.N. f.it.972). Description in Kinkeldey No. 48.

7. Anonymous: *Della Virtute et Arte del Danzare,* published by G. Messori Roncaglia, Nozze Tavani-Santucci, Modena, 1885.

8. Guglielmo and Domenico: *Otte Bassedanze,* published by M. Faloci Pulignani, Nozze Renier-Campostrini, Foligno, 1887.

9. Brussels: *Le Manuscrit dit des basse dances,* facsimile edition by E. Closson, Société des Bibliophiles et Iconophiles de Belgique, Bruxelles, 1912.

[59] No. 27, p. 149.

10. Michel Toulouze: *L'Art et Instruction de Bien Dancer*, Paris (before 1496). Facsimile edition by Victor Scholderer, The Royal College of Physicians, London, 1936.

11. Vallet de Viriville: *Chronique de la Pucelle* (1445), Paris, 1859 (contains several basse dances). See Kinkeldey No. 48, p. 367.

12. Cervera (Spain), Archivo Municipal, manuscript of basse dance steps (without music); description and facsimile in *Folklore y Costumbras de España*, Barcelona, 1931–33, II, 302–303.

13. Robert Coplande: *The Maner of Dauncing base daunces*, London, 1521. Facsimile edition by the Pear Tree Press, Flansham, Sussex, 1937.

14. Antonius de Arena: *Ad suos compagnones . . . bassas Dansas et Branlos practicantes*, Avignon, 1536.

15. Simone Zuccolo: *La pazzia del ballo*, Padua, 1549. Facsimile edition Milan, 1934.

16. Diego Ortiz: *Tratado de glosas*, Rome, 1553. Reprint by Max Schneider, Bärenreiter Verlag, 1936.

17. Rinaldo Corso: *Dialogo del ballo*, Venice, 1555.

18. Luys Venegas de Henestrosa: *Libro de Cifra Nueva*, 1557, ed. by Anglès in *La Musica en la Corte de Carlos V*, Barcelona, 1944.

19. Thoinot Arbeau (Jehan Tabourot): *Orchésographie*, Lengres, 1588. Reprint by L. Fonta, Paris, 1888. English translation *Orchesography* by Cyril W. Beaumont, London, 1925.

20. Fabrizio Caroso: *Il Ballarino*, Venetia, 1581.

21. ———: *Nobilità di Dame*, Venetia, 1600. Music printed by O. Chilesotti, *Biblioteca di Rarità Musicali*, Vol. 1, 1883.

SECONDARY SOURCES

22. H. Anglès: *La Musica en la Corte de los Reyes Catolicos*, Madrid, 1941. See also Nos. 18 and 25.

23. W. Apel: *The Notation of Polyphonic Music*, Cambridge, 2nd ed. 1944.

24. ———: "A Remark about the Basse Danse," in *Journal of Renaissance and Baroque Music*, I (1946), 139.

25. F. Asenjo y Barbieri: *Cancionero Musical*, Madrid, 1890, reprint Buenos Aires, 1945; new edition by H. Anglès, I, Barcelona, 1947.

26. H. Besseler: *Musik des Mittelalters und der Renaissance*, 1931–1935.

27. F. Blume: *Studien zur Vorgeschichte der Orchestersuite*, Leipzig, 1925.

28. Ch. van den Borren: *Guillaume Dufay*; Académie royale de Belgique, Classe des Beaux Arts, Mémoires II, 2; Brussels, 1926.

29. M. F. Bukofzer: "An Unknown Chansonnier of the 15th Century," in MQ XXVIII (1942), 14 ff.

30. E. Closson: "La structure rhythmique des basse dances," in *Sammelbände IMG* 14 (1913), 567 ff.

31. J. Dieckmann: *Die in deutscher Lautentabulatur überlieferten Tänze des 16. Jahrhunderts,* 1932.

32. A. Einstein: *Zur deutschen Literatur für Viola da Gamba,* Publikationen der IMG, Beihefte, II, 1; Leipzig, 1905.

33. ———: "Die Aria di Ruggiero," in *Sammelbände IMG* 13 (1912), 444 ff., and *Rivista Musicale Italiana* 41 (1937), 163 ff.

34. E. Gerson-Kiwi: *Studien zur Geschichte des italienischen Liedmadrigals* [Diss. Heidelberg, 1933], 1938.

35. O. Gombosi: Review of Dieckmann No. 31, in *Zeitschrift für Musikwissenschaft* 17 (1935), 118.

36. ———: Review of Kinkeldey No. 48, in *Zeitschrift für Musikwissenschaft* 17 (1935), 125.

37. ———: Review of Sachs No. 69, in *Acta Musicologica* VII (1935), 23 ff.

38. ———: "Der Hoftanz," in *Acta Musicologica* VII (1935), 50 ff.

39. ———: "Zur Frühgeschichte der Folia," in *Acta Musicologica* VIII (1936), 119 ff.

40. ———: "Italia, Patria del Basso Ostinato," in *La Rassegna Musicale* 7 (1934), 14 ff.

41. ———: "The Cultural and Folkloristic Background of the Folia," in *Papers* of the AMS, Cleveland, 1940 [1946], 88.

42. ———: "About Dance and Dance Music in the Late Middle Ages," in *MQ* XXVII (1941), 289 ff.

43. ———: "Stephen Foster and 'Gregory Walker,'" in *MQ* XXX (1944), 133 ff.

44. W. Gurlitt: "Burgundische Chanson und deutsche Liedkunst," in *Bericht über den musikwissenschaftlichen Kongress in Basel,* Leipzig, 1925, 153 ff.

45. J. Handschin: "Über die Laude," in *Acta Musicologica* X (1938), 29 f.

46. E. Hertzmann: "Studien zur Basse Danse in 15. Jahrhundert," in *Zeitschrift für Musikwissenschaft* 11 (1929), 401 ff.

47. L. Ilari: *Indice per materie della Biblioteca Comunale di Siena,* Siena, 1844–1848, VII, 96.

48. O. Kinkeldey: "A Jewish Dancing Master of the Renaissance," in *A. S. Freidus Memorial Volume,* New York, 1929, 329 ff.

49. ———: *"Fifteenth-Century Basse Danses,"* Abstract in *Bulletin* of the AMS, No. 4 (1940), 13 f.

50. M. Lattes: *Notizie e documenti di letteratura e storia giudaica,* No. IX, *Intorno a Guglielmo Ebreo* (from *Antologia Israelitica*), Padova, 1879.

51. G. Mazzatinti: *Inventario dei manoscritti italiani delle biblioteche di Francia,* Rome, 1886–1888, Vols. I–III.

52. W. Merian: *Die Tabulaturen des Organisten Hans Kotter,* Leipzig, 1916.

53. ——: *Der Tanz in den deutschen Tabulaturbüchern,* 1927.

54. K. Meyer: "Michel de Toulouze," in *Music Review* 7 (1946), 178.

55. A. Michel: "The Earliest Dance Manuals," in *Medievalia et Humanistica* I (1945), 117.

56. E. Montellier: "Quatorze Chansons du XVe siècle extraites des Archives Namuroises," in *Commission de la vieille chanson populaire, Annuaire* (Antverp), 1939, 153.

57. G. Morphy: *Les Luthistes Espagnols du XVIième siècle,* Leipzig, 1902, Vols. I–II.

58. E. Motta: "Musica alla corte degli Sforza," in *Archivio storico lombardo,* Ser. 2, 4 (1887), 29–64, 278–340, 514–561.

59. J. M. Müller-Blattau (with F. Ranke): *Das Rostocker Liederbuch,* Schriften der Königsberger Gelehrten Gesellschaft, Geistesw. Kl. 4, H. 5, 1927.

60. F. Pedrell: *Cancionero Musical Popular Espagnol,* Vol. III, Valls, 1918.

61. A. Pirro: "Deux dances anciennes," in *Revue de Musicologie* 5 (1924), 7.

62. ——: *Histoire de la Musique de la fin du XIVe siècle à la fin du XVIe,* Paris, 1940.

63. G. A. Quarti: "La danza del cinquecento," in *Scenario,* 1938, 364.

64. R. Renier: "Osservazioni sulla cronologia di un' opera del Cornazano," in *Giornale storico della letteratura italiana,* XVII (1891), 142 ff.

65. H. Riemann: "Die rhythmische Struktur der Basse Dances," in *Sammelbände IMG* 14 (1913), 349 ff.

66. ——: "Der 'basso ostinato' und die Anfänge der Kantate," in *Sammelbände IMG* 13 (1912), 531 ff.

67. ——: "Basso ostinato und Basso quasi ostinato," in *Festschrift fur Liliencron,* 1910, 192 ff.

68. C. Sachs: "Der Rhythmus der Basse Danse," in *Acta Musicologica* III (1931), 107 ff., and *Mélanges de Musicologie* (Laurencie), Paris, 1933, 57 ff.

69. ——: *World History of the Dance,* New York, 1937 (German edition 1933).

70. L. Schrade: *Die handschriftliche Überlieferung der ältesten Instrumentalmusik,* 1931.

71. J. F. R. Stainer: "An Old Book on Dancing," in *Musical Times* 40 (1899), 461 f.

72. M. Steinschneider: *Hebräische Bibliographie,* Vol. 19, Berlin, 1879.

73. J. Wolf: Review of Closson No. 9 in *Die Musik* 12 (1912–1913), 296.

74. J. Wolf: *Handbuch der Notationskunde,* Vols. I–II, Leipzig, 1913, 1919 (Kleine Handbücher der Musikgeschichte, VIII).

75. G. Zannoni: "Il libro dell'arte del danzare di Antonio Cornazano (1465)," in *Rendiconti della R. Academia dei Lincei,* Ser. 4, VI, 281 ff., Rome, 1890.

REFERENCE WORKS

76. C. W. Beaumont: *A Bibliography of Dancing,* 1929.

77. P. D. Magriel: *A Bibliography of Dancing,* 1936 (supplements).

VII

Caput: A Liturgico-Musical Study

1. THE ORIGINS OF THE CYCLIC MASS

SINCE THE early days of musical research Mass cycles of the
fifteenth century have attracted special attention of scholars and
musicians alike for reasons that are still valid today. The cyclic Mass
holds a central place in the music of the period because it embodies
the most representative and extended form of Renaissance music. Not
without justification have early historians like Ambros molded their
conception of the period after this form. Very little would be left of
the chapters on the fifteenth and sixteenth centuries in his *Geschichte
der Musik* if the sections on the Mass were omitted. It is no exaggeration to assert that the cycle of the Ordinary of the Mass was the focal
point on which all the artistic aspirations and technical achievements of the composer converged. It held as dominating and prominent a place in the hierarchy of musical values as the symphony did
in the eighteenth and nineteenth centuries.

The idea of combining the five parts of the Ordinary of the Mass
into one cycle is not as old as is generally believed. From the liturgical
point of view there was no need to unify the unchangeable items of
the Ordinary, because they are not sung in direct succession during
the celebration of the Mass, except for the Kyrie and Gloria. Even if
there were unity it would be made immaterial by the intervening
prayers and chants. It is for this reason that in medieval music only
individual movements were set to music just as they were used in the
liturgy. The first suggestions of the cyclic Mass are to be found in

the fourteenth century. The so-called Mass of Tournai, which has for a long time been regarded as the first cyclic Mass,[1] cannot strictly be regarded as a Mass cycle. Its constituent parts were composed separately and were only later arbitrarily combined. No musical relations exist between the single movements. They are, moreover, composed in different styles. The first cycle known to have been composed as a unit comes from the pen of the French composer-poet Guillaume de Machaut. There can be no question that in this work the Ordinary is in a certain sense a six-section cycle (the sixth part is the *Ite missa est,* which Machaut has included in the musical setting).[2] It has sometimes been claimed that Machaut's Mass is unified musically by recurrent motives, but this claim is open to question because the motives seem to be figures and formulae that are not characteristic enough and are not placed conspicuously enough to serve a really unifying function. Actually some of the movements are composed freely in conductus style without use of plainchant, while others are written like isorhythmic motets with the proper plainchants in the tenor. The unity displayed by this Mass is primarily that of the liturgy, not of musical material.

The distinction between musical and liturgical unity is a crucial point, the importance of which has not been sufficiently stressed in past discussions.[3] Without it the significance and spiritual background of the Mass cycle cannot possibly be understood. It takes a very bold and independent mind to conceive the idea that the invariable parts of the Mass should be composed not as separate liturgical items, but as a set of five musically coherent compositions. In the latter case the means of unification are provided by the composer, not the liturgy. This idea, which is the historical premise of the cyclic Ordinary, betrays the weakening of purely liturgical consideration and the strengthening of essentially aesthetic concepts. The "absolute" work of art begins to encroach on liturgical function. We discover here the typical Renaissance attitude—and it is indeed the Renaissance philosophy of art that furnishes the spiritual background to the cyclic Mass. The beginnings of the Mass cycle coincide with the beginnings of the musical Renaissance.

[1] Coussemaker, *Messe du XIIIe siècle,* 1861. The editor placed the work by mistake in the thirteenth rather than the fourteenth century.

[2] Editions by Machabey and de Van.

[3] Peter Wagner's *Geschichte der Messe* (1913), though out of date in many details, is still the best book on the subject.

It is therefore hardly surprising that the decisive turn in the development of the cyclic Mass occurred only in the early fifteenth century. At this time the first attempts are made to unify the movements of the Ordinary by means of the same musical material. We must distinguish here between two methods. First, the composer may use a brief characteristic motive in one or more voices which recurs at the beginning of each movement in the same or only slightly varied form and thus serves as a motto for the entire cycle. These motto beginnings, however, affect only the first few measures and have no influence on the further course and structure of the composition. Secondly, the composer may employ a borrowed cantus firmus in the tenor which underlies all movements as a structural voice and thus serves as a much more powerful and consistent unifying factor than the motto.[4] Both the motto and cantus firmus may be used in conjunction.

The two methods of unification arose independently but developed, interestingly enough, in exactly parallel stages. The first stage, the incipient cycle, comprises only two paired movements, either the Gloria and Credo, or the Sanctus and Agnus. The coupling of just these movements was probably prompted by the text, since each group has a similar text structure in common; Gloria and Credo are built in alternating lines in the manner of a psalmody, Sanctus and Agnus have a tripartite structure. The latter is true also of the Kyrie, and it is significant that in certain early cycles the Kyrie is indeed more closely related to the Sanctus-Agnus group than to the other.

According to all evidence available at present, it may be stated that incipient cycles with motto beginning originated a little earlier than those with cantus firmus. The former will therefore be discussed first. The pairing of movements by means of a motto is clearly documented by a number of sources. The first intimations are found in the Turin MS (TuB) of c. 1410–20. It records five Gloria-Credo pairs [5]

---

[4] A third possibility, unrelated to the other two, is the polyphonic plainsong Mass, which paraphrases the chants of the Ordinary. Since the musical material differs in each movement, we cannot speak here of musical unification in the strict sense, for it is really an extension and intensification of the liturgical unity which was known in medieval music. However, the plainsong Mass of the Renaissance is modeled after the unified tenor Mass and achieves artistic coherence through musical style.

[5] The MS presents at another place (fol. 139v–141v) an almost complete cycle (only the Agnus is lacking). The four movements are based on various sections of the same (secular?) tune in the tenor. This unusual and interesting piece is a later addition to TuB and would bear further investigation.

which obviously belong together stylistically. although only a few of them give indications of a motto, and even these are slight. The earliest source to carry out the pairing on a large scale is the Bologna MS (BL), written originally for Piacenza, a considerable part of which is organized exclusively in Gloria-Credo pairs.[6] Many of these stem from the same composer and have a very clear motto connection, for example those by Hugo de Lantins (fol. 84v–86) and Dufay (fol. 33v–38); others by the same composer do not have a clear motto, e.g. Antonius de Civitato (fol. 81v–84); still others consist of compositions written by different composers and have been combined more or less arbitrarily by the scribe in analogy to the genuine pairs. In the last case, obviously, there cannot be a motto. It should be noted that BL contains only Gloria-Credo pairs. Pairing of Mass fragments (Gloria-Credo as well as Sanctus-Agnus) is vaguely suggested in certain compositions by Leonel in the Old Hall MS,[7] although the scribe did not yet actually group them together. In the Aosta and Trent MSS the pairing of Gloria-Credo and Sanctus-Agnus has become a recognized practice. The scribe of Tr has sometimes pointed out the connection between the pairs by written remarks. We may infer from the manuscripts that the Gloria-Credo pair was the first one to be joined together, and that it was soon complemented by the corresponding Sanctus-Agnus pair.

The next step of the motto Mass is the combination of two separate pairs in one composite cycle, a process that repeats on a higher level the pairing of two unrelated single compositions. BL contains several such cycles by Zacharia-Dufay, Ciconia–Arnold de Lantins, and others. The cycle by Ciconia-Lantins deserves special mention, as it consists of three pairs—(1) the introit *Salve sancta parens* and Kyrie by Lantins, (2) Gloria and Credo by Ciconia, and (3) Sanctus and Agnus by Lantins again. The settings by Lantins use the plainsongs of the *Missa de B.M.V.* (*Grad. Rom.* IX) in the tenor and thus represent a partial plainsong Mass (the introit, too, is similarly treated in the tenor). Ciconia's pair, however, is not unified by a motto and is freely composed. The disparate pairs have nevertheless been grouped together to a composite cycle. The same manuscript contains, on the other hand, a few complete cycles written as a unit

6 See de Van's list in *Musica Disciplina*, II, 231.

7 See the essay on OH, pp. 44 and 60.

by one and the same composer (Lymburgia, Arnold de Lantins,[8] and Dufay [9]) which are more or less unified by means of motto beginnings. Dufay's *Missa Sancti Jacobi* includes not only the complete Ordinary but also the pieces of the Proper based on the "proper" plainsongs. This is a special Office and takes an unusual position among the early cycles in BL. The Mass cycles by Lymburgia and Lantins are clearly held together by the same motto. It is significant that the Gloria-Credo pair on the one hand and the Sanctus-Agnus pair on the other begin almost identically and form two closely related pairs within the larger cycle. In both cases the Kyrie stands somewhat apart. Thus the original pairing is still reflected in the first known examples of the unified Mass cycle with motto beginning. Since this type of cycle is associated primarily with Lymburgia, Lantins, and Dufay, we may safely assume that it was developed by the composers of the Franco-Flemish school around 1425.

The first manifestations of the tenor Mass or cantus-firmus cycle appear only slightly later, in the second quarter of the century, and are associated primarily with composers of the English school, notably Leonel Power and Dunstable. As to the date, it is characteristic that TuB, OH, and BL, while they give evidence of the incipient, and even of the complete, cycle with motto, do not show a trace of the cantus-firmus cycle, except for the above-noted addition to TuB. Mass cycles on a cantus firmus are to be found only in such later sources as the Aosta and Trent MSS and a newly discovered fragment in the Bodleian Library.[10]

The idea of writing a Mass setting on a tenor not borrowed from plainsongs of the Ordinary was prompted by a medieval form, the isorhythmic motet. The fountainhead of the development is the transfer of the isorhythmic technique to the Mass, to which many single isorhythmic Mass sections in OH and LoF attest. So far as the cyclic idea is concerned, it is important to keep in mind that the setting of the complete Ordinary is unified by an independent tenor whose liturgical function does not relate to the Ordinary. It has been pointed out above that Machaut did not take this step; his isorhythmic tenors are still chants from the Ordinary and change from movement to

8 Published in *Polyphonia Sacra* (ed. van den Borren), 1932, Nos. 1–5.

9 *Missa Sine Nomine*, printed in *Opera omnia* (ed. de Van), Vol. 3.

10 Add. MS C 87 with music by Benet, Bedingham, Plomer, and anonymous composers. I have dealt with this important fragment in "English Church Music of the XVth Century," in *The New Oxford History of Music.*

movement, as they do also in a paired Gloria and Credo by Leonel (Ao 169–170). This pair is historically important, as it is intermediate between the traditional and the new practice which Leonel himself adopted toward the end of his career. In the Mass sections under consideration here the tenors may still be liturgical, but they have as a rule nothing to do with the Mass. Significantly, these tenors continue to be isorhythmic even though the upper voices gradually abandon that device. There are, in addition, settings with non-isorhythmic tenors drawn from sources foreign to the Ordinary. These settings, too, are mostly of English origin.[11]

The decisive step toward the cycle is again the pairing of two movements on the basis of the same tenor which establishes an unequivocal element of unity and, unlike the motto, conditions the entire musical structure. Dunstable's Gloria and Credo on *Jesu Christe fili* [12] illustrates the incipient Mass cycle with cantus firmus. The two movements are built on the same isorhythmic tenor, and neither has a motto, which the English composers seem to have cultivated less extensively than their Continental colleagues, since there was no need for it if a common tenor was used. Once the idea of joining two movements by means of a cantus firmus had been established, its extension to all movements of the Ordinary lay close at hand. The first known complete cycles [13] are transmitted in the old layer of the Trent codices and the Aosta MS and include the *Missa Alma redemptoris* by Leonel Power [14] and the *Missa Rex seculorum,* ascribed in Tr to Power and in Ao to Dunstable. The former work is based on an isorhythmically repeated tenor, the latter on a tenor that presents the chant in free rhythm and varying melodic elaboration. We thus have evidence that the two types of tenor treatment, the rigid and the flexible, are as old as the form itself. The Bodleian fragment contains the remnants of Gloria, Credo, and Sanctus from a *Missa Requiem eternam,* built likewise on an isorhythmic tenor. It is not

11 See the Credo on *Alma redemptoris* by Anglicanus (DTOe, Vol. 61, 92) and an anonymous Gloria on *Virgo flagellatur* in Pemb. One of the rare Continental settings of the type is a Credo on *Alma redemptoris* by Johannes de Gemblaco (BL, Tr, Ao), which may have been prompted by English models. There seems to be no other Mass section on a foreign tenor in BL, and this one has been paired (incorrectly?) with a Gloria by the same composer in free treble style.

12 DTOe, Vol. 61, 114 and 117. The editor has obscured the isorhythmic structure of the tenor by irregular barring.

13 According to English custom the Kyrie was chanted; its omission from the polyphonic setting does not make the cycles incomplete.

14 Published in *Documenta Polyphoniae Liturgicae* (ed. Feininger), Ser. I, No. 2.

a Requiem Mass (which contains no Gloria) but a Mass cycle on the introit from the Mass for the Dead. Other cycles by English composers have come down to us in incomplete form. A case in point is Dunstable's Credo and Sanctus on *Da gaudiorum premia.*[15] Here again the tenor is isorhythmic. The two movements found in Ao probably belong to a complete cycle, now lost, because the pairing of Credo and Sanctus is rather anomalous. The earliest English Mass cycles are all based on liturgical tenors and do not particularly stress the motto beginning. Leonel Power's *Missa Alma redemptoris* has at best a slight suggestion of a motto; other works have none at all. Only later in the century does the motto become a regular feature of the English Mass cycles, doubtless in imitation of Franco-Flemish practice. That the paired arrangement of movements persisted even in the complete Mass cycle (where it was no longer necessary) can be seen in the *Rex seculorum* Mass.

What proof do we have that the above-mentioned works are actually early examples of the type? No theorist of the time tells us anything about the development of the cyclic Mass, and none of the compositions is precisely dated. All we have by way of historical data are the scant biographical facts about Power and Dunstable. If it is correct that Leonel Power died in 1445—the date has not yet been verified—he can have composed his Mass cycles only in the second quarter of the century, probably in the last decade of his life. Aside from that, we are reduced to inference—but rather conclusive inference from the repertory of the sources themselves. It is revealing that a major part of Ao groups the movements of the Mass still in the medieval manner according to classes (all Kyries together, etc.), whereas they are grouped in another part, at times incorrectly, in pairs. Leonel's *Missa Alma redemptoris* is the only complete cantus-firmus cycle of the entire manuscript, and the same cycle appears also in the oldest part of Tr (Codex 87). The partial or complete cycles with borrowed tenor are attributed in the earliest sources (Ao, Tr 87 and 92) almost exclusively to English composers, and there remains no doubt as to their essential contribution to the creation of the form.[16] The cyclic tenor Mass is the most influential achievement of the English school of Renaissance music.

---

[15] The Sanctus has been transcribed in *Musica Disciplina* II, 70.

[16] This bears out an old thesis of von Ficker (*Studien zur Musikwissenschaft,* VII [1920], 30), even though his claims rested on shaky foundations and the particulars of his position were untenable.

Once established, the form was soon generally adopted in European music. It cannot be doubted that Dufay's leadership was decisive also in this respect. Since his late Masses always employ a cantus firmus, he must have recognized at this stage of his development that the tenor cantus firmus was the safest means of cyclic unity. His cycles draw on sacred melodies (*Caput, Ecce ancilla, Ave regina*), but also on secular ones (*L'homme armé, Se la face* [17]). Not only does Dufay extend the source of the cantus firmus to the secular field (he is perhaps the first composer to do so), but he invariably opens with a motto beginning before he permits the tenor to come in. Thus he combines the two means of unification and merges the two streams leading to the cyclic Mass in one great tradition which was to dominate the second half of the century and which was to form our idea of a typical cyclic Mass.

Cycles with motto but without cantus firmus do not disappear completely—they survive in certain works of Okeghem, e.g. *Missa Quinti toni*—but they hold a subordinate place.

These are, in rough outline, the origins of the Mass cycle, a musical form that took tremendous strides within a very short time. Two points relating to the form have not yet been touched upon: how the cyclic idea manifested itself in the Gregorian Ordinary, and what criteria determined the choice of cantus firmus. The first point has been briefly discussed by Peter Wagner [18] but would deserve a more thorough study. It is well known that the medieval collections of plainchant group the melodies of the Ordinary by classes, and this arrangement persisted well into the sixteenth century. The same classification prevails in many medieval sources of polyphonic music, as may be seen in OH and as late as Ao. The arrangement of plainsongs in single Ordinaries for certain feasts or liturgical occasions, found in the current reference books, is only a recent development; indeed, even the term *Ordinarium Missae* is foreign to medieval practice. The unified classification was prompted, in the opinion of Peter Wagner, by the polyphonic Mass cycle. In the second half of the century polyphonic manuscripts generally adopt the grouping by Mass cycles, as found for example in Modena, Est. lat. 456, and this order may be called the typical arrangement of a Renaissance manuscript. However, Wagner's idea that polyphonic sacred music may

17 DTOe, Vol. 14/15, 120 ff.
18 *Gregorianische Formenlehre* (*Einführung*, III), 1921, 438.

have set the model for plainsong collections is rather startling in view of the fact that the reverse is generally true in medieval music. While most Gregorian collections of the fifteenth century do continue to lump the chants of one class together, certain sources group them in closed Ordinaries, composed probably for special occasions. It is significant that TuB, which gives the first indications of the incipient cycle in polyphonic music, contains also no less than five Gregorian Mass cycles, two *Missae breves* and three complete Ordinaries.[19] This isolated example suggests that the idea of cyclic order was in the air at the beginning of the fifteenth century. The plainsong Ordinaries do not antedate Machaut's Mass, but they do appear sooner than the musically unified Mass cycle of the Renaissance.

Let us consider, finally, the principles underlying the selection of the cantus firmus. While the recurring music of the motto beginning was as a rule freely composed, the opposite is true of the cantus firmus, which was borrowed from plainchant or a *res facta,* either sacred or secular. In certain cases the cantus firmus could also be contrived by the composer (*soggetto cavato dalle vocali,* solmization syllables, etc.). It has frequently been commented upon that Renaissance composers were apparently indiscriminate in choosing their structural voice. Many pious souls have found it shocking that love songs appear as cantus firmi of Mass cycles. This certainly is indicative of the weakening of liturgical observance, but at the same time it bespeaks the interpenetration of the secular and sacred spheres which prevailed in the Middle Ages even more strongly than in the Renaissance. Secular tenors in sacred compositions are in fact a heritage of the medieval motet. Furthermore, it should be considered that the selection of a sacred cantus firmus, for example the Marian antiphon *Ave regina,* is perhaps even more startling from the liturgical point of view. Such an antiphon was sung in the Office, not in the Mass, and, moreover, serving as cantus firmus, it was relegated to a mere scaffolding voice without liturgical function. The mixture of Ordinary and Office and the non-liturgical use of a liturgical melody betrays, perhaps, a more serious lack of liturgical propriety than the choice of a secular cantus firmus, which, at any rate, could not create liturgical confusion. The Renaissance musicians recognized the cyclic Mass as the most dignified form of composition and thus indirectly also recognized its liturgical dignity, but in their essentially artistic approach to the

[19] See the list of contents published by Besseler in AMW VII (1925), **212.**

problem, which put musical unity above all, they were no longer guided by the strictly liturgical attitude of medieval musicians. It may seem paradoxical that the Mass cycle, the most extended composition before the advent of the opera and the symphony, and regarded today as liturgical music *par excellence,* was actually the result of the weakening of liturgical ties at the oncoming of the Renaissance.

2. THE SOURCE OF THE *CAPUT* MELODY

Although the Mass cycle has been accorded recognition commensurate with its aesthetic and artistic importance, it still harbors many unresolved questions to which, despite persistent efforts, the right answer has not yet been found. As a rule, the cantus firmi furnish the general title of the composition. Only if we know the borrowed material in its original form can we properly evaluate the way the composer has utilized it and the extent to which he conforms to or departs from tradition; in short, only this knowledge sets the right perspective on the technique of compositon and on the question of what is the composer's own and what is not. In Masses such as *Ave regina celorum* by Dufay or *De plus en plus* by Okeghem the titles lead us directly to the plainchant or the *res facta* that the composer has taken over, but in a not inconsiderable number of compositions the cantus firmus carries either no designation at all or a title that cannot be identified. In the latter case the title is no more than a road sign in the middle of nowhere, because it does not lead us to the original composition. Although the melodies referred to in the incipits of the manuscripts were as a rule well known at the time, they have become enigmatic and tantalizing hints to us who are no longer familiar with the comprehensive repertory of the fifteenth century and who know it only from the limited number of compositions that have withstood the vicissitudes of nearly five centuries. Many a musicological Sherlock Holmes has tried to solve the puzzles of Mass titles by piecing together circumstantial evidence and clues from widely scattered sources. In Masses in which incipits are completely lacking the identification of the cantus firmus is made even more trying and is reduced to the chance that the tune may accidentally be recognized. If the composer employed melodic coloration, it is not even always possible to determine definitely whether or not there is a cantus firmus at all. It is indeed difficult to decide which one of the two predicaments is less desirable, to have no indication at all (in which case it can at least be assumed that the structural voice was not borrowed but written by the composer himself), or to have merely a title of some unknown source.

The Masses with which this study proposes to deal belong to the second category. The three famous Masses on *Caput* come from the pens of the three leading composers of the fifteenth century, Dufay, Okeghem, and Obrecht. They all use the same cantus firmus, designated by the single enigmatic word *Caput* (head). Although the three compositions have been generally accessible for many years, if not decades,[20] all attempts at identification of the cantus firmus have failed. A certain aura of mystery hovers over the *Caput* Masses. As far as we know, only these three composers have written an entire Mass on this particular melody, though it was common practice to borrow cantus firmi and set them time and again. It is also striking that only this triumvirate of the Flemish school should have used it, and in a fashion that discloses unmistakable similarities, if not direct dependencies, in the treatment of the tenor melody, many of which have passed unnoticed so far. The *Caput* melody itself is puzzling, not only because of its unknown origin, but also for its extraordinary melodic characteristics, which have raised doubts as to its supposedly sacred origin.

Various assertions and theories have been advanced about the mysterious melody; these, however, have helped little to clarify the issue. In the introduction to the edition of the Austrian *Denkmäler* Franz Schegar has drawn attention to three liturgical texts in which at least the word *caput* occurs.[21] The list of such texts could indeed be extended indefinitely, but not one of them shows in its music any relation to our cantus firmus. Schegar leaves open the question whether or not the three texts quoted by him have any bearing on the *Caput* melody, and, apparently dissatisfied with his own references, he

[20] The Masses are available in the following editions: Dufay, DTOe, Vol. 38 (1912), ed. by Adler and Koller; Okeghem, *ibid.;* and also in *Collected Works,* ed. by Plamenac, Vol. II, American Musicological Society, 1947; Obrecht, *Werken,* I, No. 18, ed. by Johannes Wolf. The *Denkmäler* edition is untrustworthy in many details, but it reproduces the Masses by Dufay and Okeghem in facsimile, so that the editorial mistakes can at least be checked. The errors in the transcription of Okeghem's Mass are listed in the editorial notes of Plamenac's edition, which is reliable and after which the music will be quoted here.

[21] DTOe, Vol. 38, p. xiii.

rather abruptly asserts that the character of the melody points to a secular origin. While the Latin timbre of the cantus firmus does not exactly favor this opinion, it must be admitted that certain features of the melody, especially the frequent use of disjunct motion, is not very characteristic of a typically "Gregorian" chant, so that secular, or at least non-Gregorian, elements may well have played their part in it. Unfortunately, our knowledge of what constitutes "secular style" in fifteenth-century music as apart from "sacred style" (if such a distinction can be made at all) is as yet so limited and so strongly colored by unconscious prejudices (which we are apt to take for facts) that it would be precarious to make a categorical assertion.

All other scholars who have discussed the question take the sacred origin of the melody for granted, but this is the only point in which they agree. Peter Wagner, with the trained eye of a specialist in plainchant, recognized the melismatic character of the cantus firmus and suggested that it could very well be the *jubilus* of an alleluia in the Mixolydian mode.[22] However, no alleluia with this melody exists. In his edition of Obrecht's Mass, Johannes Wolf maintains, on the other hand, that the cantus firmus is probably derived from a section of the tract *Eripe me,* sung on Good Friday. Indeed, its verse *Caput circuitus* does start with a melisma on the crucial word, but not by any stretch of the imagination can the two melismas be called similar.

Still another suggestion, and a very ingenious one, has been proffered by André Pirro in his last book.[23] Reiterating that the melody must have been well known at the time, he suspects, on the basis of the word "Head," that it may have belonged to a special Office, composed for a beheaded martyr, or possibly for the translation of relics—for example, those of St. Andrew, who was specially honored in the diocese of Cambrai. Pirro's brilliant deduction takes the liturgical situation into account (which his predecessors failed to do), but nevertheless has not led to a palpable result. Plamenac, in his editorial notes,[24] merely reports the divergent opinions of Wagner and Wolf. My own search for the melody was guided by the suspicion that the melody was possibly a sequence. This hypothesis was suggested by the inner repeats of the melisma and also by the atypical

[22] *Geschichte der Messe,* 95.
[23] *Histoire de la musique de la fin du XIVe siècle à la fin du XVIe.* Paris, 1940, 77.
[24] Okeghem, *Collected Works,* II, xxvi.

behavior of the melody. Both features are common in sequences, though they are normally built much more regularly than the *Caput* melisma. However, the consultation of several medieval sequentiaries was fruitless.[25] All attempts to determine the origin of the *Caput* melody have had a negative result.

The first clue that led eventually to the discovery of the real source came from a liturgical manuscript of the fifteenth century, the so-called "Processional of the Nuns of Chester," now at the Huntington Library. The text of this collection has been edited by the Henry Bradshaw Society,[26] but, as usual in liturgical publications of this and most other learned societies, the music has been regarded as a troublesome accessory and has therefore been excluded from the publication.[27] The customary omission of music is most unfortunate, not only for the musicologist, who is thus forced to turn to the originals, but also for the liturgiologist, who deprives himself of some valuable evidence as to local variants or differences between the Roman and non-Roman rites which may not be apparent in the texts.

The particular section in the Chester Processional that arrested my attention was the antiphon *Venit ad Petrum*, conspicuous for its long melisma on the final word *caput*. With my senses sharpened by a prolonged period of "Head"-hunting, my interest was aroused at once. So far as I could tell from memory—the *Denkmäler* were not accessible at the time—the melisma sounded vaguely familiar, but it did not seem to be identical with the melody of the Masses. However, my curiosity was sufficiently stimulated to investigate whether

[25] There is a deplorable lack of publications in the field of sequence. The editions of Schubiger, Clément, Misset-Aubry, Drinkwelder, Bannister-Hughes, and Moberg are limited in their scope; individual sequences are scattered in numberless articles and studies, but not a single major sequentiary has ever been published with the music. Unfortunately many plainchant specialists still persist in regarding the sequence as an intruder not worthy of serious study. They forget that many a Kyrie and such celebrated antiphons as *Alma redemptoris*, often quoted as classical examples of genuine "Gregorian" chant, are of a much later date than many sequences. The Monks of Solesmes, to whom we owe so much by way of publications, show a strong disinclination to include the sequence in their research, for it does not belong to the "classic" period of Gregorian chant, and, what is worse, it may not bear out or may even upset their rhythmic theories. Many of the manuscripts they have worked on contain large sections dedicated to tropes and sequences, but these sections have been consistently omitted from their publications.

[26] Vol. XVIII, 1899, ed. by J. Wickham Legg.

[27] The superficial treatment of music is even more pronounced in many manuscript catalogues. The excellent catalogue of the French liturgical manuscripts by Leroquais deals with music very inadequately, and the *Census* by De Ricci-Wilson does not even indicate, in every case, the presence of music.

or not variants of the same antiphon existed. A perusal of several Italian Processionals and Graduals [28] of the fifteenth century elicited nothing, for the collections did not even contain the piece. But a search in Sarum Processionals and Sarum Graduals was at last amply rewarded: they not only contain the antiphon but present a version of the *Caput* melisma that coincides verbatim with the cantus firmus of the same name. The *Caput* Masses are therefore founded on a section from the antiphon *Venit ad Petrum* of the Sarum use, more specifically on its final word, which is adorned by a huge melisma (see Plates 6 and 7).

It is easy to be wise after the event and to see why the cantus firmus has eluded identification for so long. Only a single and, as we shall see later, a most significant word has been borrowed from the antiphon, and since this is the very last one it cannot be found in any alphabetical index. Moreover, Sarum Processionals have not been reprinted with their music, though a modern text edition is available.[29] Had the music been accessible, the source of the tenor would probably have been discovered much sooner. It must be admitted, however, that the antiphon appears also in the facsimile edition of the *Graduale Sarisburiense,* where it has remained unrecognized since 1894. The mystery of why the melody carries a single word reveals itself now as an apparent one because this word is indeed the only one rightfully associated with it. The discovery of the source of the cantus firmus solves one puzzle in fifteenth-century music but raises, on the other hand, several new questions which could not be seen before.

3. LITURGICAL ASPECTS OF THE ANTIPHON
VENIT AD PETRUM

Before we turn to the music of the antiphon we must deal with the liturgical aspects, important not only in themselves but also with regard to the music. As we shall see, they actually elucidate certain unusual musical features. The antiphon belongs to the ritual of the washing of the feet during Holy Week, instituted in commemoration of the fact that Jesus washed the feet of the Apostles at the Last Supper (John, 13). This *pedilavium* takes place, usually after Vespers,

[28] The capitalized form of the word will refer to liturgical collections as a whole, the other to single chants.

[29] *Processionale ad usum Sarum, Leeds,* 1882, ed. by W. G. Henderson.

on Maundy or "Shere" Thursday and appears, therefore, in the rubrics of the liturgical books under *Feria V in C(o)ena Domini.* During the ceremony a number of antiphons are sung, of which the first one, *Mandatum novum,* has given the name to the entire rite, commonly referred to as *Mandatum* in the Missals or Processionals. It is the same word, incidentally, from which Maundy Thursday derives its name, Maundy being the "Englished" form of *mandatum.* The words of the antiphon are a compilation from the Gospel according to St. John, 13, 6–9, and run as follows:

Venit ad Petrum; dixit ei Petrus, Non lavabis mihi pedes in aeternum; respondens Jesus dixit, Si no lavero te, non habebis partem mecum; Domine, non tantum pedes meos, sed et manus et *caput.*

The text concentrates on the dialogue between Peter and Jesus and directly juxtaposes their utterances with omission of some of the narrative parts. It contains two important statements: "If I wash thee not, thou hast no part with me," and "Lord, not my feet only, but also my hands and my head." It should be noted that the last word receives, for no apparent reason, the greatest musical emphasis through the melisma, the only one of the entire antiphon, which is set otherwise in the ordinary neumatic style.

The series of antiphons sung during the *mandatum* was not rigidly prescribed and varied greatly in different countries and even in different localities. It is precisely our antiphon that is frequently omitted; in fact, it is missing in most liturgical books and manuscripts that have been consulted for this study. If we consider only those liturgical sources that have been published with their music (in facsimile), there are no more than three containing the antiphon. They are listed here in chronological order: (1) the Gradual of Saint-Yrieix [30] of the eleventh century, fol. 67 v; (2) the Gradual of Rouen [31] of the thirteenth century, fol. 89; and (3) the Sarum Gradual [32] of the thirteenth century, fol. 98.

To these manuscripts a large group of unpublished sources can be added. A *Missel plénaire* of the thirteenth century (Paris, Bibl. Nat., MS. lat. 1112, henceforth quoted as the Paris Missal) preserves a version of *Venit ad Petrum* on fol. 90 v. There are, furthermore,

[30] *Pal. mus.* XIII, 134.
[31] *Le Graduel de l'église cathédrale de Rouen,* Rouen, 1907, ed. by Loriquet, Pothier, and Colette.
[32] *Grad. Sar.,* 1894.

numerous English sources which belong to the Sarum use and therefore essentially duplicate the Sarum Gradual. These Sarum Missals and Processionals range from the thirteenth to the sixteenth century. It may suffice here to refer to the manuscripts that Legg used in his text edition [33] of the Sarum Missal, notably the Crawford Missal, Manchester, John Rylands Library, MS lat. 24, fol. 90 (see Plate 6); MS 135 of the Bibliothèque de l'Arsenal, Paris; and Bologna, Bibl. Univ., MS 2565. Mention should also be made of the printed Sarum Missal of 1507 (fol. xcvii v, Pollard 15862) which has been made accessible in the microfilm series *Books printed in England before 1600*.[34] The list of manuscript Processionals includes British Museum, Harleian MS 2942, fol. 48–48v (14th c.) and the Processional of the Nuns of Chester (15th c.).[35] The printed Processionals of 1519 (Pollard 16235) and 1530 (Pollard 16240), the only two with music accessible in the microfilm series,[36] omit our antiphon, but other printed Processionals—e.g., those of 1508, 1517, 1555—do contain it. The reason for the omission is simply that in the Sarum use only five antiphons were mandatory, while the others, including *Venit ad Petrum,* were optional. They are listed under the rubric "si necesse fuerit"—*i.e.,* if the length of the ceremony made additional chants necessary.

The sources listed above are all of either French or English origin. The first French one, Saint-Yrieix, belongs to Saint-Martial, the second to the Norman use of Rouen, the third to the use of Paris, the English sources to the Sarum use. The fact that the Norman and English liturgies share certain unusual antiphons is not surprising in view of the intimate historical connections between the Norman and Sarum rites.[37] It has not been possible to determine how widely the antiphon was disseminated in France, but its occurrence in three important centers (Saint-Martial, Paris, and Rouen) implies a fairly wide distribution. The question would be worth further study.

While the search for the antiphon *Venit ad Petrum* has been successful in French and English sources, it has had, so far at least, a com-

[33] *The Sarum Missal,* ed. by J. Wickham Legg, Oxford, 1916, 108.

[34] University Microfilms, Ann Arbor; Carton 135.

[35] Huntington Library, San Marino, California, MS EL 34 B 7, fol. 42v; for the text edition see note 26.

[36] Carton 95.

[37] See Edmund Bishop, "Holy Week Rites of Sarum, Hereford and Rouen Compared" in *Liturgica Historica,* Oxford, 1918, 276 ff.

pletely negative result in those of the Roman use. The *mandatum* ceremony itself appears of course regularly in the Roman liturgy, often with a great number of antiphons, but *Venit ad Petrum* is contained neither in the medieval Graduals and Processionals nor in those of the current Roman use. Apparently, then, the antiphon does not belong to "Gregorian" chant proper, *i.e.* to the Roman codification of the liturgy. This startling and highly unexpected conclusion is confirmed from the strictly musical point of view by the non-Gregorian character of the melody.

Although a comparative study of the *mandatum* in the Roman, French, and English rites cannot be carried out at this time because it would call for a much wider documentation, a listing of the sets of antiphons according to the various sources readily demonstrates the difference between the non-Roman and Roman liturgies. It will not be necessary to list separately the various Sarum sources, as they all substantially agree in the order and number of antiphons. We can restrict ourselves to the following five series, which all include our antiphon:

TABLE 1

Saint-Yrieix

1. Mandatum novum
2. Postquam surrexit
3. Si ego Dominus
4. Domine tu mihi
5. In diebus illis
6. Diligamus nos
7. Ubi fratres in unum
8. Maneant in nobis
9. Manete autem
10. In hoc cognoscent
11. Deus caritas est
12. Ubi est caritas
13. Tunc percinxit se
14. Mulier quae erat
15. Maria ergo unxit
16. Dixit autem Jesus
17. Congregavit nos Christus
18. Congregavit nos in unum
19. Caritas est summum
20. Surgit Jesus
21. Vos vocatis me magister
22. Misit denique
23. Postquam ergo
24. Coena facta
25. *Ante diem festum*
26. *Venit ad Petrum*
27. Benedicat Dominus
28. Tellus ac aetherea [versus]
29. Domum istam

Rouen

1. Mandatum novum
2. Si ego Dominus
3. Vos vocatis me magister
4. In hoc cognoscent

5. In diebus illis
6. Maria ergo unxit
7. Diligamus nos
8. Ubi fratres in unum
9. Ubi est caritas
10. Domine tu mihi
11. *Ante diem festum*
12. *Venit ad Petrum*

Sarum

1. Mandatum novum
2. Diligamus nos
3. In diebus illis
4. Maria ergo unxit
5. Postquam surrexit
———[si necesse fuerit]
6. Vos vocatis me magister
7. Si ego Dominus
8. *Ante diem festum*
9. *Venit ad Petrum*

Chester

1. Mandatum novum
2. Si ego Dominus
3. Postquam surrexit
4. In diebus illis
5. Accepit Maria
6. *Ante diem festum*
7. *Venit ad Petrum*
8. Tellus ac aethera [versus]
9. Congregavit nos Christus
10. Congregavit nos in unum
11. Domum istam

Paris

1. Mandatum novum
2. Diligamus nos
3. Postquam surrexit
4. In diebus illis
5. Si ego Dominus
6. In hoc cognoscent
7. Vos vocatis me magister
8. *Ante diem festum*
9. *Venit ad Petrum*

The above lists should be compared with the Roman set of antiphons, for which we adduce here only three representative series. The first is taken from the first printed edition of the Missale Romanum (1474).[38] The second comes from a Continental, probably Italian, manuscript collection of the early fifteenth century (Cambridge, Univ. Lib. Add. MS. 6668)[39] the contents of which have not yet been described. It follows, by and large, the Roman use and has been selected here because it contains a greater number of antiphons than many other Continental sources of the time. The third, finally, gives the antiphons of the current use as noted in the *Liber Usualis*.

[38] Henry Bradshaw Society, Vol. XVII, 1899.

[39] The exact place of origin of this source is not known, but the Latin text shows some influence of Italian spelling. The manuscript, listed as an antiphonary in the catalogue, contains a mixed repertory of great variety destined, apparently, for special occasions. Aside from sequences, the responds for the Nocturns are most notable. In the series of *mandatum* antiphons the scribe has erroneously listed some of the subsidiary psalms as antiphons proper, a very common mistake which occurs also in some of the French and English sources of Table I. The errors have been corrected in our lists.

TABLE 2

Roman (15th c.)	*Italian (15th c.)*
1. Postquam surrexit	1. Dominus Jesus
2. Dominus Jesus	2. Postquam surrexit
3. Benedixisti Domine	3. Si ego Dominus
4. Exemplum enim dedi	4. Vos vocatis me magister
5. Quam dilecta	5. Mandatum novum
6. Deus miseriatur	6. In hoc cognoscent
7. Congregavit nos Christus	7. In diebus illis
8. Mulier quae erat	8. Maria ergo unxit
9. Domine tu mihi	9. Domine, tu mihi
10. Quod ego facio	10. Caritas est summum
11. Si ego Dominus	11. Ubi est caritas
12. In hoc cognoscent	11a. Christus descendit (continuation)
13. Benedicta sit	12. Diligamus nos
14. Ubi caritas et amor	13. Ubi fratres in unum
	14. Congregavit nos in unum
	15. Maneant in nobis
	16. Benedicat nos Deus

Roman (current use)

1. Mandatum novum
2. Postquam surrexit
3. Dominus Jesus
4. Domine tu mihi
5. Si ego Dominus
6. In hoc cognoscent
7. Maneant in vobis
8. Benedicta sit sancta
9. Ubi caritas et amor

Comparing the various series, we find that most sources agree in putting *Mandatum novum* at the beginning. The Italian collection does not conform to the rule and gives first place to *Dominus Jesus postquam cenavit.*[40] This text narrates the first phase of the footwash-

---

[40] The same is true of the Worcester Antiphonary, *Pal. mus.* XII, 213, and of a Carthusian Gradual of the fifteenth century, Brit. Mus. Egerton 3267, which is of English origin but does not follow the Sarum use. For further *mandatum* antiphons see the references in the introduction to *Pal. mus.* XII, 65. Still another arrangement is to be found in manuscripts of the Beneventan use, *Pal. mus.* XIV, 284; they begin with the antiphon *Postquam surrexit*, which normally takes the second place in the series.

ing at the Last Supper and contains the significant words "Exemplum dedi vobis." It thus emphatically establishes the precedent for the *mandatum* ceremony and can therefore fittingly replace the antiphon from which the *mandatum* has borrowed its name. It should also be noted that in the Sarum use the text *Dominus Jesus postquam* likewise appears. It precedes the *mandatum* as *communio* of the foregoing Mass and thus leads directly to the *mandatum* itself. Aside from the first antiphon there exists between the various uses a surprising lack of uniformity in the order and selection of antiphons. This diversity is rare in the regular liturgy and typical only of special occasions. The closest analogies exist between Paris and Sarum; the two sets agree not only in the number of antiphons, but, with one exception, even in the chants themselves. Whether or not this implies a general kinship of liturgies it is difficult to say; the agreement is, at any rate, very striking. The Gradual of Saint-Yrieix with its tremendous number of antiphons encompasses nearly all the chants of the other sources and gives us an idea of how extended the ceremony must have been in the monastery for which the manuscript was written.[41]

The antiphons do not necessarily relate the story of Jesus washing the feet of the Apostles. For example, *Accepit Maria* of the Chester series combines passages from John 12:3 and Luke 7:38, which deal with the anointment of Jesus' feet by Mary Magdalen; *In diebus illis* (Luke 7:37–38) and *Maria ergo unxit* (John 12:3) refer to the same event. Strictly speaking, the Mary Magdalen episode does not belong to the *mandatum;* the point of the latter is precisely that Jesus washes the feet of others, but the similarity of subject accounts for the association.

Several other antiphons have no bearing on footwashing at all. In Saint-Yrieix we find *Benedicat Dominus* and in the Italian series *Benedicat nos Deus,* both of which are prayers for benediction, but which are not identical in text or melody. In the Roman lists the antiphon *Benedicta sit sancta Trinitas* stands quite apart from all others. It belongs rightfully to the Feast of Trinity, where it is sung today as an introit with a different melody but the same words. Its insertion in the *mandatum* series seems to be a peculiarity of the Roman use. It can also be found in the Beneventan manuscripts,

[41] *Pal. mus.* XIII, 26.

which record it as early as the eleventh century.[42] While it cannot
be ascertained at what time the antiphon was connected with the
mandatum, it is at any rate evident that the chant stands in strange
surroundings. The French and English sources recognize this fact
by simply omitting it. In the Chester Processional the antiphons are
divided into two groups, of which the second begins with *Tellus et
aethera.* This chant carries no designation in Chester and differs
from all the others in that it is not an antiphon but a processional
hymn or *versus,* as this type is called in many medieval sources.[43]
Saint-Yrieix and Chester also have the last antiphon in common,
Domum istam, a prayer for the protection of the "house." The latter
antiphon appears only in the two manuscripts compiled for a monastery, which accounts for the use of a chant that has no inner connection with the *mandatum.*

A close examination of the five sets of antiphons in Table I reveals
that they belong to two types of sources which may be briefly distinguished here as "monastic" or conventual and "cathedral" or diocesan
groups. The sources of the first type, Saint-Yrieix and Chester, put
Venit ad Petrum in the middle and conclude the set with *Domum
istam,* while those of the second—Rouen, Paris, and Sarum—end
directly with *Venit ad Petrum.* Both types show great diversity as
to number and selection of antiphons, but they all agree in one important point: they invariably present *Venit ad Petrum* preceded by
Ante diem festum. That the two chants always appear in this order
is easily explained by the words. *Ante diem* stems from John 13:1–5
and forms the exact complement of *Venit ad Petrum,* which begins,
as will be recalled, with verse 6 of the same chapter. As far as the
words are concerned, the antiphons are therefore continuous. In the
Antiphonary of Worcester [44] the two chants are actually contracted
into a single antiphon, and for this reason *Venit ad Petrum* is not
listed in the alphabetical index. This particular version of *Venit*

42 *Pal. mus.* XIV, 283.

43 The general form of the processional hymn is similar to that of the Latin cantilena
and English carol; see the discussion of this point on p. 149. Spanke (*Zeitschrift für
französische Sprache,* LIV [1931], 285) has proposed classing the *versus* under the general
term "conductus," as certain later medieval MSS do. It is true that many conductus
served as processionals, but they do not necessarily have the verse structure and choral
repetenda of the *versus.* In view of the difference in musical and literary form it seems
advisable to retain the terminological distinction, at least in specialized writings. See
further Ellinwood, "The Conductus," in MQ XXVII (1941), 165.

44 *Pal. mus.* XII, 213.

ad Petrum differs in its music somewhat from the Sarum use, and does not contribute anything to our subject because the word *caput* is not set to the final melisma in which we are interested here. Another version of the contracted form is to be found in a *cantatorium,* now in the British Museum (Add. MS 23922, fol. 31v–32).[45] Here the word *caput* carries a fairly long melisma, but it cannot be transcribed because the music appears in staffless neums.

In the majority of sources *Ante diem* and *Venit ad Petrum* appear as two independent chants with distinctly different melodies. They agree, however, in one respect: they both end with a long melisma on the words *discipulorum* and *caput* respectively. Since in plainchant melismas are not inserted haphazardly but usually lend emphasis, the two words must be of special significance. The melismas differ melodically, but they have two exceptional features in common: (1) the wide range and disjunct character of the melody, and (2) the fact that they appear at the end of an antiphon—a liturgical form in which long melismas are most unusual. Even more striking is the fact that precisely these two antiphons are as regularly omitted in the liturgical sources of the Roman use as they are present in those of the French and English use. They belong apparently to a pre-Gregorian and certainly non-Roman stratum of the chant like the *Christus vincit* formulas of the *Laudes Regiae.*[46] The absence of the two decisive antiphons from Roman sources cannot be explained on musical grounds, nor can they account for the strange circumstance that the musical stress falls on the word *caput*. There seems to be a confusion of extremities, for it would be more appropriate to emphasize the word *pedes* in a foot-washing ceremony. At this point of the investigation the help of a specialist in liturgical history was needed.[47] The next paragraphs briefly summarize his findings.

The washing of the feet was not only an act of humility, but was associated in most of the non-Roman rites with the sacramental sphere, more specifically with the sacrament of baptism. The footwashing formed part of the baptismal ceremonies in the Mozarabic,

[45] The MS has been described by A. Wilmart, *L'Ancien Cantatorium*, Strasbourg, 1928. The contracted version without melisma appears also in Brit. Mus., Egerton MS 274, fol. 158v.

[46] See Bukofzer, "The Music of the Laudes," in Ernst H. Kantorowicz, *Laudes Regiae*, University of California Publications in History, Vol. 33, Berkeley, 1947, 209.

[47] It was my good fortune to be able to turn for advice to my friend and colleague Professor Ernst H. Kantorowicz. Full details will be given in his forthcoming study on the Baptism of the Apostles.

Gallican, Ambrosian, and Irish rites, the African Church, and some Eastern churches. The connection of foot-washing and baptism, which is far from being self-evident, goes back to the interpretation of the washing of the feet on Maundy Thursday as symbolizing the Baptism of the Apostles. Scattered evidence for this concept, which tends to raise the foot-washing into the sacramental sphere, can be found in both Eastern and Western sources. St. Ambrose is one of the main authorities for the sacramental character of the *pedilavium*. To him it is not merely an act of humility; he calls it also "a work of sanctification" and "a sacrament" [48] and consciously sets Milan against Rome, where the ceremony, then as now, was regarded only as an act of brotherly love. The direct association of the washing of the feet with baptism has survived in the West in the decretals of Pseudo-Isidorius, which belong to the ninth century and are most likely of Gallican origin. This author succinctly states: *"Lavatio pedum nostrorum significat baptismum."* [49] The difference between the non-Roman and Roman interpretations could not be outlined more clearly. In most non-Roman rites the ceremony was an act of humility, but at the same time it was associated with the sacramental sphere of baptism. Not so in Rome, where it had no sacramental connotation and was "no more than a pious imitation of Christ's action at the Last Supper," [50] a demonstration of brotherly love.

This divergence of interpretation is reflected also in the choice of antiphons. In the Roman form of the *mandatum* the idea of brotherly love (*caritas*) prevails, as is shown beyond doubt in the antiphon *Ubi caritas et amor*. Significantly, this chant appears in the Roman series prominently at the end; it takes, in other words, the same place as *Venit ad Petrum* does in the series of the non-Roman rites. The text of *Ubi caritas* refers to the mandate of brotherly love which is designated as a *mandatum* in the Bible (John, 1. Epistle, 4:21). It could therefore fittingly be sung in the *mandatum* of the washing of the feet, which is clearly interpreted here in the spirit of *caritas*. In the non-Roman tradition this idea is relegated to the background. Saint-Yrieix and Rouen, it is true, do contain the anti-

[48] Edward J. Duncan, *Baptism in the Demonstrations of Aphraates, the Persian Sage*, Studies in Christian Antiquity, ed. by Johannes Quasten, The Catholic University of America, Washington, 1945. See especially the chapter "The Washing of Feet as a Baptismal Rite," p. 67.

[49] *Decretales Pseudo-Isidorianae*, ed. by P. Hinschius, Leipzig, 1863, 160.

[50] Duncan, *op. cit.*, 72.

phon *Ubi caritas,* but they consign it to a less prominent place, whereas the English sources go even a step further and omit it altogether. The sources of the "cathedral" group, Rouen, Sarum, and Paris, testify to a shift of accent from *caritas* to the *pedilavium* itself. They conclude the series with *Ante diem festum* and *Venit ad Petrum* and thus point to the "sacramental" interpretation of the *mandatum* in the non-Roman tradition.

The twofold interpretation is countenanced by iconographical evidence. The washing of the feet was a favorite subject for medieval artists, and, as in all pictorial representations of biblical scenes, they usually tried to give faithful illustrations of the Scriptures. There are two iconographic types representing the scene. One shows Peter raising both hands in a gesture of remonstrance and deprecation as Jesus stoops to wash his feet. It corresponds to the words "non lavabis mihi pedes in aeternum" and reflects the idea of humility and *caritas.* The other type represents the scene in a different spirit. Here Peter is shown pointing with his right hand to his head. The gesture corresponds to the words "non tantum pedes meos sed et manus et caput" and reflects the idea of baptism.[51] The first type was predominant in the Roman sphere, whereas the second type, which came to the West from the orbit of Byzantine art, seems to have been practically unknown until the tenth century.

It now becomes easily understandable that the word *caput* should receive emphasis. It is the key word of a special liturgical interpretation and consequently is given musical prominence by the melisma. The exact parallel between pictorial representation and music is a point of supreme interest. The hand of Peter points to *Caput* as obviously as the melisma does in the antiphon, and what the one makes clear to the eye the other makes clear to the ear. We have here a striking example of how the fields of liturgical history,

[51] See Plates 4 and 5. From the great number of pictures of the second type I have selected only an early and a late one. The first is taken from Paris, Bibl. Nat. MS lat. 17325, fol. 27v (see Ph. Lauer, *Les Enluminures Romanes,* Paris, 1925, Pl. LXXVI). The manuscript dates from the late eleventh century, and although it is of German origin the Byzantine influence on the miniatures is unmistakable. The second illustration is Dürer's eloquent woodcut of the Washing of the Feet in his *Kleine Passion* (1510), which shows that Renaissance artists were well acquainted with the second type. That it was known also in England as early as the beginning of the twelfth century is proved by a Psalter written for St. Alban's in London, now in Hildesheim. A description of the miniature (fol. 19v) is found in Adolph Goldschmidt, *Der Albanipsalter in Hildesheim,* Berlin, 1895. It should be noted that the learned historian of art did not understand the meaning of Peter's gesture. Interpreting it as a utilitarian gesture, ill suited to the solemn occasion, he says that the picture shows Peter "resting his head."

iconography, and music elucidate one another, how the one becomes intelligible only through the other. Our starting point was a musical one: an unusual melisma called for an explanation which could come only from the liturgy. If these fields are brought together they can solve a problem that any one of them, taken separately, would not be able to explain. Thus they profit from each other. Hitherto it was not known that the "sacramental" interpretation of the *mandatum* existed also in the Sarum rite. We do not know whether this interpretation still affected the liturgy in the fifteenth century, when the *Caput* Masses were written, or whether it had already faded away. At any rate it is clearly preserved in the music. The manifestations of the history of music and art may be shaped by liturgical concepts, but, once established, they may assume a life of their own and persist longer than the liturgical use that prompted them. Thus a time lag between the artistic and liturgical forms results which enables us to discover in the former the vestiges of the latter.

A history of the antiphon *Venit ad Petrum,* which would be highly rewarding, lies beyond the scope of this study and would be possible only if a vast number of liturgical sources were accessible. Future research will have to determine at what time the antiphon first appeared in this particular musical form, where it was introduced, and how it spread through the different local rites. Furthermore, it must be investigated whether the antiphon was from the beginning associated only with the *mandatum* or whether it had other functions. The origin and the variants of the *Caput* melisma would be of special interest. Since musical sources with readable notation date back not earlier than the eleventh century, it is probable that the Gradual of Saint-Yrieix is one of the earliest sources to contain the melisma in a form that can be accurately transcribed. The editor suggests that the Gradual contains survivals of Gallican chant.[52] Our antiphon may possibly belong to the Gallican group, although we have no positive and direct proof for that assumption because our knowledge of Gallican chant is as yet too restricted. The antiphon occurs neither in the Ambrosian antiphonary of the twelfth century [53] nor in the modern edition of the *Antiphonale Mediolanense* of the Milanese

[52] *Pal. mus.* XIII, 30.
[53] *Pal. mus.* V and VI; British Museum, Add. MS 34209.

rite.[54] It is likewise absent in the *Missale Mixtum* [55] of the Mozarabic rite. The antiphon is therefore not traceable in the Roman, Ambrosian, and Mozarabic chant. Its presence in comparatively late sources of the Gallican and Sarum use suggests a French origin, but may, on the other hand, be due solely to the fact that the musical sources of the other non-Roman rites are at present only very incompletely known.

Before we conclude the discussion of the liturgical aspects of our antiphon we must consider whether it has any relation to the time of the liturgical year at which the *Caput* Masses were sung. It would be natural to assume that they were performed, like the antiphon on which they are based, on Maundy Thursday, but this assumption is open to question. The *Caput* Masses are settings of the complete Ordinary, including the *Gloria,* which was regularly omitted during the Lenten season. The Sarum Gradual, however, does permit the singing of the *Gloria* when the bishop himself celebrates the Mass. It could be surmised, therefore, that the *Caput* Masses were sung at such a solemn occasion on Maundy Thursday. On the other hand, it should be borne in mind that cantus firmi of Mass cycles do not necessarily indicate the liturgical season. This is obvious in those cases where a secular tune serves as cantus firmus, but even if such antiphons as *Ave regina caelorum* are used, no definite conclusion about the performance can be drawn. A Mass on *Ave Regina* could be sung on the Feast of the Holy Virgin, and similarly the *Caput* Masses could have been composed in honor of St. Peter. A third possibility— namely, that the antiphon had no influence whatsoever on the liturgical destination of the Mass—should not be ruled out altogether, because a certain disregard for liturgical propriety is a characteristic of the musical Renaissance.

4. MELODIC VARIANTS AND STRUCTURE OF THE *CAPUT* MELISMA

The antiphon *Venit ad Petrum,* reproduced in facsimile in Plates 6 and 7, stands as a whole in Mixolydian but cannot be easily classified as to authentic or plagal mode because it displays the characteristics of both at different sections of the melody. The "dominant" or

[54] Rome, 1935. The edition is based in part on the manuscript just cited.
[55] Migne, *Patrologia Latina,* LXXXV–LXXXVI.

tone of recitation is at the beginning unquestionably not *d,* but *c,* which makes the melody plagal; however, toward its end the melody rises, especially in the melisma, to *g,* the recitation tone shifts to *d,* and the melody becomes authentic. In the index to the *Graduale Sarisburiense* Frere has correctly assigned the antiphon to both the seventh and eighth modes. While the modern classification matters little in itself, the obstacles the chant sets to classification are in themselves noteworthy because they point at a layer of the chant that may antedate the establishment of the modal system. The melody encompasses both the plagal and the authentic range and has an exceptionally wide *ambitus* comprising an octave plus a fourth. The Rouen version differs from the others in that the major part of the antiphon is transposed to the upper fourth, which makes the key signature of one flat necessary; the dominant is *f,* and sometimes even *e* (corresponding to *b,* the original tone of repercussion in Mixolydian). At the words "non tantum pedes," where the Sarum version proceeds by unison, the Rouen version suddenly drops a fourth to the original untransposed position, so that the melisma itself appears at the same pitch as in all other sources. As a result the antiphon does not exceed an octave. The fact that the compass is reduced in Rouen to exactly an octave is very likely due to the desire to eliminate melodic irregularities and to adapt the antiphon by means of transposition to the normal compass of a mode required by a typically Gregorian melody. If this inference is correct, the Rouen version would represent a later revision of the original melody.[56]

We turn now to a discussion of the *Caput* melisma itself. In Ex. 1 the five main variants have been juxtaposed to facilitate comparison.[57] The unusually complex internal structure of the melisma can be grasped most easily in the Sarum version, which is more regularly organized than any other variant. It consists of five phrases of uneven length, marked a, b, c, d, and e, which follow one another in the order a b a b a c c d d e. The melisma receives its characteristic shape from the internal repeats, which can be set forth in the following diagram:

$$a \, \|{:} \, b \, a \, {:}\|{:} \, c \, {:}\|{:} \, d \, {:}\| \, e$$

Not only the rational and lucid organization, but also a melodic peculiarity, distinguishes the Sarum version from the others. It should

---

[56] The variant of Rouen throws some light on the relations between the Norman and Sarum rites: the two liturgies are closely akin, but there are nevertheless musical differences, the extent of which has not yet been studied.

[57] The manuscript references are given on p. 231 f.

be noticed that the Sarum variant prefers at times wider intervals than those that occur at analogous places in the other variants: it goes to the high *g'* in phrase b (similar in this respect to Rouen and Paris, but unlike Chester and Saint-Yrieix), and goes up to *e'* at the end of phrase d so that the fourth *e'-b* results, while most other sources have only a third *d'-b*.[58] The use of wide intervals, the replacement of seconds by thirds and similar melodic changes, are characteristics of the northern dialect of Gregorian chant. In connection with the *Christus vincit* acclamation [59] I have had occasion to point out similar manifestations of northern dialect in the Sarum rite; their reappearance in the *Caput* melisma supports the view, tentatively expressed in my earlier study, that the chant of Sarum as a whole should be grouped with the northern dialect, not, as Peter Wagner held, with the Romanesque dialect.

The Sarum version in Ex. 1 is drawn from five sources: (1) the Sarum Missal (Manchester, John Rylands Library, MS lat. 24, fol. 90); (2) the *Graduale Sarisburiense* (fol. 98); (3) a manuscript Processional of the fourteenth century (Brit. Mus., Harley 2942, fol. 48–48v); (4) the printed Sarum Gradual of 1507; and (5) the printed Sarum Processional of 1555 (Pollard 16248). The sources substantially agree in their readings. There would be no point in recording all the minor variants were it not that they demonstrate the degree of accuracy with which melodies were copied and preserved in liturgical books. Most of the variants are, in fact, scribal errors or misprints; the latter are especially numerous because of the comparative novelty of music print.

In the Sarum Missal (Plate 6) the third note of phrase c (a repeated *d*) is omitted and replaced by a liquescent neum; moreover, phrase c as a whole is stated only once; finally, the fourth note of phrase d (a repeated *c*) is omitted and replaced by a liquescent neum exactly as in the following manuscript.

The *Graduale Sarisburiense* inserts in phrase c after the first ligature one more repeated *d'*, and omits in the repeat of phrase c the first group *e-f*, *g-d* (correctly given in the first statement); it lacks in phrase d the fourth note, a repeated *c* which is replaced by a liquescent neum. Furthermore, the syllable *ca* stands a little too far to the left;

[58] It should be noted *pro contra* that the last interval of the melisma is an exception in that it is a third in Sarum, a fourth in the Continental variants.

[59] See the study quoted in footnote 46, 205, n. 57.

Ex. 1. Five variants of the *Caput* melisma.

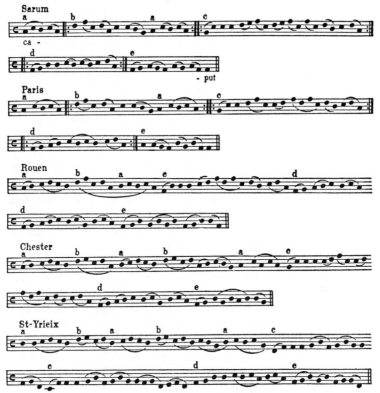

the melisma begins on *b* and not on the preceding ligature, as the other sources prove.

The Sarum Processional of the fourteenth century comes closest to the version that Dufay used (see Plate 7). It differs only in one minute detail: it omits from phrase d the fourth note (a repeated *c*).

In the Gradual of 1507 the first *d* in the initial statement of phrase a is misprinted as *c*, another repeated *d* is inserted in the second statement of phrase c after the fourth note, and the last ligature *g-d*, present in the first statement of the same phrase, is omitted in the second statement.

The Processional of 1555 inserts in phrase c another repeated *d* after the fourth note, erroneously indicates the first *g-d* of phrase c a third too low (correctly given in the first statement), and does not repeat phrase d at all. The last reading, the only major disagreement of this source, is significant in view of Dufay's treatment of the cantus firmus. Since most irregularities occur but once and are not repeated in another statement of the same phrase, they are evidently the result of carelessness or confusion. The frequent repetitions of melismatic groups and of single tones are indeed confusing, as will be evident to those who take the trouble of copying out the melisma. The ligatures vary among all sources; the ones given here are those of the latest source, the printed Processional. No set of ligatures agrees exactly with that of Dufay's tenor.

The comparison of the Sarum version with the four others readily discloses that the discrepancies can be interpreted neither as accidental deviations from the same melody nor as conscious variations of it. Unlike the slight internal differences among the Sarum sources, which are merely various readings of the identical melisma, the Continental versions are genuine variants of a melody that was adopted in the various local rites in different ways. Some of these variants seem to be related to one another, but there are as yet not enough of them to distinguish distinct groups according to their origin. In Example 1 all versions have been analyzed according to the five constituent phrases in order to indicate the analogies to the Sarum melisma. It should be noted that the letters "a," "b," etc., do not correspond to the Sarum version in all particulars. The phrases differ not only melodically but also formally, because the repeats are often not exact, or may be lacking altogether.

The variant of the Gradual of Saint-Yrieix, remarkable not only for its age but especially for its exceptional features, cannot be read very accurately as to pitch and is transcribed here with due reservations. In the manuscript (see *Pal. mus.* XIII, Pl. 134) only one clefless line, drawn by dry point, is given round which the neums are grouped more or less diastematically. The tonal significance of the clef line varies according to the mode of the piece; in the seventh mode it would indicate a *b*, in the eighth mode a *g*.[60] The context makes it clear that it signifies in our case a *g*, which means that the scribe classified the melody as Hypomixolydian. The highest note of the melisma is probably *f'*, if we can trust the spacing of the scribe. The note stands so high that it breaks into the line of text directly

[60] *Pal. mus.* XIII, 160.

above. It could have been transcribed as a *g'* were it not for the fact that the spacing suggests a second rather than a third, and for the parallel we find in the Chester version. The Saint-Yrieix melisma differs from all others in its extreme range. It encompasses a tenth, while the other versions do not go beyond an octave. The most striking feature in the melody is perhaps the final cadence *a-e,* which defies any strict classification according to mode.

It would be precarious to assume a scribal error (*a-e* for *c'-g*) merely on the ground that the cadence does not fit the mode, because this irregularity might be precisely the characteristic of the melody. It could also be argued that the scribe forgot to insert the sign *eq* [= *equaliter*], which is used in the manuscript to transpose phrases by shifting the tonal meaning of the pitch line by a third. Thus the final cadence could possibly read, with transposition of the last two notes, *a-c'-g.* This formula occurs twice before in the melisma, but, on the other hand, so does the original cadence *a-e.* So far as the inner consistency of the melody is concerned both solutions would therefore be possible. Another change of clef, which can likewise not be proved (though it is perhaps a little more plausible than the one just suggested), concerns the repeated phrase c which stands here exactly a fifth lower than in the other sources. If we assume a shift of a fifth the extreme range and the discrepancy with the other sources would be eliminated. A return to the original pitch would then have to be assumed at the beginning of phrase d, which would not be too forced, since that phrase starts on a new line. However, both suggestions are too uncertain to be included in the transcription.

Aside from the wide range of the melisma, its florid line is noteworthy. The basic five phrases are fairly well defined and recognizable in themselves, but not a single repeat of any phrase is strictly literal; there is always some melodic change or extension of the phrase (as in the repeat of phrases a and c). The lack of strict repeats bespeaks an early stage of development in which the rational order of the melisma was not yet carried out rigidly.

We find a similar lack of formal integration in the versions of Rouen and Chester. The former is the least satisfactory of the variants published here. It is probably corrupt, since its beginning stands on extensive erasure, which makes it difficult to decipher the ligatures. Phrases b-a are neither clearly defined nor repeated; phrase c also is stated only once; it begins a tone below the Sarum version, but resumes normal pitch in its second part. Only phrase d is sung twice, but here again the repeat is not exact. The final cadence falls on c'-g-g. The Chester variant rises only to f' in phrase b, omits the repeats of phrases c and d, and comes to the cadence on a instead of g. Both versions are rather short because of the omissions of repeats.

The variant of the Paris Missal comes closest to the Sarum version. Formally it is strictly organized so that the restatements of phrases can be indicated by repeat marks; melodically it agrees with Sarum more nearly than any other variant, and even in the ligatures it corresponds closely to the reading of the *Graduale Sarisburiense,* which is all the more noteworthy as the Sarum sources show no uniformity in this respect. However, there are some important deviations even between these two versions, and they cannot be fortuitous because they appear unchanged in the repeats. Phrases a and b are identical in both versions with regard to melody and ligatures. Phrase c of the Paris version reduces the three repeated d's at the beginning to only two, and then the following ligature reads e-g-d, instead of e-f-g-d. The four-note ligature of the same phrase reads g-f-g-d in the repeat, probably by mistake. We have here the only instance where the Paris version prefers a smaller step (a third, or possibly a second) to the interval of a fourth in the Sarum variant. Phrase e, finally, begins on b instead of g and thus eliminates the wide spacing of the northern dialect. The final cadence occurs as in the Rouen version, on c'-g-g, as against b-g-g of the Sarum version.

The variants fall into several overlapping groups with regard to their melodic features. Rouen and Chester change the characteristic turn b-d-c-d-b of phrase a to a stepwise figure which rises to e; Saint-Yrieix does the same and even modifies the first note to c, which removes the modal ambiguity of the melisma. The versions of Rouen, Paris, and Sarum all reach the high g' in phrase b, whereas those of Chester (and Saint-Yrieix?) go only to f'. The variants of Sarum and Paris, on the other hand, are obviously closely related in their formal articulation and show that the melisma had crystallized by the thirteenth century in a definite and rational pattern of repeated phrases which remained unchanged to the fifteenth century, when it was borrowed as a cantus firmus. The Sarum use presents the most strictly organized and lucid variant. The significant internal discrepancies between the different versions of the *Caput* melisma and the antiphon as a whole reveal that *Venit ad Petrum* was less clearly established and stereotyped than antiphons of the regular liturgical repertory, in which we meet, as a rule, with fewer and less incisive variants.

The *Caput* melisma belongs to the group of melismatic extensions of antiphons generally called *neuma* or *cauda.* They were appended to antiphons on solemn occasions for festal splendor and markedly contrast in their melismatic nature with the usual neumatic style of antiphonal chant. Exactly when the custom of adding festive melismas to antiphons originated is not known, but it is, according to Peter Wagner,[61] an old and very probably Oriental heritage. Several theorists record whole series of such melismas [62] in the order of the church modes, but these examples are much more restrained and modest than our *Caput* melisma or that on *discipulorum* in the antiphon *Ante diem.* In their dimension and musical style the latter resemble much more the elaborate melismas of responsorial chant. The fact that our antiphon shares this characteristic with the responds indicates a confluence of antiphonal and responsorial styles. Now such merging of styles is typical of pre-Gregorian and non-Roman chant. The clear stylistic distinction of Gregorian chant proper, first expounded by Peter Wagner, appears in it only to a very limited degree. In suggesting that the *Caput* melisma is reminiscent of an alleluia, a responsorial chant, Peter Wagner himself has unwittingly confirmed this point—unwittingly because he did not know that the melisma actually belongs to an antiphon. Melismas of similar character are to be found as a rule only in responds, not in antiphons. Jacobus of Liége [63] quotes eight long responsorial melismas, one for each mode, and these examples are indeed as extended and florid as the *Caput* melody. As early as the ninth century the Carolingian theorist Amalarius mentions in his fundamental *De Ordine Antiphonarii* [64] the famous *triplex neuma* on the words *Fabrice mundi,* the final melisma to the respond *Descendit de celo.* Since that time there has been, according to Peter Wagner, a growing tendency to adorn re-

---

[61] *Gregorianische Formenlehre (Einführung in die Gregorianischen Melodien,* III), Leipzig, 1921, 321.

[62] See the treatise by Odington, in Coussemaker, *Scriptores,* I, 219; further references in Wagner, *op. cit.,* 321.

[63] Coussemaker, *Scriptores,* II, 339 ff.—at that time erroneously ascribed to Johannes de Muris.

[64] Migne, *Patrologia Latina,* CV, 1273 ff.

sponds with melismas.[65] In Hartker's Antiphonary of Saint-Gall (tenth century) [66] only a limited number of responds for certain seasons or feasts (Advent, Christmas, and Trinity) are supplied with them, but they are already more numerous in the Lucca Codex (twelfth century).[67] However, in the latter source they are restricted to chants in the first and eighth modes; it may or may not be coincidental that the latter mode is also that of the antiphon *Venit ad Petrum*. The latest stage of development, of which Jacobus of Liége is a witness, was reached when responsorial *caudae* were added to all modes indiscriminately.

One of the decisive reasons why the *Caput* melody must be associated with melismas of responsorial chant is its internal structure. In his path-breaking work on the form of Gregorian chant Peter Wagner has brilliantly analyzed the melismatic sections of responsorial singing and shown that they consist, as a rule, of internal repeats of the same or similar phrases which are followed, in turn, by one or two subsequent phrases that are stated only once.[68] The structure can be schematically represented as follows: a a b b [c c] d [e]; it corresponds in principle, though not in detail, to that of the *Caput* melisma. Internal repeats occur in two kinds of responds, in the alleluias and, less frequently, in the offertories. This group Wagner has set off against another group of responds, the tracts and graduals, which operate in the florid sections with what he has aptly called "migrant melismas." The latter have no or very few internal repetitions and are organized in a florid if vague and improvisatory manner. They rely on certain fixed formulas, which reappear unchanged in a great number of tracts and graduals in different context and are joined together like a mosaic. Wagner has associated the migrant melisma with Oriental practices, characteristic of the archaic layer of the chant, and the formal rationalism of the clearly organized melisma with the Roman stage of the development.[69] We can infer, as has already been suggested above, that the indistinctly organized variant of Saint-Yrieix represents an early stage of the melisma, and the concise and lucid Sarum version the latest stage.

[65] *Formenlehre*, 345.
[66] *Pal. mus. Ser.* 2, I.
[67] *Pal. mus.* IX.
[68] *Formenlehre*, 347 and 410 f.
[69] *Op. cit.*, 417.

It is, however, very unlikely that the Sarum version should owe its organization to "Roman" influence, since the antiphon does not belong to the Roman repertory. Wagner's distinction between "Oriental" and "Roman" ought not be taken too rigidly, but rather as a tendency toward greater rationalization inherent in any trend toward formal clarity. The distinction cannot claim absolute validity, as the two purportedly opposed techniques, the mosaic of the migrant melisma and the organization by varied or literal repeats, cannot always be clearly distinguished. Wagner himself has proved this point very convincingly by inadvertently drawing on the same music while demonstrating the two alternatives. He has listed the same melody once as migrant melisma (No. 21) and then again as an example of the opposite, the rational Roman technique.[70] He took the music from the gradual *Domine praevenisti* and the alleluia *Surrexit Dominus* respectively, but overlooked the fact that in spite of the different text the melismas of the two *versus* are identical. This is not the only case where a gradual and an alleluia have certain passages in common, nor is it the only case in which this particular melisma has been used.[71] We must conclude, therefore, that the two groups of responsorial chant are more closely akin than has so far been realized. Both go back to early Christian chant [72] and thus indirectly to Oriental practices. It would be incorrect to disclaim Oriental survivals in the one type and admit them in the other; rather, both of them preserve them in various degrees. We cannot enter here into a discussion of the very intricate relations and affinities between the melismas of graduals and those of alleluias. Such an investigation would throw new light on the historical development of the chant and probably entail certain modifications of Peter Wagner's position; but it ought not to be forgotten that a study of this nature has become possible only through his fundamental research.

In the absence of a thorough stylistic study of plainchant it is as yet impossible to determine, on musical grounds, how old the *Caput* melisma is. It cannot have originated as one of the *neumata* that were

[70] *Op. cit.,* 383 and 416.

[71] For example, the graduals *Dolorosa (Grad. Rom.* 442) and *Benedicta et venerabilis (Grad. Rom.* [98]) have in their *versus* the same melody and in part even the same text. Our melisma appears in both to the word *Virgo.*

[72] See also the remarks about the pre-Gregorian alleluia in Egon Wellesz, *Eastern Elements in Western Chant,* Monumenta Musicae Byzantinae, Subsidia, Vol. II, No. 1, American Series, Oxford, 1947, 175 ff.

appended to antiphons from the beginning of the twelfth century,[73] because it is at least a century older and, moreover, differs from them in style. It strongly resembles the melismas of responsorial singing, and its melodic features suggest relations to a pre-Gregorian or at least non-Roman stratum of the chant. Exuberant melismas of a peculiar melodic style are frequent in Mozarabic as well as Ambrosian chant,[74] which did not go through the Roman rationalization and therefore retain pre-Gregorian characteristics even in compositions written long after the time of the "Gregorian" reform. These melismas are generally not as rationally constructed by means of symmetrical repeats as the Sarum variant is; rather, they resemble the freely organized version of Saint-Yrieix. The melisma *vellus* from the *cantus* (the Ambrosian term for tract) *Suscipiant Domine*[75] gives a good idea of a typical Ambrosian melisma (Ex. 2). It is similar to the *Caput*

Ex. 2. Melisma from an Ambrosian tract.

melisma not only in the use of disjunct intervals and inner repeats but especially in the emphasis on the fourth, which is more characteristic of Ambrosian than of Roman chant.[76] Melismas of this type are very common in the Ambrosian repertory; several of them far exceed the *Caput* melisma in florid writing and show many more inner repeats.[77] The general resemblance between the *Caput* melisma and Ambrosian style cannot be denied, but the point should not be pressed too much; all we can infer from it is the commonplace that non-Roman dialects are more closely related to one another than they are to the Roman chant.

The mode of our antiphon gives at least a few hints as to the age

[73] Wagner, *Ursprung und Entwicklung der liturgischen Gesangsformen (Einführung in die Gregorianischen Melodien*, I), 1911, 151.

[74] That Ambrosian chant can be considered, at least in part, as pre-Gregorian has been emphasized by Bannister (after Dom Morin: *Les véritables origines du chant Grégorien*, 1901, 13); see Henry M. Bannister, "Ordine 'Ambrosiano' per la Settimana Santa," in *Miscellanea Ceriani*, Milan, 1910, 129. Unfortunately, the article does not discuss the Ambrosian liturgy of Maundy Thursday, which would be of interest for our subject.

[75] *Pal. mus.* VI, 48, or *Antiphonale Mediolanense*, 22–23.

[76] Wellesz, *op. cit.*, 119; but see also Bukofzer, *Speculum* XXIII (1948), 522.

[77] Compare the melismas on *eius* and *rex* in *Pal. mus.* VI, 29–30 and 41.

of the composition. We have seen above that when melismas were first inserted, the responds of the first and eighth modes were singled out, and there is reason to believe that these modes are older than the others. This point is confirmed by the tracts, which are among the earliest and most strongly Oriental chants of the Mass.[78] To the present day they belong exclusively to either the second or the eighth mode. In the opinion of Peter Wagner both modes are of a venerable age,[79] but Ferretti has adduced strong, though perhaps not yet conclusive, evidence on the basis of early liturgies that the eighth mode is the more ancient of the two.[80] However this may be, there can be no doubt that the latter belongs to an archaic layer of the chant. The fact that *Venit ad Petrum* stands also in the eighth mode [81] proves, of course, nothing positively as to the age of the antiphon, but it does not contradict an ancient origin either. Its mode, at any rate, continues the oldest tradition of plainsong.

There is a striking stylistic difference in melody type between the *tractus* of the second mode and those of the eighth mode. Wagner has correctly seen that the latter are on the whole short, have fewer verses than those of the second mode, and are distinguished by fresh and energetic lines. Yet neither Wagner nor Ferretti has stressed the fundamental contrast in melody style and defined it by stylistic criteria. Tracts in the second mode move in their highly melismatic sections within the compass of a comparatively small interval, often in conjunct and circular motion within a third, whereas those in the eighth mode generally superimpose two fourths and thus encompass a seventh, which is often extended to an octave or a ninth.[82] Feretti's claim [83] that tracts in the eighth mode are "simpler in construction" than those in the second mode is open to challenge. The same is true of his assertion that the melismas in the tracts of the eighth mode can

---

[78] Wagner, *Formenlehre*, 366, calls them "die Erstlinge des christlichen Messgesangs"; see also Wellesz, *op. cit.*, 140, where the thesis of the Oriental origin of the tract is confirmed.

[79] *Formenlehre*, 367.

[80] Paolo Ferretti, *Esthétique Grégorienne*, 1938, 148 ff.

[81] The mode of *Ante diem festum* varies in the sources; the Sarum Gradual puts it clearly in the fifth mode, but the Paris Missal, and apparently the Saint-Yrieix Gradual also, present it in the same mode as *Venit ad Petrum*, the eighth. In view of the liturgical connections between this pair of antiphons the sameness of mode is not surprising, but it would require a special study to determine which of the modes is the original one.

[82] The reader is referred to the following tracts from the *Grad. Rom.*: *Filii hominum, Ad te levavi, Qui confidunt, Saepe expugnaverunt,* and especially *De profundis* and *Commovisti.*

[83] See the quotation in Reese, *Music in the Middle Ages*, New York, 1940, 178.

be reduced to a few formulas.[84] Actually, they are quite numerous; moreover, they are complex in structure and more disjunct in their interval progressions than those of the second mode, they prefer fourths as structural intervals, and they adopt sweeping melodic designs which are indeed of great musical interest. The *Caput* melisma conforms in its wide sweep and disjunct motion precisely to the melody type of the eighth mode and thus once again displays the characteristics of responsorial rather than antiphonal singing. The general similarity of interval progression between tracts of the eighth mode and the *Caput* melisma will be seen in the melisma *est* (Ex. 3)

Ex. 3. Melisma from a Gregorian tract in the eighth mode.

est

from the tract *Commovisti*.[85] There are, on the other hand, noticeable dissimilarities. The melodic style of the tracts is characterized by formal freedom and irrational flow with few or no inner repeats indicating, like the style of Ambrosian melismas, a pre-Gregorian stage of development. It should be noticed that the quoted excerpt is based on two superimposed fourths, *d-g* and *g-c'*, which are linked by the final *g* of the mode; the same fourths play a decisive role in the antiphon *Venit ad Petrum*, with the difference that they are spaced here more widely in opposite fashion as *g-c'* and *d'-g'*, an arrangement that does not occur in the tract.

Interrelations between the tracts and our antiphon exist, finally, also with regard to the *tuba* or tone of repercussion. Like several other types of Gregorian chant, the tracts have a multiple tenor, that is to say more than one tone of recitation. The double tenor of the eighth mode falls on *c* or *b* (the latter tone occurs only in archaic pieces), and on *g*, which serves a double function as tenor and final. We have seen on page 243 that our antiphon, too, has a multiple tenor; in the first section the *tuba* falls on *c* and *g*, and at the end it shifts to *d*. Such

---

[84] Ferretti's statement that the formulas of the second mode are more numerous and more complex than those of the eighth mode seems to be exaggerated, to say the least, but I am not prepared to make a categorical assertion to the contrary. Even if his statement were true, it would be no sufficient proof for his claim that the eighth mode is the more ancient of the two. The argument, the more variety in the formulas the more recent the mode, is not convincing.

[85] This is a typical migrant melisma which recurs repeatedly in varying context. See the *versus Montes* of the tract *Qui confidunt*.

double (or even triple) tenors appear in various archaic types of plainchant, not only in tracts, but also in the *tonus peregrinus* and the responsorial psalmody of the Office. It is this characteristic which, perhaps more strongly than any other, implies that the antiphon must be old. Since chants with multiple tenor do not adhere to the usual limitations of a mode, they probably antedate the codification of the modal system with its stereotyped tenors and ranges, which took place in the course of the ninth and tenth centuries. It follows that the antiphon can hardly be later than the ninth century.

Looking back on the above musico-liturgical discussion, we cannot help feeling how uncertain the ground is on which we have moved. At almost every turn of the argument an impasse has been reached which reflects the incomplete state of our present knowledge, especially in matters of chronology. Nevertheless, it has been possible to arrive at certain fairly definite conclusions which may be summarized as follows.

The antiphon *Venit ad Petrum* holds an exceptional position in the liturgy. It belongs neither to the Mass nor to the Office, but to a special service, the *pedilavium* or *mandatum* on Maundy Thursday. The conspicuous melisma on *caput* which has prompted the discussion stresses a "sacramental" connotation of the ceremony according to which the washing of the feet symbolizes the Baptism of the Apostles. Pictorial representations of the scene depict St. Peter pointing at his head, a gesture that is precisely analogous to the melisma. The "sacramental" interpretation is common in the "marginal" liturgies, but is foreign to the Roman church. The music of the antiphon does not belong to the Roman repertory. Its non-Roman origin is confirmed by its unusual musical style. Although the chant must be classified as an antiphon, it bears in its melisma the earmarks of responsorial chant and thus parallels in the music its exceptional liturgical position. It does not observe the conventions of the modal system. Emphasis on fourths and disjunct motion falls in with features of Ambrosian chant and those responds of the Roman liturgy that bear the stamp of Oriental origin, such as the tracts, which are not yet touched by the Roman normalization and rationalization of plainsong. The multiple tenor, too, points to an archaic style. The melodic type of the melisma is only inaccurately described as "eighth mode." The melisma shares its melodic type, but not its structure, with the tracts of the eighth mode. Its clear formal organization suggests a later date of origin than that of the tracts. It seems to have been composed at a time when the tradition of *tractus* composition was on the wane but not yet quite extinguished. It represents an extension of archaic practices to antiphonal chant.

These conclusions are based on observations of facts; unless we indulge in far-fetched speculation we cannot, at present, go further. The elucidation of such exacting questions as the age of the antiphon, its place of origin, and its mode of dissemination must be left to a specialist who has a vast body of liturgical manuscripts at his disposal. A study of the migrant melisma in responsorial chant, as yet unwritten but urgently needed, would doubtless narrow down the wide scope of problems relating to responsorial melismas and substantiate or modify what has been suggested here, of necessity, in fragmentary and tentative fashion.

5. THE *CAPUT* MELISMA AS MASS TENOR

The transformation of a plainchant into a Mass tenor involves certain modifications of the borrowed material in respect to both rhythm and melody. Above all, the *cantus planus* must be turned into a *cantus mensuratus,* that is to say a melody with a distinctly measured rhythm. The composer is confronted with two alternatives: he may either present the borrowed chant in even note values as a rigid cantus firmus in the strict sense and retain in the polyphonic setting something of the effect of not strictly measured plainchant rhythm; or he may impose on the notes rhythmic patterns of his own choosing which have no connection with plainchant and which are conditioned merely by the polyphonic setting. It is the latter alternative that applies to the three *Caput* Masses.

With regard to melody we can again distinguish between two possibilities. The composer may either respect the borrowed melody and take it over unchanged, or turn it into a real *cantus figuratus,* paraphrased or modified by melodic elaboration, which ranges from a few ornaments at the cadence to extended insertions and melodic protuberances which may at times all but obliterate the course of the original melody. It is clear that in the latter case the rhythm must be as free as the melodic treatment. In the *Caput* Masses, however, the borrowed material remains melodically untouched, so that freedom in rhythm is counterbalanced by strict observance with regard to melody.

The discussion of the *Caput* tenor must begin with the Mass by Dufay, the earliest of the three. We do not know what prompted Dufay to select the antiphon *Venit ad Petrum*. Neither do we know from which liturgical source he borrowed. When Dufay composed the Mass he was Canon at Cambrai Cathedral, and we might expect to find a clue in fifteenth-century Graduals from Cambrai. Unfortunately, no such liturgical collection has been published. The only missal from Cambrai that I have been able to consult [86] does not contain the antiphon and, moreover, follows on the whole the Paris use. It seems unlikely that the comparison of other Graduals from Cambrai will help us, because the tenor of Dufay's Mass differs from any of the known French versions of the antiphon. In fact it agrees so exactly in every detail with the Sarum version that Dufay must have borrowed it directly or indirectly from the Sarum use. The dependence on the Sarum version can be explained by three hypotheses: (1) the liturgy in Cambrai may have been influenced by the Sarum use; (2) Dufay may have taken the cantus firmus directly from a Sarum book, perhaps because the work was commissioned for England; (3) Dufay may have borrowed his tenor as a *res facta* from a pre-existing composition, an earlier *Caput* Mass by an English composer, and thus have merely followed an English model in the same way as Okeghem and Obrecht do that of Dufay. The latter hypothesis assumes the existence of an English *Caput* Mass, now lost, which would be apparent, like a mirage, only by way of reflection. It cannot be proved that the prototype actually existed, but it would very naturally account for the Sarum version of the tenor and explain certain indications of English influence in Dufay's work.

For a long time it has been known that Dufay's stylistic development received a decisive stimulus from the English sixth-chord style in general and the panconsonant style of Dunstable in particular. This English influence is clearly borne out in his early works, and also in the testimony of Martin le Franc, who, in his *Champion des Dames*,[87] explicitly refers to the composer's indebtedness to England. While this experience belongs to Dufay's early period, the *Caput* Mass

[86] Paris, Bibl. Nat. MS lat. 17311.
[87] A. Piaget, *Martin le Franc,* 1888, 121–122.

acquaints us with other forms of English influence which pertain to his late period and which are not usually considered when his artistic debt to England is assessed. We must mention here above all the form of the cyclic Mass itself. In adopting the tenor Mass Dufay followed a precedent that English composers had set, and this would be true even if the cantus firmus were not of English origin. Another facet of English influence comes to light in the omission from the Credo of certain sections of the text, which seems to be characteristic of English Mass composition, and which has as yet not been explained from the liturgical point of view.[88] Dufay omits the passages from *Et in spiritum sanctum* to *Confiteor,* and from *Tertia die* to *Et ascendit,* or we should perhaps say more cautiously that these sections do at any rate not appear in the Trent Codices. Although the editor has supplied part of the missing words, there still remain gaps. It is, however, very likely that beginning with *Et resurrexit* (m. 151) the words should be divided up between the voices so that alto and bass should have the missing passages. Exactly this arrangement is to be found at the analogous place (m. 144) in Okeghem's Mass, which in general faithfully imitates Dufay's work in the distribution of the words.[89] If this inference is correct, Dufay and Okeghem would agree in giving not an abbreviated but merely a telescoped version of the text, such as occurs much more frequently in English than in Continental Mass settings.

English influence is suggested also, as Professor Strunk has pointed out to me, in the fact that Dufay uses the Kyrie trope *Deus creator omnium,* an English favorite which appears almost invariably in troped Sarum Graduals.[90] The English features just discussed may have been derived from the hypothetical English *Caput* Mass, and in borrowing its tenor for what may be his first cyclic Mass on a

---

[88] See Peter Wagner, *Einführung* I, 105, and Dom A. Hughes, "The Text-Omissions in the Creed," in *Missa O quam suavis,* ed. by H. B. Collins, Plainsong and Mediaeval Music Society, 1927, xxxiii. The idea that the omissions were made for the sake of brevity provides no satisfactory explanation, though brevity may have been a secondary consideration. See also Otto Marxer, *Zur spätmittelalterlichen Choralgeschichte St. Gallens,* 1908 (*Veröffentlichungen der Gregorianischen Akademie,* III).

[89] Only the Chigi version of Okeghem's Mass gives the correct division of words *Et resurrexit* and *Et in spiritum.* The Trent version gives only rough cues of the text. At the analogous place in Dufay's Mass the two incipits read *Et resurrexit* and *Et incarnatus,* of which the latter is probably a scribal error for *Et in spiritum.* The editors have compounded the error by reading *Et resurrexit* in all voices without indicating the change in the *Revisionsbericht.* Thus they destroy the only hint of telescoped treatment.

[90] On the other hand, the inclusion of a polyphonic Kyrie in the cycle is not typical of English music.

cantus firmus Dufay possibly acknowledges the English origin of the type. To be sure, all this is hypothesis, since there is no direct trace of an English *Caput* Mass. For practical purposes we shall henceforth consider Dufay's work as the original one, but it should be kept in mind that the selection and manipulation of the cantus firmus reflects perhaps the work of an English composer.

The fact that the Mass is based on an unusual cantus firmus of English origin is less significant than the way in which it is turned into a *cantus figuratus.* The entire cantus firmus as it appears in the tenor voice is given in Ex. 4 (all note values have been halved). In every movement the melody is stated twice [91] in what may be called a "double *cursus,*" first in perfect time (statement A) and then in changed rhythm in imperfect time (statement B). The two statements differ melodically only in one particular: the repeat of phrase d occurs only in cursus B.[92] The notes of the two statements have been aligned in Ex. 4 so as to make the identity of pitches directly apparent to the eye. The tenor agrees with the Sarum version of the melody (Ex. 1) in all respects except for two single notes, marked in Ex. 4 by asterisks: *c* (A 40 or B 44), which has been inserted in the first statement of phrase c, and *a* (A 69 and B 78) at the very end. Study of the context reveals that both notes are cadential insertions.[93] The *c* is necessary in order to arrive at the cadence on *a* by means of a suspension. As to the second inserted note, it is evident that Dufay merely corrected a shortcoming of the cantus firmus. The final turn *b-g-g* of the plainchant would have prevented him from using the stereotyped tenor cadence—a descending step to the final—which at this time was absolutely *de rigueur.* It could perhaps be argued that the composer borrowed from an unknown variant of the chant that contained even the two additional notes. This hypothesis must be dismissed as highly improbable because the inserted *c* appears only once where it is needed in the cadence, not in the repeat of the same phrase, which moves right on to a cadence on *g* and for which the plainchant provides the necessary stepwise progression. If the original plainchant had contained a *c,* it would occur twice like all the other notes of phrase c. It is therefore safe to conclude that the two liberties were taken solely for the sake of the cadence. Aside from that the

[91] Pirro, *Histoire,* 77, erroneously asserts that the tenor of the Kyrie is stated only once.
[92] The repeat marks in Ex. 4 have been drawn according to the original phrase division of the plainsong. They clearly show how arbitrary Dufay's grouping of the notes is.
[93] Another such case is the *a* in A 52, not found in statement B.

Ex. 4. The tenor of the *Caput* Masses.

plainsong appears without any melodic change or elaboration strictly as it is found in the liturgical source.

This observation invalidates Schegar's analysis of the cantus firmus in the preface to the edition of the Austrian *Denkmäler*. He maintains that the cantus firmus consists of several melodic "Veränderungen" or "Umspielungen" of what he calls various "Grundformen." His analysis is based on preconceived ideas of variation; they may be suited to the late quartets of Beethoven (which probably prompted them in the first place), but cannot be applied to fifteenth-century music. The alleged "results" of such unhistorical methods cannot as a rule be refuted because of their inherent vagueness, but the identification of the cantus firmus permits us in this case to disprove them for once in conclusive manner.

Although statements A and B are melodically strictly the same, they differ radically in their rhythmic arrangement. This is not merely the natural consequence of the change from perfect to imperfect time but is due to the deliberate design of the composer. In turning the plainsong into a *cantus mensuratus* he completely disregarded the original arrangement of the ligatures as well as the original phrase divisions. Even if we did not know the original ligatures of the Sarum variants, it can still be proved that the composer ignored them because they are not the same in the two statements. Had the ligatures been of any importance to him they would agree. The disregard for the original phrase divisions of the plainsong is even more conspicuous. The letters indicating the plainsong phrases in Ex. 1 have been added to the mensural version in Ex. 4, but it is obvious that they no longer fit, and that the cadences at analogous places in the two statements do not correspond. It is significant in this connection that the cadence tones are chosen arbitrarily; for example, phrase a is made to end on *d* (A 7) and *b* (B 7) respectively. Even more divergent is the treatment of phrase c, as can be seen if A 29–30 is compared with B 31–32. Here the same passage is brought to a full cadence the first time and treated as a continuous section the second time; both statements run directly counter to the phrase division of the plainsong, which would call in either case for a cadence *before* the beginning of phrase c. The phrase begins with the ligature *a-d'*, which the composer does not hesitate to split in two, making its first note the last one of the preceding phrase.

The comparison of the two freely rhythmicized *cursus* of the cantus

firmus makes it evident that the *Caput* tenor depends on the plainsong only with regard to the notes, but does not respect its ligatures,
phrases, or rhythmic patterns. This point must be emphasized in
view of certain false analogies that have been drawn between cantus
firmus and plainchant rhythm.[94] It is of course the rule rather than
the exception in fifteenth-century music that the plainsong was thoroughly recast in order to serve as a fitting cantus firmus. This is confirmed not only by Dufay's *Caput* Mass but also by his Masses on *Ave
regina celorum* and *Ecce ancilla;* the same is true of the works of
Busnois, Regis, Okeghem, Obrecht, Josquin, and others. Only in
comparatively few compositions is the plainsong ever presented literally as *cantus planus* in even note values; more often it is modified by
both rhythmic patterns and, at times, highly individual melodic elaboration which may or may not recur in every movement of the cycle.
The cantus firmus served merely as a scaffolding of the composition
which the composer was free to set up in accordance with his own
imagination and the exigencies of the movement. Just as the beams
and joists form the scaffold of a house but are nevertheless cut to the
shape of the building they support, so does the cantus firmus establish
the framework of the musical structure but nevertheless takes its shape
from the composition it underlies. The distinctive rhythms the composer imposed on the cantus firmus formed a vital part of the process
of composition and actually mattered more than the inherent structure of the borrowed material. The lack of concern for the latter applies, however, mainly to plainsongs; if a voice from a polyphonic
res facta was incorporated, the original rhythm was generally left
untouched; but even in the latter case there are enough examples
dealing arbitrarily with the tenor of a chanson.[95]

The rhythmic shape of the *Caput* tenor was probably determined
by the type of counterpoint and "harmony" the composer envisaged.

---

[94] Russel G. Harris, "An Analysis of the Design of the 'Caput' Masses by Dufay and
Okeghem in their Metric and Rhythmic Aspects," in *Hamline Studies in Musicology*, ed.
by Ernst Krenek, I, 1945, 27 ff. In this study the rhythmic theories of the Solesmes school
are mistaken for facts and expanded by further hypotheses. The decisive point, the
rhythmic identity of the tenors in Dufay's and Okeghem's Mass, has been missed by the
author.

[95] See for example the first and third Mass on *O rosa bella* (DTOe, Vol. 22), the
Masses on *Le serviteur* by Faugues (not Okeghem) and an Anonymous (DTOe, Vol. 38),
and Bedingham's *Deuil angoisseux* (DTOe, Vol. 61).

Once established, the rhythm of the cantus firmus does not change. Except for such slight divergencies of notation as variants in the ligatures, or notes that appear one time sustained and the next time subdivided, the tenor appears in each movement in the same rhythmic configuration. It is, in other words, an isorhythmic tenor the *taleae* of which have grown to gigantic proportions, namely an entire movement. The only liberties Dufay takes concern certain deliberate omissions of rests or phrases and the long rests that separate the main sections of the immutable tenor. In a strictly isorhythmic Mass even these interruptions would, of course, be included in the rhythmic pattern.[96] The old tradition of mapping out an arbitrary rhythmic pattern in the *talea* survived longest in the rhythmic arrangement of Mass tenors. It is indeed in the tenors of the Mass cycle that the vestiges of isorhythmic procedure were kept alive to the end of the fifteenth century, when the isorhythmic motet proper had long since run its course.

The mathematical precision with which the tenor sections return in the *Caput* Mass is significant not only in itself but especially with regard to the interdependence of the three Masses. It conclusively proves the existence of a single pattern. Okeghem must have been familiar with Dufay's Mass, and Obrecht in turn with the works of his predecessors. The two younger composers took over not only the melody of the cantus firmus, but also its exact rhythmic shape and phrase structure; moreover, they cut up the text in the same manner as Dufay and adhere to the major divisions of each movement. In a word, Dufay's Mass served as model and springboard for the later works. In order to make this point clear it is necessary to compare Dufay's cantus firmus measure for measure and note for note with that of the two other Masses. In Table 3 a condensed analysis of the three tenors is given, indicating (1) time signature, (2) measure numbers of statements A and B, (3) the number of inserted rests before or between the tenor sections (the number of breves appears in parantheses), and (4) occasional inserted notes which Okeghem or Obrecht added at the end of sections. Underscored measures indicate diminution.

---

[96] It may be remarked that arbitrary phrase division and isorhythmic structure characterize also the tenor of Power's Mass on *Alma redemptoris.*

TABLE 3

Scheme of the *Caput* Masses

Dufay

Kyrie   O (21) A 1–30 (4) 31–42 (9) 43–70
Christe   C (40) B 1–46 (20) 47–79

Gloria   O (16) A 1–30 (1) 31–42 (2) 43–70
Qui tollis   C (40) B 1–79

Credo   O (19) A 1–30 (2) 31–42 (3) 43–70
Et incarnatus   C (56) B 1–46 (16) 47–79

Sanctus   O (17) A 1–30 (4) 31–42 (3) 44–54, 56–70
Benedictus   C (24) B 1–46 (6) 47–79

Agnus I/II   O (16) A 1–30/(4) 31–42 (4) 43–70
Agnus III   C (20) B 1–32 (4) 33–46, 63–79
                         [phrase d not repeated]

Okeghem

Kyrie   O (1) A   1–13, 24–30, d
Christe   ₵ (14) B 33–46
Kyrie   O   A 56–70, d

Gloria   O (17) A   1–30 (1) 31–42 (2) 43–70 (1) d d
Qui tollis   ₵ (26) B   1–79 (4) d

Credo   O (20) A   1–30 (2) 31–42 (2) 43–70, d
Et incarnatus   ₵ (48) B   1–46 (16) 47–79 (4) d

Sanctus   O (18) A   1–30 (4) 31–42 (3) 44–54, 56–70 (2) d
Benedictus   ₵ (29) B   1–46 (6) 47–79 (3) d

Agnus I/II   O (13) A   1–30/(4) 31–39, 52–70
Agnus III   ₵ (19) B   1–14, 26–43, 60–79 (6) d
                         [phrase d not repeated]

Obrecht

Kyrie   O (2) A 1–27
Christe   ₵   B 28–32 (1) 33–46 (1) 33–37, 54–66
Kyrie   ₵   B 66–79

Gloria   O (16) A 1–30 (1) 31–42 (2) 43–70
Qui tollis   C (38) B 1–79

Credo	O	(16)	A	1–30	(1)	31–42	(2)	43–70	
Et incarnatus	C	(42)	B	1–79	(2)	c			
Sanctus	O	(18)	A	1–30,	(4)	31–42	(3)	44–54,	56–70
Benedictus	¢	(24)	B	1–46	(6)	47–79			
Agnus I/II	3/2	(16)	A	1–30/(4)		31–42	(3)	43–70	
Agnus III	¢	(20)	B	1–32	(4)	33–46, 63–79, c			

[phrase d not repeated]

In the table identity of rhythm and melody is indicated directly by the identity of measure numbers, which always refer to Ex. 4. For example, A 1–30 in the Credo of the three Masses means that each movement is based on the identical section of the cantus firmus, namely section A 1–30 of Ex. 4. In any one of the compositions the actual measure numbers may be different because the rests vary at the beginning of each piece. The identity of tenors can be shown only if the basic version is taken as the standard of reference.

We turn now to the tenors of the individual Masses in order to discover in what respect they differ. Since they are identical in melody and rhythm, differences can arise only in the grouping of sections and the number of inserted rests. Table 3 reveals at a glance that the divisions agree, on the whole, in all three Masses. Dufay subdivides statement A into three sections, each of which is articulated by rests, and statement B into two. The divisions recur in nearly all movements in the same manner, except that the rests vary, or are even omitted, as in the *Qui tollis.* Agnus III is the only movement that breaks through the isorhythmic pattern of the tenor; it omits measures B 47–62 and, moreover, the repeat of phrase d. Tracing these measures in Ex. 4, we find that they consist only of phrase repeats. Dufay (or his English predecessor) shortened the cantus firmus in order to adjust it to the brief text, yet he made his omissions not arbitrarily but merely dropped repeats so that the melody is still presented once in its entirety. This proves that the composer was well aware of the internal structure of the melisma; and although his phrase divisions, as will be remembered, do not exactly coincide with those of the chant, he still manages to leave all essential intervals intact and to shorten the melody without doing violence to it. One further slight irregularity characteristic of the Sanctus only should be noted, namely the omission of measures A 43 and A 55. These gaps are insignificant in them-

selves—they include only measures with two rests and one upbeat—
but are nevertheless important in connection with the two other
Masses.

So long as the source of the *Caput* melisma was not known it could
not be determined who was responsible for its rhythmic organization.
Now that the cantus firmus has been recognized as an arbitrarily
rhythmicized plainsong, it is clear that the appearance of the same
rhythm in the later Masses is not an inherent feature of the tenor;
rather, it proves that Okeghem and Obrecht borrowed the structural
voice from Dufay, faithfully preserving its rhythm and altering it
only by making selections from it and by varying the number of
intervening rests. Theoretically, both Okeghem and Obrecht were
under no obligation to follow Dufay's model and could have cast the
plainsong in an entirely different rhythmic mold. However, with
the decisive role of tradition and of composition after models in
Renaissance music it is not surprising that the very existence of Dufay's Mass should have prompted the younger composers to write
Masses on the same cantus firmus, and their reliance on a "voice of
authority" expressly acknowledges this fact. Okeghem and Obrecht
borrowed the *Caput* melody as a *res facta* from a pre-existing composition and not as a plainsong from a liturgical source. This may be
true also of Dufay, but it is certain in the case of the two younger
composers.

If the tenor of the later works is compared with that of Dufay
it will be found that, the same rhythm notwithstanding, there are
certain signs that with the passage of time the ties of tradition began
to slacken. Okeghem keeps closer to the authoritative voice than
Obrecht. There is ample external and internal evidence for this statement. Unlike Obrecht, Okeghem, in this notation of the tenor, leaves
the ligatures as well as the clef of the borrowed voice essentially
unchanged. He places Dufay's tenor in the bass by means of a curious
"canon" which directs the singer to read the original alto clef of the
cantus firmus an octave lower. It would have been at least as simple
to write the voice at pitch in the bass clef and to dispense with the
written direction altogether. Why, then, did Okeghem resort to a
device of which he has made much more significant use in other
works? There is only one possible answer to this question: he wanted

to preserve the characteristic alto clef of the original and keep the melody untouched *in its external appearance* although it is actually transposed to the bass register. The canon is therefore only ostensibly superfluous; it is a subtle means of indicating that the tenor was a borrowed *res facta.*

Aside from the "canonic" transposition, the tenor deviates from the model only with regard to the introductory and intermediary rests, the few added *d*'s in the cadence, and the time signature ¢ in statement B.[97] The general arrangement of the tenor sections in the Gloria, Credo, and Sanctus duplicates the original one in every single particular: the *Qui tollis* runs through continuously without any subdivision, and the sections *Et Incarnatus, Pleni sunt,* and *Osanna* fall at exactly the same places. It is of special interest that the Sanctus retains even the trifling irregularities of Dufay's Sanctus, the omission of A 43 and 55. The correspondence of such minute traits is of no musical significance whatsoever for the composition, but precisely for this reason it cannot be a coincidence. It proves conclusively that Okeghem did not copy the cantus firmus once, as though it were a fixed entity, but took it over movement by movement, simply copying the tenor as he went along. This gives us a revealing insight into the completely empirical manner of borrowing that was practiced in Renaissance music.

The Kyrie and the Agnus do not reproduce the tenor in its entirety. Here Okeghem selects his sections and, like Dufay, shortens the cantus firmus in a highly judicious fashion. In the Kyrie the cantus firmus is presented only once, with omission of all internal repeats of the melisma; this accounts for the seemingly arbitrary and discontinuous measure numbers in Table 3. A further complication arises from the fact that he combines statements A and B. Phrases a b a c d e appear in correct succession, but phrase c belongs to statement B, all others to statement A. In the choice of phrase divisions Okeghem follows Dufay again as much as possible. For example, the phrase of the *Christe* consists only of B 33–46, exactly the same measures that Dufay singled out in the abridgment of his Agnus III. The cantus

[97] In the *Denkmäler* the time signatures are incorrectly reproduced in several movements; moreover, the note values of the second part have been halved in each movement. Since the reduction is not indicated, the reader gets a false impression of the tempo relation between the first and second parts, especially since the ¢ signature is retained in the reduced transcription. The exact relation between C and ¢ with regard to tempo presents some problems in those cases where the note values in *alla breve* are twice as long as those in C; see Apel, *The Notation of Polyphonic Music,* 2nd ed., 1944, 191.

firmus has been shortened also in Okeghem's Agnus, but less severely than in the Kyrie. The melody is actually stated twice, but again with omission of phrases that are normally repeated. These condensations leave no doubt that Okeghem, though he did not draw the *Caput* melisma directly from plainchant, was fully conscious of its internal structure and was careful not to destroy the essence of the melody in his adaptation of it.

The most significant conclusion we can draw from the above comparison is that there is not a single measure in Okeghem's cantus firmus that does not go back to Dufay. What may appear to the superficial observer as melodic variants turn out to be the result of selection and combination. This observation could have been made regardless of whether or not the source of the tenor was identified, for it concerns only the notes and rhythm of the tenor. In his analysis of the tenors in the *Denkmäler* Schegar [98] has missed this crucial point and consequently lists what he calls phrase C_6 as a "variation" peculiar only to Okeghem; it is actually no more than the combination of B 33–43 and 60–62 of Dufay's tenor. Misled by this analysis, other scholars have likewise failed to notice Okeghem's slavish dependence on Dufay, and their remarks are sometimes at variance with the facts. Gombosi is mistaken in saying that the tenor is stated only once in each movement; [99] this is true only of the Kyrie. Van den Borren erroneously considers the rhythm of the tenor as "free"; [100] and Pirro falsely asserts that the last Agnus contains the tenor "tout entier." [101]

The comparison of the tenors warrants another important conclusion with regard to the chronological sequence of the Masses. We know from an archive record [102] that Dufay's *Caput* Mass was entered in the choir books of Cambrai in 1463. It stands to reason that the work was composed in the same year or shortly before that time, a conclusion which the late style of the piece confirms. Gombosi has, on general stylistic grounds, placed Okeghem's Mass in the early period of the composer and has suggested a date of sometime before 1470.[103] Van den Borren has maintained, in view of certain archaic

---

[98] DTOe, Vol. 38, xi and xiv.

[99] Johannes Gombosi, *Jacob Obrecht, eine stilkritische Studie,* Leipzig, 1925, 81.

[100] Charles van den Borren, *Etudes sur le quinzième siècle musicale,* Antwerp, 1941, 198.

[101] *Op. cit.,* 107.

[102] Jules Houdoy, *Histoire artistique de la cathédrale de Cambrai,* 1880; see the extracts from the archives for the year 1463.

[103] *Op. cit.,* 82.

characteristics, that it may even antedate Dufay's Mass.[104] Up to now his hypothesis has passed as improbable, but not impossible. Now that the dependence of Okeghem's tenor on that of Dufay can no longer be doubted, it has become untenable. Since Okeghem makes selections from the complete cantus firmus, and since it is most unlikely that partial presentation should precede integral presentation, Okeghem's Mass must be the later work. The identification of the cantus firmus thus enables us to clear up a point of chronology.

Furthermore, it throws new light on a biographical question. In nearly all reference works Okeghem is said to have been a pupil of Dufay, although there is no documentary proof in support of this claim. The works of Okeghem show in their borrowings direct relations only to the music of Binchois, and this is probably the reason why Plamenac considers it likely that the latter was Okeghem's teacher.[105] The tenor of the *Caput* Mass establishes beyond doubt that a direct contact between Dufay and Okeghem existed. While this is not sufficient evidence to decide the question, it adds at any rate a new facet to the relation between the two composers.

That the *Caput* Mass of Obrecht is the latest of the three has never been questioned, since it bears all the earmarks of a later style. Careful scrutiny of Obrecht's tenor discloses several remarkable relationships to the two earlier works which imply that Obrecht was familiar with both of them. By and large Obrecht, too, respects the rhythm of Dufay's tenor and borrows it literally. But he no longer slavishly retains externals, such as notation and ligatures. It will be seen in Table 3 that three movements (Gloria, Credo, and Sanctus) duplicate exactly the phrase divisions of Dufay (and Okeghem), including even the slight irregularity of the Sanctus. It should especially be noted that the inserted rests correspond very closely to those of Dufay, particularly in the Gloria, Sanctus, and Agnus; Okeghem displays more independence from Dufay in this respect.

On the other hand, Obrecht takes more liberties than Okeghem permits himself. The time signatures of statement B waver between C and ₵, the former being reserved for the Gloria and Credo. Here Obrecht follows in part Dufay, in part Okeghem. He releases the

---

[104] *Op. cit.,* 197.
[105] See the article on Okeghem in Baker's *Biographical Dictionary of Musicians,* 1940.

cantus firmus from its fixed position in one voice and shifts it about in successive movements. The Kyrie presents it in the tenor; the Gloria in the soprano; the Credo in the tenor again, but transposed a fifth down; the Sanctus in the alto, again transposed a fourth up; and the Agnus finally in the bass, transposed to the lower octave. Furthermore, it is significant that the tenor of Agnus I and II is stated in strict diminution. These modifications are symptomatic of Obrecht's attitude; he experiments with new possibilities and plays with the borrowed voice as only a later composer will do. There are, moreover, several minute discrepancies as to rhythm and even melody which bespeak a somewhat relaxed attitude toward the voice of authority. It will not be necessary to list them all, but a few examples must be given. In the Gloria A 14 and 24 are changed from ♩ ♩ 𝅗𝅥 to 𝅗𝅥 𝅝; in the *Benedictus* B 72 is doubled in length, but only the first time, not in the repeat of the phrase; and in the *Et incarnatus* (m. 67 of the composition) Obrecht changes at B 25 the notes *f-d* (*c-a* of the untransposed version) to *f-g*. The context makes clear that the changes are far from being mistakes, but are, on the contrary, deliberate alterations which the composer made in order to accommodate the particular musical progressions he had in mind. Here we catch Obrecht "cheating" for the sake of convenience. Finally, with regard to the selection and abridgment of phrases from the cantus firmus, Obrecht betrays a more independent spirit than Okeghem. Like the latter he shortens the Kyrie, but his selection of phrases is rather arbitrary: measures B 35–37 appear twice. The repeat is out of order, and a glance at Ex. 4 informs us that the second time they merely take the place of B 47–53 which present the same notes, but in a different rhythm. In spite of the irregularity the cantus firmus runs through once in its entirety.

The Kyrie and the Agnus are the two movements that give us definite clues for Obrecht's acquaintance with the two earlier Masses. That his cantus firmus is identical with that of Dufay would not in itself prove his familiarity with Dufay's work, for conceivably he could have borrowed it from Okeghem and thus only indirectly from Dufay. Conversely, he could have taken it directly from Dufay without knowing Okeghem's work. However, neither alternative seems to hold. As has already been pointed out, the number of rests agrees in most movements so nearly with those of Dufay that it can hardly be explained by anything but direct dependence. The Kyrie, on the other hand, is patterned after Okeghem. It has only one tenor statement (as against Dufay's two), and combines in the single *cursus* sections from statements A and B.[106] These are precisely the distinguishing features of Okeghem's Kyrie, which Obrecht followed in principle though not in detail. The Agnus, finally, is nothing less than a unique combination of the salient traits of Dufay's and Okeghem's Agnus. So far as the general pattern of the tenor is concerned, it exactly duplicates that of Dufay, with inclusion even of the initial and the first set of intermediary rests. Conversely, the ₵ signature and the striking shift of the cantus firmus to the bass is obviously taken over from Okeghem. The Agnus stands apart from all other movements of the Mass not only for these borrowed features, but also for an original one, the diminution of statement A, which neither Dufay nor Okeghem ever employs. Obrecht displays in this last movement, the fitting climax of the whole work, how he could retain distinctive characteristics of the two earlier works, yet arrive at a new and individual result. Indeed, his Agnus is a perfect example of the "Art of Borrowed Composition," as this type of Renaissance music might be called. In his handling of the borrowed voice he strikes the balance between tradition and originality. The very specific features that his Mass has in common with one or the other of the earlier works clearly imply that Obrecht knew the two other *Caput* Masses. It will be seen below that this conclusion is supported by stylistic comparison.

The analysis of the tenor structure has disclosed many more and much closer interrelations between the Masses than have been suspected up to now. It opens up a new perspective and reveals an unbroken line of handing down the same material—that is to say, of *traditio* in the strict sense of the word, running from the late period of Dufay over Okeghem to the days of Obrecht at the end of the century. All this can be gathered from the mere mechanics of the tenor. The structural voice can be built into a composition in many different ways and has in itself little bearing on the musical style of the work; precisely for that reason it establishes purely structural and abstract relations which furnish conclusive internal evidence of direct interdependence.

---

[106] A minor point may be presented here for what it may be worth: Obrecht prescribes in this movement, and also in the Agnus, the ₵ signature which Okeghem always employs. These two movements borrow also other structural features from Okeghem.

6. STYLISTIC ANALYSIS OF THE *CAPUT* MASSES

DUFAY

In the preceding section our attention was directed to the voice the Masses have in common which made it necessary to concentrate on the unifying element. This is only one aspect of the music, and not even the decisive one. A stylistic analysis discloses fundamental differences with regard to individual style and the manner in which the tenor is incorporated in the composition, although there are also stylistic features that tie the works even closer together.

Dufay's *Caput* Mass clearly represents, like the Masses on *Ecce ancilla* and *Ave regina celorum,* the style of his later period. What strikes the ear immediately is the lucid organization of melody, which he achieves by directing his patterned, yet gracefully curved and swelling line toward the cadence. Frequent brief rests within the line serve to endow the phrase structure with his wonted rational clarity of design, which distinguishes even the melodies of the early period. The melodic interest of the composition rests squarely in the highest voice, which is the leading one throughout. This is true not only of the extended duets, where it lies openly at the surface, but also of the four-part sections, in which the melody rises freely above the cantus firmus, which serves merely as a foil for the unimpeded flow of the treble. The melody moves primarily in thirds and fourths, which are the points of rest and the structural intervals. They are filled in and embellished by means of the stereotyped melodic formulas of ornamentation which give the melody its typical rhythmical flexibility and at the same time its ornamental and formalized lucidity and grace.

The melody is firmly supported by cadences which are conceived in an essentially harmonic manner and which supply, as it were, the pillars for the melodic garlands. The second contratenor functions in the full sections no longer as a traditional contratenor but as the real bass of a harmonic setting, as may be seen in a typical excerpt from the *Qui tollis* (Ex. 5). The quoted section presents the beginning

Ex. 5. Dufay: *Caput* Mass, from the Gloria.

of statement B, harmonized exclusively in what can only be called pure bass progressions. The emergence of such a harmonic bass line is the corollary of the new type of part writing in four voices which represents the greatest stylistic advance of Dufay's late period. In the section in which the cantus firmus drops out, the second contratenor has a less bass-like and more melodic appearance and serves as counterpoint to the upper voice or voices. The first contratenor is indispensable only in the duets where it furnishes the melodic counterpart to the soprano; in the four-part passages it functions more or less as a filler or *vagans,* as the frequent skips and rests indicate. The fact that it could possibly be omitted in the full sections without doing violence to the essential progressions bespeaks an early phase of four-part writing. Even in his late style Dufay was not yet able to equalize and balance the four voices in their melodic importance.

The preponderance of the treble accounts for the lucid phrase structure, which can be readily grasped by the ear. As he developed from his early to his late style Dufay proved himself more and more the past master of the well-turned phrase. The transparency of the musical weft is greatly enhanced by the composer's resourceful use of textural contrast. He goes further in this respect than his followers, as neither Okeghem nor Obrecht has written such extended duets in his *Caput* Mass. Dufay utilizes pairing of voices in almost every possible permutation and thus produces sections of varied texture which follow each other directly in succession or in alternation with full four-voice passages. It is Dufay who set the precedent for Josquin's systematization of the device.[107]

The cadences of the *Caput* Mass differ strikingly from those of Dufay's early period. Nearly all of them retain in their melodic contour a stereotyped formula, the ornamental sixth cadence, commonly but misleadingly called the "Landini sixth." In his late works Dufay harmonized this ubiquitous melodic figure not by the archaic VII$_6$-I

Ex. 6. Typical cadences of the fifteenth century.

[107] See also the pairing of voices in Dufay's late motet *Ave regina coelorum* (ed. Bukofzer, Music Press, 1949).

or sixth-chord cadence which had prevailed since the days of the *ars nova,* but by the modern V-I cadence. The latter came slowly to the fore in the fifteenth century and took first a form in which the contratenor skips up an octave (Ex. 6a). In its fully developed form in four parts (Ex. 6b) the bass moves up a fourth or down a fifth. Significantly, it is the latter form that prevails in Dufay's *Caput* Mass. In the following the most important cadences have been listed, namely those from the end of the first and second statements of the cantus firmus. All of them stand in the G mode.

Kyrie:	G V-I	G V-I
Gloria:	" V-I	" V-I
Credo:	" V-I	" V-I
Sanctus:	" VII$_6$-I	" V-I
Agnus:	" VII$_6$-I $(+3)$	" V-I

The final cadences of all movements employ the modern V-I progression, and so do the cadences of the first parts. Only the Sanctus and Agnus close the first part with the old sixth-chord cadence. Precisely the two latter cadences introduce the third, which is, however, sustained only in the Agnus. The use of the full triad in the final chord is a touch of modernism in Continental music that brings, as it were, the older type of cadence up to date. All the V-I cadences, on the other hand, end on the open fifth. The similar cadences in the Sanctus and Agnus are only one of several traits suggesting the survival of the paired arrangement of Mass movements.

The harmonies by which Dufay articulates the cadence consist of no more than a plain dominant-tonic progression which may be approached from almost any degree. The chord progressions between cadences are planned not according to functional logic but according to a melodic—that is, a linear—principle. Gombosi has rightly emphasized that the spacing of the cadences depends essentially on the melody.[108] The flow of each movement is, in fact, not so openly differentiated by cadences as it is in the more fully developed harmonic style of later Renaissance music. The melodic rather than harmonic function of the cadence discloses that harmonic part writing was still in its incipient stage; though the cadence itself is clearly defined and established, it does not as yet affect its wider context. Its organizing power does not yet radiate beyond its immediate surroundings. In

[108] *Op. cit.,* 80.

Dufay's music the harmonic form of the cadence is modern, but it is as yet restricted to its bare essentials and is localized within a narrow space; its melodic form, on the other hand, harks back to the old ornamental cadence figure. In its combination of progressive and retrospective features Dufay's cadence can be taken as the symbol of his Janus-faced late style. It sums up the exact historical position of the composer in a single formula (see Ex. 6b).

The harmonic style of the Mass conforms by and large to the normalization of dissonance treatment which is one of the outstanding accomplishments of Renaissance music. Dufay's contribution to this normalization cannot easily be overestimated, and not by accident does Tinctoris like to demonstrate his "rules" of counterpoint from the works of that composer. The dissonance treatment of Dufay recognizes the triad as the main harmonic combination. Chords on primary beats must be either consonances or suspensions that resolve to a consonance. Dissonances are relegated to secondary beats or subdivisions of the beat and occur mostly in passing. It is true that there are also some exceptionally rough dissonances in the Mass. These frictions indicate that four-part writing was still a novelty and that the unwonted number of parts sometimes created a situation that could only be solved forcibly. The occasional parallel fifths between upper voices bespeak the same difficulty. It is usually the fourth part that is the troublemaker and that gets in the way of the other parts. If it is omitted, the underlying consonant harmony will usually emerge intact. It may be added that some of the unaccountable dissonances turn out to be misprints or incorrect editorial emendations. For example, the first contratenor of the Agnus (m. 178–179) is corrupt and has been incorrectly emended by the editor. Another faulty passage, which Professor Strunk has pointed out to me, occurs in the bass of the Sanctus (m. 72–76). Here the editor has erred in his transcription. The first note of m. 72 must be a perfect breve; when this change is made all the dissonances, including the unprepared six-four chord in m. 75, disappear. The fact that the arbitrary editorial changes have not been noted in the *Revisionsbericht* may speak for itself.

Imitation plays a very minor role in Dufay's Mass. On the whole, the texture is non-imitative, and whenever imitation occurs it is incidental and has no structural function, as can be seen in the *Christe* (m. 190 ff.) and Agnus (m. 9–12 and 100–104). It does not affect the cantus firmus and takes place only between the freely composed voices.

At times it is worked in so inarticulately as to become almost inaudible. Passages of this kind occur in the *Christe* (m. 138–140) and Gloria (m. 112–115). The imitations, such as they are, show in their motives complete independence from the cantus firmus. This statement differs from the view of Schegar, who has tried to show in an exceedingly detailed analysis in the Austrian *Denkmäler* that the soprano, and to some degree the other voices also, are nothing but a continuous paraphrase and melodic elaboration of the cantus firmus. His claim falls in with an old theory of Schering which has long since been discredited. In spite of the impressive tables Schegar's analysis is untenable in both method and result.[109] The same faulty method which purported to prove "variations" within the cantus firmus itself is applied here to the other voices. The alleged similarities between the cantus firmus and the treble are the result of far-fetched manipulations. Schegar first divides the cantus firmus into his hypothetical "Grundformen" and then forcibly reduces the other voices to motivic material of such elementary intervals as occur in literally every melody of the time. Furthermore, he not only allows for partial transpositions of his "motives" but lifts the intervals he considers essential out of context and even from stereotyped and ubiquitous melodic figures. It goes without saying that such contrived resemblances can be discovered in almost any group of voices of the period. Schegar's method of analysis is unhistorical because it is incompatible with the procedures of Renaissance music. It must be written off as a classical example of pseudo-scholarly thoroughness and misapplied ingenuity.

In Dufay's Mass the cantus firmus serves only as a general framework of the composition; it divides the movements into their constituent parts and gives the bass directions for various harmonizations, but does not otherwise condition the melodic design. The penetration of the freely composed voices with the melodic substance of the cantus firmus which can sometimes, if rarely, be discovered in the music of Okeghem, is not typical of Dufay, though there are a few exceptional examples in his music. The assimilation of the composed voices to the cantus firmus arises only in a later phase of the cyclic Mass. The supporting function of the tenor holds true not only in form but also in melody. Although the cantus firmus is the pre-existing voice, its melody is made indistinct in order to serve as contrapuntal

---

[109] See also van den Borren, *op. cit.*, 146.

prop to the treble. Precisely because this support is borrowed material the treble can become the focal point of the composition.

Let us finally consider the Mass as a whole. The cyclic unity which pervades all five movements is guaranteed essentially by two factors: the cantus firmus with its double *cursus,* which unifies the inner structure of the composition, and the motto beginning of the introductory duets which recurs in all movements.[110] Since the motto has no strictly structural function, it merely enables the listener to recognize at once that the movements belong together even before the structural voice has entered. The introductory duets start invariably on *c,* and the movements end as invariably on *g.* In his harmonization Dufay observes the Mixolydian mode, the proper mode of the cantus firmus, and whenever it enters, a triad on *g* is sounded. Only the Kyrie forms an exception in that the tenor is harmonized for once in E minor. Thus the Kyrie stands somewhat apart from the other movements in respect to harmony. We have seen above that the Sanctus and Agnus are also set apart by their sixth-chord cadences. A further differentiation comes to light when we compare the duets preceding the second statement of the cantus firmus. In the Gloria and Credo they are about twice as long as in the Sanctus and Agnus because of the text. Musically, the five movements are subtly differentiated and can be grouped like this: Kyrie; Gloria and Credo; Sanctus and Agnus. Thus the original pairing of movements which we found in the earliest complete Mass cycles is still faintly suggested in Dufay's work.

The paired arrangement is, however, not reflected in melodic recurrences between movements. It attests to Dufay's rich melodic imagination that he, after having stated the motto, clothes the invariable scheme five times in a new melodic garb, as variegated in its phrases, cadences, and melodic design as in its rhythmic patterns and contrapuntal combinations. Even though all these means are somewhat formalized, they unfold in ever new permutations and are made subservient to the spontaneous flow of the melody. Certain patterns could be taken out of their context and cited as "proof" of melodic recurrence, but this method would miss the point by elevating a formula to the rank of a characteristic motive. Only very exceptionally do

---

110 The fact that the motto motive bears no relation whatever to the cantus firmus may be taken as an incidental argument against the alleged dependence of the soprano on the tenor.

the same melodic turns appear at analogous places in the various movements. The recurrences easily escape attention because of the continuous unfolding of the melody. The most conspicuous and also most extended repeat, which has so far been overlooked, is to be found in the Gloria and the Agnus. At exactly the same place, the beginning of statement B, Dufay writes virtually the same twelve measures of music in all voices (Gloria m. 130–142 = Agnus m. 115–127). The correspondence is closest, as is to be expected, in the soprano and bass, and least exact in the alto. Even in this "double take" the melody is differently articulated at the end by means of a varied cadence and thus takes a different aspect the second time. The Mass as a whole attests to Dufay's felicitous inventiveness and remarkable fecundity of melodic ideas.

OKEGHEM

In the discussion of Okeghem's *Caput* Mass we shall, reversing the procedure applied to Dufay, begin with the larger formal aspects and then turn to the internal stylistic differences. Okeghem's Mass is short in comparison with that of Dufay, mainly because the introductory duets, if present at all, are much more concise. Although all five movements are linked up by the same cantus firmus, a close cyclic unity obtains only in the last four. The Kyrie stands distinctly apart; it is extremely brief, presents the cantus firmus only once in a shortened combination of statements A and B, omits the introductory duet altogether, and lacks the motto beginning which all other movements have. The motto itself is almost literally borrowed from Dufay, but is transposed to the lower third (Ex. 7). The resemblance is not

Ex. 7. Motto beginnings of the *Caput* Masses.

equally patent in all movements, but it can hardly be fortuitous in view of the other borrowed features. The correspondence is most convincing in the Sanctus-Agnus group, less so in the other pair.

Pairing of movements comes to light also in a peculiar feature of the introductory duets. Those of the Gloria and Credo fall into two sections which are separated by a full-measure rest. This strange halt in duet sections is fairly typical of English compositions of the Leonel-Dunstable generation.[111] Possibly Okeghem, too, was subject to English influence. Van den Borren has already suggested that the melodic lines of the *Caput* Mass recall English style.[112] English influence can be inferred also from the isolated position of the Kyrie, a movement the English preferred to exclude from polyphony. Okeghem may have written his Mass originally in the English manner as a four-movement work, adding the Kyrie only as an afterthought to bring the work in line with Continental practice; or he may have taken his cue from the hypothetical English *Caput* Mass, which may have been composed without Kyrie and motto.

The paired arrangement of the four subsequent movements is accentuated by harmonic means. The Mass as a whole stands in the Dorian mode, which obtains, however, only sporadically, as it covers a wide range of harmonic fluctuation. The harmonic ambiguity enables the composer to incorporate the Mixolydian plainsong in a Dorian composition without any change or transposition. He solves the discrepancy of modes simply by adding a *d* to the cantus firmus after it has run its course—a device that Dufay did not need because no modal conflict existed. Examination of the main cadences at the end of the two tenor statements gives the following result:

Kyrie:	D VII_6 [or V] –I	D VII_6-I
Gloria:	" VII_6-I	" VII_6-I
Credo:	" VII_6-IV-I	" VII_6-I
Sanctus:	G VII_6-I	" VII_6-I
Agnus:	G VII_6-I	" VII_6-I

In striking contrast to Dufay (see p. 274), Okeghem cadences consistently by means of the sixth chord, which in his day had already become somewhat archaic. The Trent Codices and the Chigi MS, the only two manuscripts preserving the work, differ with regard to the first cadence of the Kyrie. In the former source the last note of the cantus firmus is sustained; in the latter manuscript a semibreve rest has been inserted before the added *d*. As a result, the VII_6-I cadence of the Chigi MS appears in the Trent Codices as V-I. The latter

---

111 See the reference in "The Beginnings of Choral Polyphony," p. 188.

112 *Op. cit.,* 199.

cadence may be the more accurate variant, because the rhythmic value of the sustained note agrees with Dufay's tenor. The Kyrie stands harmonically apart from the other movements, as it is the only one to contain the modern form of the cadence at this prominent place. It would be far-fetched to take this as confirmation of our suspicion that the Kyrie was composed later than the rest, because the sixth-chord cadence is employed as a deliberate archaism and is therefore no valid criterion for the date. I say "deliberate" because Okeghem concluded his movements always with a freely composed coda which did not bind him to any progression; yet he still chose to avoid the modern cadence.

In respect to melodic form the cadences stand in equally sharp contrast to those of Dufay. Without exception they no longer employ the conservative formula of the ornamental sixth but substitute for it the modern cadence of leading note to final (7–8). Okeghem's cadences show, therefore, a Janus face: they are retrospective harmonically and progressive melodically; they are, in other words, the exact complement of Dufay's cadences, but the two constituent elements have exchanged places. While the older composer is looking ahead from an earlier stage of development the younger is looking back from a later stage.

As in Dufay's Mass, the cadences divide the last four movements into two groups. The Gloria and the Credo end on *D* in all sections, while the Sanctus and the Agnus have in their first parts half-cadences on or "modulations" to G. If we take into account the differentiation of movements by means of harmony, introductory duets, and motto, the Mass as a whole falls again into three groups: Kyrie; Gloria and Credo; Sanctus and Agnus. The pairing is much more pronounced in Okeghem's work than in that of Dufay, and may be regarded also as an archaic feature.

With regard to musical style the two Masses are worlds apart. Despite the identity of the scaffolding voice, Okeghem's individuality bursts forth in the general approach as well as in the smallest details. It is difficult to capture in words the specific flavor emanating from the work. Van den Borren has justly asserted that the first thing that strikes one about Okeghem is that "il n'a pas de système." [118] Yet, while there is no system, there is a very distinct guiding principle: the thoroughly linear conception of part writing which profoundly affects

[118] *Op. cit.*, 168.

and modifies all other factors of his technique.[114] This principle assumes seemingly self-contradictory aspects in Okeghem, for it fuses retrospective and progressive features in paradoxical manner. On the one hand, the independence resulting from the linear conception of each voice seems to be a relic of Gothic polyphony with its strata of successively composed parts; on the other, the parts are no longer superimposed in layers, but are intertwined in a rich contrapuntal fabric which is possible only if the voices are conceived simultaneously. One of the outstanding traits of this music is the noteworthy advance over Dufay in the treatment of four very nearly equivalent voices. No part could be omitted without impairing the whole. While Dufay concentrates the musical interest in the treble, which determines both phrase structure and harmonization, no such single determinant exists for Okeghem. This constitutes one of the main obstacles to the understanding of his music.

Okeghem's linear counterpoint is essentially non-imitative and belongs to a type of contrapuntal writing that has been minimized, if not ignored, in both historical and practical books on counterpoint. Non-imitative counterpoint, a little-traveled byway in the development of contrapuntal art, is difficult to grasp and a challenge to the imagination. In the contrapuntal instruction of today it has become almost axiomatic, for reasons that cannot be discussed here, that counterpoint is practically synonymous with and inseparable from imitation. Okeghem's counterpoint is perhaps the best example of the opposite concept. He is far from being the "father" of continuous or structural imitation, as Riemann [115] has been trying to make us believe on the basis of inadequate knowledge of the music and premature generalizations. On the contrary, Okeghem's sacred works are characterized by sparseness of imitative entries, and the few that can be found are restricted to motto beginnings, which may not even be Okeghem's own, or to transitory and sometimes singularly vague imitations without structural function.[116] Only in his secular music does he approach, at least occasionally, a more systematic and consistent use of the device, for example in his strikingly imitative chanson *Petite Camusette.*[117] If any claim for Okeghem's contribution to the development of imitation can be made, it can be supported by his

[114] Gombosi, *op. cit.,* 81.
[115] *Handbuch der Musikgeschichte,* II: 1, 233.
[116] See also van den Borren, *op. cit.,* 166, 170.
[117] Printed in Gombosi, *op. cit.,* App. 8.

chansons; but in this form the device had been used since the early days of the Franco-Flemish school.[118] Even in such late works as the *Missa Fors seulement,* which shows an unusually high degree of imitation, the device does not attain a dominant position. The *Missa Prolationum,* which uses mensuration canon, represents a unique case because the canonic voices start together, so that the imitative structure remains practically inaudible.

In the *Caput* Mass imitation is virtually nonexistent, and the rare instances where it can be discovered confirm the rule. The clearest case is perhaps the introductory duet of the Sanctus (m. 10–12), which brings in imitation at the fifth. A typical example of the composer's vague use of the device occurs in the Credo (m. 68–73), in which the three free voices loosely imitate one another without strictly observing the rhythm of the pattern. Nevertheless the imitative connection is obviously intentional, because the voices enter successively after several rests. For another case of imitation see Ex. 9 below.

In general, however, the voices move independently of one another without offering the ear sharply profiled motives which can be easily recognized or retained. That Okeghem was quite capable of inventing precise motives in imitation is proved by his chansons, but in his sacred music he chose a different path, more in keeping with his non-imitative polyphony. This observation brings us to the crucial point: imitation as such presupposes well-defined and profiled motives, without which it cannot operate successfully. The absence of imitation is therefore only the logical corollary of the absence of such motives. An attendant stylistic factor is Okeghem's apparent aversion to melodic sequence. This device, which is nothing but the projection of imitation into a single voice, needs clearly stated patterns in order to be audible and recognizable in the repeat. The whole complex of imitation and sequence depends on such patterns, and precisely these Okeghem eschews with striking consistency.

The reader will not have failed to notice that Okeghem's counterpoint has been described so far in negative terms only. This negative approach is not just a precious literary device but the logical conse-

---

118 The reference works and music histories that tell us otherwise are out of date. In the 11th edition of Riemann's *Musiklexikon,* for example, Okeghem figures as the "Altmeister des durchimitierenden a cappella-Stils," with the specific reservation that the epithet applies probably only to his sacred works; the secular compositions are said to continue in the older (non-imitative) tradition. This information has made the rounds in the numerous works based, admittedly or not, on Riemann.

quence of the fact that our present-day nomenclature lacks the positive terms that would adequately describe Okeghem's music. This lack, a telling symptom of the narrowness of our musical terminology, is a serious obstacle to stylistic analysis. It is therefore not easy to state positively what Okeghem's counterpoint is. We have seen that its main principle is linear part writing, and only through it can his counterpoint be properly understood. In the absence of circumscribed patterns and the customary means of articulation each voice flows on smoothly, subject only to its own linear direction. This effect results from writing each line as a counterpoint against now the one, then the other part, and not necessarily against the cantus firmus as the master voice. This technique may be illustrated by a short passage from the Credo (Ex. 8), which begins with statement B of the cantus

Ex. 8. Okeghem: *Caput* Mass, from the Credo.

firmus in analogy to the quoted excerpt from Dufay (Ex. 5). It will be noticed that the voices are very nearly equivalent with regard to contrapuntal texture and rhythmic pace. While Dufay keeps the leading voice florid and sets it off against cantus firmus and bass, Okeghem distributes florid passages more evenly over all free voices and minimizes their rhythmic contrast with the borrowed voice by adjusting their rhythmic pace to that of the cantus firmus.[119] This rhythmic equalization grows out of the contrapuntal interrelations. The voices serve each other mutually as springboards for counterpoints, so that it becomes impossible to say which is the "melody" and which the "coun-

[119] In the *Denkmäler* this point is somewhat obscured by the reduction of only one part of each movement, so that it seems as though the pace of the bass had been stepped up to adapt it to that of the upper voices. The result, lack of differentiation, is of course the same.

terpoint" or countersubject. The voices or subjects are often paired, either in contrary motion (see treble and tenor in m. 148–149), or in parallel motion (see bass and alto at the beginning of the example). In the latter case the parts move in tenths, one of Okeghem's favorite intervals for this purpose. By the very nature of Okeghem's writing the treble is rarely the dominant part; it is not even *primus inter pares*, but just one of four autonomous, yet correlated parts. Alternating in importance, each one in turn relinquishes its leading position to another. Independent in rhythm and melody, none is in itself characteristic enough to stand out against the others for its motivic formation. The subordination of the single voice to the total effect of their interplay creates a certain uniformity, not to be confused with dullness, which is the natural result of the equalization of parts. The difficulty in composing in this style is precisely that each voice must be autonomous enough to be an individual line, yet not so much so as to encroach on the others.

The interdependence of autonomous lines is clearly reflected in the unusually complex phrase structure. In part writing such as this the voices do not coincide in their points of repose; the phrases are of uneven length and cannot, therefore, cadence together. The asymmetrical and individual phrase structure of each part strongly reinforces the independence of lines. The continual stream of overlapping phrases brings us to the most striking single factor in Okeghem's music: the avoidance of cadences. He has a veritable *horror vacui* and betrays a strong disinclination to interrupt the continuous intertwining and overlapping of lines or to arrest the flow of voices in simultaneous halts. The section given in Ex. 8 reproduces only the beginning of a four-voice passage that contains not a single conclusive cadence for forty-six measures, and when the cadence finally arrives it is distinctly light and not emphatic. The fact that the cantus firmus appears as the lowest voice greatly facilitates the avoidance of cadences, and this is evidently the main reason why Okeghem put it in the bass. There are essentially two cadential devices which sustain the flux of the voices. One is what Zarlino calls the interrupted cadence, in which one voice behaves as though it came to a cadence while the other either moves on to a note foreign to the cadence or pauses briefly. The other is the deceptive cadence, such as we find in Ex. 8, m. 155–156, or similarly deceptive progressions which Okeghem uses incessantly, sometimes even as a means to introduce the cantus firmus.

The avoidance of cadences (again a negative term!) accounts for the restless continuity so highly characteristic of Okeghem's music. As to the major divisions, there is an unmistakable tendency to soften contrasts and to bring about smooth transitions between duets and full sections. Even if he concludes a duet with a cadence, he keeps up the motion in one voice and runs it directly into the tutti (see, for example, the Gloria); or he introduces the two lower voices successively a measure apart, not simultaneously, as Dufay prefers to do (see the beginning of the Credo). The Sanctus illustrates both possibilities in conjunction. Still more conspicuous are those transitions which completely ignore the cadence and gradually expand the setting from two to four voices. This case is exemplified by the beginning of the *Qui tollis,* in which the cantus firmus enters almost imperceptibly.

The desire to create a ceaselessly flowing style manifests itself strongly in the melodic design. While Dufay's melody progresses in neatly juxtaposed phrases and receives direction from, and in turn sets a goal to, the cadence, Okeghem's overlapping lines hover in midair because they are not securely anchored at the fixed points the cadence would normally provide. For this reason they lack the directive forcefulness of Dufay's motives, undulate in seemingly contourless and irrational fashion, and are bound only to their own intervallic progressions. Their peculiarly restive yet gentle quality and their endless floating would perhaps be most fittingly described by the term "endless melody," which is actually more appropriate here than in Wagner's music.

The floating quality of the lines is caused in turn by the placid rhythms without sharp edges and by the absence of sequential or repetitive patterns, which makes it difficult for the ear to anticipate or retain the ever-new interweaving of asymmetrical phrases. Since the flow is not regulated by cadences, the major sections seem to originate spontaneously and rhapsodically without a premeditated plan. There is, however, one exception to this prevailing rhapsodic impression: the final cadence. Okeghem takes great care to build up tension toward the end and to create a feeling of expectancy leading up to the final cadence. He steps up the melodic pace and the harmonic rhythm, increases the contrapuntal complexity, and by joining these devices achieves a distinctly climactic *stretto* effect. This "drive to the cadence," as the phenomenon may be called, seems to be a characteristic of only the middle phase of Renaissance music (1480–1530) and seems to be restricted to composers of the Franco-Flemish school.[120] It begins with Okeghem, is carried to perfection by Obrecht and Josquin, and declines soon thereafter. Okeghem's Masses furnish several convincing examples of this drive; it is introduced in the *Caput* Mass most prominently at the end of the last *Agnus* (Ex. 9). Here the melodic pace is

Ex. 9. Okeghem: *Caput* Mass, end of the Agnus Dei.

faster than at any other place in the composition and the voices are unified by motivic fragments in imitation, but it is so narrowly spaced and so loose that it easily passes by unnoticed. It may seem strange that the bass does not participate in the drive. However, this is far from being an isolated procedure with Okeghem.[121] He likes to permit the bass, or sometimes another voice, to drop out completely for most of the drive and to make it re-enter again only for the final chords. Apparently, the composer feared that the increased pace in all voices might be confusing rather than climactic. Nevertheless a drive to the cadence for as many as five voices can be found occasionally, e.g. the *Missa Fors seulement*.

The cadence, or rather its absence, has been discussed so far with regard to melody and phrase structure, not yet with regard to har-

---

[120] A comprehensive study of this phenomenon has not yet been made. For a preliminary account see Mary Clement, *The Approach to the Cadence in High-Renaissance Music*, University of California, Berkeley, M.A. Thesis 1945 (typewritten).

[121] *E.g., Missa Mi-Mi, Collected Works*, II, p. 9.

mony. The restive floating which characterizes the music in respect to melody is even more pronounced in the constant shifts of harmony and the iridescent interplay of vertical combinations which cannot properly be called "chords," though this term will be retained for convenience here. In view of Okeghem's thoroughly linear approach it is not surprising that he completely subordinates harmony to polyphony and shows little concern for harmony as such. His chord progressions grow out of his contrapuntal combinations of intervals, and as they are not guided by a specifically harmonic plan or logic they seem erratic and arbitrary. However, their ostensibly illogical character is merely another aspect of the fact that cadences, the principal means of a clear harmonic logic, are missing. Since the harmony is not directed by distinct bass progressions, as it is in Dufay's music, Okeghem can afford to put the cantus firmus in the lowest voice, although it is, as van den Borren has pointed out,[122] anything but a satisfactory bass in the modern harmonic sense. But precisely this very characteristic answers Okeghem's needs because it does not prescribe or imply typically harmonic progressions.

An additional reason for placing the cantus firmus in the bass is Okeghem's propensity for dark colors and low range in general. It was he and his followers who took the first significant steps toward the exploration of the bass register in choral music. This is externally expressed also in the clefs of the *Caput* Mass. They circumscribe a much lower range [123] than do the soprano, alto, and tenor clefs of Dufay's Mass. Dufay also calls sometimes for the bass clef, but he does it mostly in works of his late period, as for example in the Mass *Ecce ancilla.* He ventures into the lower region for a harmonic reason—to gain a solid support for his harmonies. Okeghem does it for a coloristic reason—to attain somber and mysteriously blending sonorities.

In his vertical combinations of intervals Okeghem favors triads in root position alternating frequently with sixth chords. Chains of parallel sixth chords are restricted in the *Caput* Mass primarily to short sections, especially to the last few progressions before the final cadence. It would be precarious to interpret these survivals of sixth-chord style as a direct English influence, since it had become common property in Franco-Flemish music as early as Dufay's "second period."

122 *Op. cit.,* 197.
123 A cursory glance at the Collected Works will show how frequently the bass clef and even the unusually low gamma clef appears in Okeghem's Masses.

Okeghem's affinity to English music lies less in his sixth chords than in his melodic style. He likes to couple his voices in parallel tenths, especially in three-voice sections. This device is suggestive of what has been called "non-quartal harmony," [124] but there is actually little evidence of this type of writing in the *Caput* Mass.

His treatment of the dissonance does not essentially differ from current practice. Dissonances on strong beats are usually prepared or are introduced in stereotyped melodic formulas, such as the ornamental sixth, the cambiata, and the inverted cambiata, all of which add a great deal of savor to otherwise consonant progressions. He resolves his suspensions sometimes irregularly by skip, or again in typically ornamental fashion by means of an échappée formula, such as we find in m. 4–5 of the Sanctus (Ex. 10) or m. 14–15 of the Gloria.

Ex. 10. Okeghem: Irregular resolution of suspension.

The most startling dissonances in the *Caput* Mass are only apparent ones and are due to editorial mishaps. An entire section of the last Agnus [125] has been inaccurately transcribed and arbitrarily altered in the edition of the Austrian *Denkmäler*, but is given in correct form in the edition by Plamenac. The latter has, however, overlooked one or two small scribal errors in the Chigi MS which produce unlikely or impossible combinations.[126] He has retained in his transcription of the Agnus (m. 72–73) a corrupt reading of the cantus firmus and has relegated to the editorial apparatus the correct version of the Trent Codices. That only the latter reading is correct could easily have been ascertained from other statements of the cantus firmus. Also in the contratenor of the Credo (m. 24) the variant of Tr seems preferable.

124 See the interesting study of Charles W. Fox, "Non-Quartal Harmony in Renaissance Music," in MQ XXXI (1945), 33, which draws attention to a hitherto neglected aspect of Renaissance music.

125 DTOe, Vol. 38, 78, m. 84–87; the editorial changes have not been recorded in the *Revisionsbericht*.

126 See the review in *Notes*, Music Library Association, V (1948), 415.

Although the prevailing mode of Okeghem's Mass is obviously centered in *D* (a distinction between Dorian and Hypodorian cannot be made here) the combination of lines results in progressions of triads that are incompatible with any one of the established modes. *Musica ficta* [127] is frequently prescribed, several times at strategic places, in order to prevent the singer from flattening the *b* which gives the first part of the cantus firmus its strange physiognomy. This *b* in the bass brings about the remarkable cadence on *b* in the Agnus (m. 93), which composers of the period took pains to avoid as much as possible. The *b* entails, furthermore, harmonic as well as melodic tritones which should not be edited out of existence; their frequency indicates that they were intended. Even when the triads are perfect they alternate in a most peculiar fashion, with deliberate disregard for dominant-tonic progressions. At the entry of the cantus firmus they swing back and forth between D minor and B minor (see Ex. 8). This highly characteristic progression involves a very closely spaced cross relation (*f-f♯*) which breaks through the limits of any one mode.

Some of the intricate questions raised by Okeghem's work with regard to mode have already been discussed by Seay.[128] The difficulty arises from the fact that Okeghem has introduced a Mixolydian cantus firmus into a Dorian composition. In her article the author proposes to recognize such combinations as an "over-all mode" standing somewhere between and above the two modes and having a special flavor of its own. While it is certainly true that Okeghem's music has a strong modal flavor, it is questionable whether the total effect of combined modes can be understood in purely modal, that is to say melodic, terms and whether the term "over-all mode" is tenable. She criticizes Tinctoris for dealing inadequately with the problem of mode in polyphonic music and refuses, on the other hand, to work with the conception of "modal harmony" because it would be anachronistic to apply this invention of the nineteenth century to Okeghem's music.

In his treatise *De Natura et Proprietate Tonorum* [129] Tinctoris defines modes as exclusively melodic entities which apply only to single

[127] The reader should be forewarned that the *Denkmäler* edition, while it makes in principle a distinction between original and editorial accidentals, does not consistently adhere to it.

[128] Virginia Seay, "A Contribution to the Problem of Mode in Mediaeval Music" in *Hamline Studies in Musicology*, I, 47. Some of her observations regarding the *Caput* cantus firmus must be corrected according to the new material presented here.

[129] Coussemaker, *Scriptores*, IV, 24 and 28.

voices of a polyphonic composition. He expands his definition by what he calls the *mixtio* and *commixtio modi*.[180] The first refers to the mixture of authentic and plagal modes, the second to the inter-mixture of various species of fourths and fifths characteristic of each mode. Quite consistently with his strictly melodic conception, he de-termines the mode of a polyphonic piece from the tenor and deals with the other voices, which may be in a different mode, separately. Their "over-all effect," which is merely another word for their simul-taneous use, remains for Tinctoris a combination of melodic entities, which he expressly recognizes as a *compositio ex diversis partibus di-versorum tonorum effecta*. The musical result of this *compositio* pro-duces, however, intervallic combinations which transcend the con-cept of mode and lead into the realm of harmony in a large sense. Tinctoris should therefore not be accused of inconsistency or of hav-ing evaded the issue. He could not go further in modal analysis with-out destroying his own premise. A theory of harmony did not exist and was not yet necessary because the combination could be explained in terms of intervals. For this reason composers and theorists of the time had an entirely empirical attitude toward chord progressions and cadences. The treatises of the period list them casuistically by way of numerous examples for virtually all imaginable cases without any regulatory principle other than intervallic considerations.

Since the musical thinking of today is dominated (or should one say tyrannized?) by harmonic interest, the incipient harmonic pro-cedures of Renaissance music have of late attracted considerable at-tention. The attempt to discuss them in terms of an "over-all mode" is in itself a symptom of this preoccupation with harmony. It seems advisable to keep the term "mode" free of harmonic connotations and to recognize the "over-all mode" as what it really is: a special type of modal harmony. This modal harmony must, of course, be distin-guished from that of the nineteenth century. The latter operates with autonomous chords, derived in analogy to those of the major and minor keys from scales; by interpreting the modal patterns as scales it clearly proves itself as an extension and expansion of tonality. The modal harmony of the Renaissance operates with intervallic com-

[180] The same distinction is made in the fifteenth-century treatise of Ugolino de Orvieto or Urbevetani, printed in De la Fage, *Essais de diphtérographie musicale,* Paris, 1864, 125; see also Wolf, *Mensuralnotation,* I, 339, and Kornmüller, "Die Musiklehre des Ugo-lino de Orvieto," in *Kirchenmusikalisches Jahrbuch,* 1895.

binations which depend on part writing and thus reflect the linear approach.

The progressions of triads in Okeghem's music are in their lack of tonal direction perfect examples of such modal harmony. Both Dufay and Okeghem combine modes in their music in the manner described by Tinctoris. However, they differ so strongly in regard to harmony because Dufay, in his late works, adumbrates incipient tonality by means of his modern cadences whereas Okeghem avoids them, subordinates chords to part writing, and creates the impression of all-pervading "modality." His modal harmony is directly bound up with his melodic design, his avoidance of cadence, and his conception of counterpoint; it is thus part and parcel of his general style.

Okeghem's sacred music has been justly associated with the ecstatic fervor of the *devotio moderna*,[181] the "contourless, mystical Neo-Gothic," and the late Gothic efflorescence of the North which "once more resurrected all the fantastic richness of Gothic art." [182] If this parallel is to be more than a simile, if the music has the power to evoke or represent mysticism, which is traditionally inarticulate, there must be distinct, palpable, and describable technical features which create that impression. What are these traits—or, to put it bluntly, how does Okeghem manage to be "mystical" in music? Looking back on the salient characteristics of his style, we find that he renounces with amazing consistency all customary means of articulating a composition: cadences, profiled motives, symmetrical phrase structure, lucid interrelation of parts, imitation, sequences, prominence of one voice over others, and so forth. Even the larger structural aspects of the composition are made subservient to this end. The cantus firmus, though it is the structural voice, is hidden in the bass as in the *Caput* Mass, or embellished beyond immediate recognition. Also the canon, ordinarily the most rational means of musical organization, is utilized by Okeghem in a peculiarly irrational fashion. It is symptomatic that he introduces it in his *Missa Prolationum* as mensuration canon, that is to say in its least perceptible form. His music avoids precisely those features that would enable the listener to grasp the details or the large

181 Besseler, *Musik des Mittelalters und der Renaissance,* 237.
182 Paul H. Lang, *Music in Western Civilization,* New York, 1941, 184, 186.

structural units and to integrate them in his mind. We have here no less than a far-reaching renunciation of rational organization in music, and that is why we are justified in speaking of musical mysticism. Okeghem's methods of composition can be rationally analyzed, however irrational their effect may be. The listener is deprived of any regularity that sets up the feeling of anticipation; he can only passively follow the unfolding of lines and be carried by their unpredictable rise and fall. Just as in the flamboyant style of late Gothic cathedrals the structural pillars and supports are hidden beneath an infinite network of ribs which branch out and interlace in delicate and seemingly endless ramifications, so is, in Okeghem's Mass, the cantus firmus covered up by the unending and irrational flow of lines. Significantly, the lack of rational articulation can be described only in negative terms, which assumed prime importance also in the "negative philosophy" of the time—in the *docta ignorantia* of mysticism, which found its last great representation in Cusanus, whose connection with the *devotio moderna* is well known.

The unfamiliar features of Okeghem's style have baffled past generations. Today we are in a better position to appreciate them properly because of certain developments in modern music, notably the revolution in harmony and the so-called "athematic" style. These have nothing to do with mysticism, but they have deepened our understanding and perspective, and have opened our minds to the fact that the strange features of Okeghem's compositions are far from being deficiencies; that they are positive qualities for which adequate terms have not yet been evolved. How Okeghem was able to weave out of his restricted material so permanent and dense a musical fabric will always remain a cause for marvel and admiration.

OBRECHT

In regard to style Obrecht can be said to stand on the shoulders of Dufay and Okeghem, to use a much-abused phrase. He combines certain features from both, but in so novel a fashion as to make the result something entirely individual. What he takes over from Dufay is above all the emphatic use of the cadence, which he develops into one of the foremost means of harmonic, melodic, and formal articulation. What he borrows from Okeghem is the art of freely unfolding polyphony, though he organizes the linear interplay of voices in an entirely different way. What, finally, sets him apart from either composer is his preoccupation with sequence and all it implies. It assumes in his music a truly structural function, pervades his melodic imagination and rhythmic patterns, and thus places him directly beside his great contemporary and rival Josquin Des Prez.

As Obrecht's Mass has been analyzed in some detail by Gombosi,[133] it will suffice here to outline the essential points and to draw attention to aspects of his style that have not yet received their due. When one turns from Okeghem to Obrecht the first impression is that of boundless exuberance and inexhaustible vigor. In sharp contrast with Okeghem's predilection for irrational and bodiless motion and somber sonorities, Obrecht's lines are robust and earthy, and breathe the same lusty virility which characterizes the Flemish canvases of the time. Continual high-pitched activity and ceaseless rhythmic drive pervade his music. The peculiar melodic vitality is the result of a thoroughly patterned organization relying essentially on melodic sequence and even direct repeats of identical or slightly varied ideas. Obrecht is the master of clearly profiled themes, memorable equally for their rhythms and for their intervals. Spinning round within a frame of a fourth or fifth and filling it in by conjunct motion, the themes are interminably and continuously expanded by means of sequences in asymmetrical patterns which are often closely juxtaposed in imitation. The complete interpenetration of sequence and imitation in the musical texture reveals here once more that the two devices are only different aspects of the same principle of varied repetition. The motives are characteristic enough to carry long phrases, although they are ubiquitous in late fifteenth-century music and can be reduced to a few basic figures which appear likewise in the music of Josquin. In the process of spinning out his lines Obrecht utilizes the skip of the octave in an especially resourceful manner and achieves surprising variety.[134]

The dynamic vigor of the rhythmic drive springs from an incessant pulse of strong beats and is heightened by the division of the beat into small units. The steady and sturdy pulse that underlies all of his music

---

[133] *Op. cit.*, 82.

[134] Imaginative use of the octave is, incidentally, a fascinating and telling characteristic of style. The octave is remarkable for the fact that in it melodic significance and harmonic implication can be more clearly distinguished than perhaps in any other interval. The relative importance and mutual dependence of the two aspects varies greatly in music history. A study of the changing position of the octave in the history of styles, which still remains to be written, would give us an insight into the fine mechanics of style formation.

enables him to bring into play, in triple meter, all sophistications of hemiola rhythm and, in duple meter, the innumerable possibilities of subtle syncopations, durational accents on and off the beat, and rhythmic patterns that start on the weak beat and gather momentum as they move to the strong beat. The pace of his music is much more rapid and emphatic than that of Dufay or Okeghem. This can best be seen in the relationship of the cantus firmus to the other voices. Obrecht writes the cantus firmus in what may be called implied augmentation; although its note values are the same as in Dufay's and Okeghem's Mass, he writes about twice as many notes of shorter duration against it, so that in effect the cantus firmus seems augmented. Even if the number of measures is nearly equal to that of Okeghem's Mass (in the Gloria it is even smaller), it takes almost twice as much time to perform the music.

The phrase structure is rather complex, like that of Okeghem, but for an entirely different reason. In Obrecht each of the free voices may have its own phrase division; they overlap mainly because of sequential and imitative organization. Very frequently, however, two voices are coupled together, moving in the same rhythm in parallel or contrary motion and arriving at the cadence simultaneously. Obrecht likes to make the transition from one phrase to the next very smooth and fluid; he often elides them by making the last note of the first phrase serve as the first note of the next one. The texture, always dense and deftly wrought, becomes very taut in the drive to the final cadence. In these drives Obrecht achieves heights of climactic tension that are comparable only to those of Josquin. The end of the Kyrie may be quoted as one of the most finished examples of the drive to the cadence (Ex. 11). Here all free parts move over the sustained *g* of the cantus firmus in very closely spaced imitation. The broadly sweeping sequential motive which Obrecht introduces owes its peculiar charm to the fact that melodic design and sequential treatment are so completely fused together that it is impossible to separate them even for the purpose of analysis.

Throughout the *Caput* Mass imitation is restricted to the free voices; the cantus firmus does not participate in it, nor does it supply motives for the other parts. Obrecht stresses the textural contrast between borrowed and composed voices by keeping them consistently apart as to melodic substance. It should be noted that this subtle differentiation of voices does not always obtain in his other Masses.

Ex. 11. Obrecht: *Caput* Mass, from the Kyrie.

Even though the imitation is very compact and approximates perpetual stretto effects, it is rationally organized, clearly audible, and precise in comparison with Okeghem's vagueness in this respect. The close spacing of imitative entries (see Ex. 11) creates an interesting ambivalence of rhythm, for the motives start on successive beats, so that the distinction and the relative weight of strong and light beats is consciously suspended for a certain time, only to be reaffirmed all the more forcefully at the cadence (see Ex. 14 below). Aside from varied repetition in sequence and imitation, Obrecht draws extensively on purely rhythmic imitation within melodically progressing lines, and on ostinato patterns—that is to say, direct and untransposed repetitions of the same motivic figure. He manages the ostinato with Purcellian facility and charm and betrays in passages of this kind more clearly than anywhere else his playful originality. The ostinati are often subservient to the drive to the cadence; in the *Et incarnatus* (m. 116–125), for example, the inexorable repeats of the bass motive have undoubtedly a climactic function. The simple bass figure *c b c e d c* of the same movement (m. 57–70) appears five times with different counterpoints and serves as a means of formal expansion.

Motivic recurrences also play an important part in extended passages in syncopation, very typical of Obrecht's music. In his propensity for this device he is somewhat of an outsider in Renaissance music. Syncopation may take two forms: it appears either in a single voice as a highly intricate and "crotchety" rhythmic configuration, or in a group of voices as simple off-beat patterns that constantly upset the normal beat of the other voice or voices. The former type operates with the infinite permutations of complex mensural notation, the inexhaustible source of delight to all Renaissance composers. Obrecht took no small pride in such sophistications, as can be seen in several striking passages of the alto part in the Gloria and Credo (Ex. 12). In the

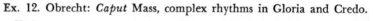

Ex. 12. Obrecht: *Caput* Mass, complex rhythms in Gloria and Credo.

quoted excerpts there are three beats to a measure of three semibreves; Obrecht not only shifts the main units to the off-beat but, with almost diabolical ingenuity, contrives a pattern in which the subdivisions straddle the main beat as well as the off-beat. Such passages as these presuppose strict adherence to the *tactus* and come off only if performed with the greatest metronomical precision. It should be noted that the mensural intricacies are concentrated in this Mass almost exclusively in the alto. This voice was probably performed or at least doubled by an instrument.

The second type of syncopation puts less weight on studiously difficult mensural patterns but plays off displaced beats in one group of voices against the regularly progressing *tactus* of the other group. The Credo contains a passage (m. 51–54) in which all free voices move together for nine beats in syncopation against the cantus firmus. In effect the beat seems to shift radically from strong to weak as though the cantus firmus were suddenly displaced. Such massive syncopations occur frequently in Obrecht's music and are in fact a characteristic of his style. In their directness and their spontaneous, if somewhat uncouth, vigor and vitality they stand equally far from Dufay's formalized grace, Okeghem's subdued intensity, and Josquin's sparkling finish.

Related to these devices is what may be called motivic syncopation, which is characterized by the conflict between *tactus* and the metrical unit of the motive. A section from the *Et incarnatus* very aptly illustrates this procedure (Ex. 13). The *tactus* contains here an even num-

Ex. 13. Obrecht: *Caput* Mass, from the Credo.

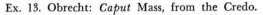

ber of semibreves, but the motives of the alto [135] and bass comprise five semibreves which run as a unit against the *tactus*. Repeated several times without rest in ostinato fashion, the motivic units shift back and forth between strong and light beat and produce an exciting overlap of patterns (indicated in the example by brackets). The impression of excitement is intensified by the fact that the two motivic units are spaced a semibreve apart, so that the shifts occur at different times. In the quoted excerpt from the Gloria (Ex. 12) motivic syncopation appears even in conjunction with mensural sophistication. Motivic syncopation has been rediscovered and extensively used in certain "motorial" compositions of modern music, but has held a subordinate place in the intervening periods.

Although the linear approach of Okeghem is still a living force in Obrecht's music, it takes on a new significance because of the essential role of harmony. The flow of the music is consciously articulated by strong harmonic cadences, and from them the sequentially spun lines received their direction and force. As the cadence is no longer as strictly localized as it is in Dufay, Obrecht can build more extended phrases, arch them more widely, and sustain them longer. It is revealing to compare his sweeping and broad lines with Dufay's formal-

---

[135] Ex. 13 differs from Wolf's edition in reading *c* instead of a rest for the third note of the alto in m. 38. This note is demanded by the context, as has already been suggested by Gombosi.

ized phrases, which are short-winded and neatly set off by intermediary cadential formulas, and, on the other hand, with Okeghem's unending melodic mosaic which hardly ever comes to a cadence. As far as the number of cadences is concerned Obrecht stands midway between the two, but he surpasses both in the breadth of his phrases. Like Okeghem, Obrecht observes polyphonic principles, but with this difference: Okeghem's lines are passive and float, those of Obrecht are active and drive.

The forceful function of the cadence can easily be seen in the excerpt from Agnus III (Ex. 14), which presents the beginning of

Ex. 14. Obrecht: *Caput* Mass, from the Agnus Dei.

statement B in correspondence with Ex. 5 and 8 above. The vigorous breath and the stepped-up pace become immediately apparent in the increased use of short notes against the unchanged values of the cantus firmus. It should not be overlooked that Obrecht introduces a motive of a descending fifth (m. 27) that appears in exactly the same rhythmic form (in doubled values) and at the same place in Dufay's Mass; but this similarity is probably just a coincidence. It is, however, not coincidental that our excerpt is taken from the Agnus. This movement has been selected because it imitates Okeghem in placing the cantus firmus in the bass and thus lends itself to an interesting comparison. Although the bass voice [136] imposes on Obrecht chord pro-

[136] Wolf flats the *b* of the cantus firmus in the Agnus in order to avoid harmonic tritones, but he leaps from the frying pan into the fire, because the flats produce very awkward melodic tritones; besides, the cantus firmus should be the last voice to be altered by *musica ficta*. Another editorial emendation should be corrected: in m. 24 of the Agnus I the last note of the bass must read *b* in spite of the resulting friction. In this

gressions that are essentially the same as those of Okeghem, they are articulated in a totally different fashion. Their retarded pace and the implied augmentation of the cantus firmus supply only a partial explanation of the change in articulation. More important is the fact that the chord progressions, far from being solely by-products of the part writing, are treated as harmonic turns in their own right. They resemble in this respect those of Dufay, but on a more highly developed level. They are directed toward a carefully prepared half-cadence (m. 30), which, though it is resolved deceptively, clearly marks off the end of a period. Such strategic cadences give the music its rational clarity of design.

In general it can be stated that Obrecht's music falls into well-defined harmonic periods of varying length but often symmetrical proportions. Linked together by melodic means and unified furthermore by imitation, they follow each other in an orderly procession. The *Et incarnatus* illustrates this period structure in an especially convincing fashion.[187] The first period (m. 1–9) is written in a note-against-note counterpoint and corresponds to the second period (m. 10–17), written in similar texture. With m. 17 there begins a sequence of three and a half measures which starts in the bass on *c* and then rises in strictly analogous sections over *d, f,* and *g* to *a.* Each section is set off by a cadence without interrupting the drive of the sequence. The sequential period is then spun out (m. 34–42) by means of the ostinato figures quoted in Ex. 13. Without breaking the continuity a new period begins with the entry of the cantus firmus (m. 43–49). At this place the bass drops out and the tenor takes over. The subsequent period (m. 49–59), in which the bass re-enters, is elided with the preceding one and is imperceptibly linked up with the following large period (m. 59–70) by means of a bass motive which appears first in m. 57–59. It then becomes an ostinato motive that pervades the entire period. The rest of the movement, too long to be fully analyzed, proceeds in similar fashion. Obrecht superimposes the period structure of his music on the cantus firmus, which runs its course unperturbed and unaffected by the artful organization of the other voices. He thus creates the impression of sweeping yet gradated continuity and avoids any suggestion of repetitiousness. As a matter

---

particular case we can be sure that Obrecht intended a dissonance, because the note in question is called for by the cantus firmus, correctly given in the manuscript.

[187] For another example see Gombosi's analysis of the *Qui tollis, op. cit.,* 82.

of fact, the ostinato figures are very nearly submerged in the stream of music and serve only to articulate the prevailing drive. The remarkable balance between the two opposed principles of periodic structure and continuous expansion, which Obrecht shares with Josquin, represents the most significant factor in his music. It is a veritable *coincidentia oppositorum,* the ultimate musical achievement of the High Renaissance.

The rapid advance in harmony from the late Dufay period to the end of the century comes to light in the type of cadences with which Obrecht concludes the major parts of his Mass.

Kyrie	G VII$_6$♯-I	(+3)	C V	-I
Gloria	G IV-II$_6$-I	(+3)	" (II♯)V-I	
Credo	C VII$_6$ -I	(+3)	" V	-I
Sanctus	C V -I	(+3)	" V	-I
Agnus	G VII$_6$♯-I	(+3)	" V	-I

Obviously, his cadences are more advanced and much more varied than those of Dufay and Okeghem, tabulated on pp. 274 and 279. All final cadences use the modern dominant-tonic progression in conjunction with the progressive leading-note cadence. They are modern in harmonic as well as melodic structure. Another progressive feature is noteworthy: Obrecht concludes the first part of each movement invariably with full triads, which he obviously considers as half-closes. They occur in Dufay only once, and in Okeghem not at all at this place, though he uses them in other places.[188] The prevailing mode of Obrecht's Mass is *C,* as all movements end consistently with an authentic cadence in the Ionian mode.[189] Characteristically, the Mixolydian mode of the cantus firmus does not affect the final cadence; Obrecht merely adds a final *c* when necessary. Only at the end of the first part does the original mode of the plainsong come to the surface, untransposed or in transposition.

Obrecht's advance over Dufay, his greater awareness of harmonic values, is mirrored also in his resourceful manner of introducing the cantus firmus. The tonal vagueness of the initial *b* is well suited to Okeghem's harmonically ambiguous style but much less so to the in-

---

[188] See the end of the *Christe* and the first major cadence of the Sanctus.

[189] Obrecht's Mass shows that the Ionian mode existed in practice long before it was theoretically recognized by Glareanus (1547).

cipient harmonic style of the other two composers. Dufay, as we have seen, always introduces the first tone of the cantus firmus as part of a triad, but this chord has no direct connection with the preceding progressions. Obrecht, bent on greater harmonic continuity, prepares the entry with a suspension (Credo) or a simple authentic cadence (Sanctus). The Kyrie and Agnus—the two movements that stand most closely to Okeghem—make this point even more emphatic by introducing the cantus firmus with a deceptive cadence which moves in both cases from A major to B minor. Through it the melody acquires a strikingly new harmonic shade which can hardly be reconciled with its Mixolydian mode.

While the movements of the cycles by Dufay and Okeghem fall into more or less distinct groups, no such arrangement can be discovered in Obrecht's Mass. It is thoroughly unified as to harmony, though the harmonies themselves are richer and more variegated than in the other works. The movements of Obrecht's Mass owe their coherence to sequential and imitative devices; the high degree of *internal* integration explains why Obrecht can completely dispense with motto beginnings, which had been, next to the cantus firmus, the principal means of *external* integration. Although highly unified, the individual movements differ from each other not only by virtue of the successive shifts of the cantus firmus but also in their closeness to their respective models. As we have seen in the comparison of Mass tenors, the three middle movements, Gloria, Credo, and Sanctus, are fashioned after Dufay, while the Agnus combines features from both models. The Kyrie stands by itself, abbreviates the cantus firmus to a single statement, and lacks a free introductory section. All these traits it has in common with Okeghem's Kyrie. One very important facet of Obrecht's borrowing has been completely overlooked up to now. He quotes at the beginning of the Gloria [140] the first eight measures from the treble of Dufay's Gloria, but gives it an entirely new set of lower voices. The quotation is exact but for a few ornamental notes and encompasses considerably more than the motto beginning. It proves irrefutably that Obrecht knew Dufay's Mass.

Even though no definite date has been assigned to Obrecht's work, it seems certain, in view of the prominent role and the assured treatment of harmony, that it was written after his first stay in Italy

[140] An engraver's error should be corrected: m. 10 of the alto must read *c*, not *a*.

(1474).[141] At about this time his style must have gone through a phase of formal and textural clarification which has left its indelible impression on his later works. His contact with the lucid texture and rational clarity of Italian music brought him that modicum of transparency and airiness which, modifying his robust Flemish counterpoint, distinguishes his later music. The most probable date for the Mass is, as Gombosi has suggested, the period between 1483 and 1485, when Obrecht served as *magister puerorum* of the chapel at Cambrai Cathedral. Here he had the best occasion to become acquainted with Dufay's Mass, which was at that time only twenty-odd years old and may still have been part of the then current repertory.

The complete edition presents as a supplement to Obrecht's Mass another Agnus on the *Caput* tenor. This movement directly follows Obrecht's work in the only extant manuscript, and since no author's name is given it is not clear whether it is an alternative movement by Obrecht or the work of another composer. Opinions about this point are divided. Wolf, in his prefatory comments, doubts that it can be ascribed to Obrecht, mainly because of several clumsy, if not faulty, progressions. Gombosi maintains on grounds of general style that it is "unquestionably authentic" and groups it, therefore, with the genuine works of Obrecht. He admits the existence of mistakes and suggests that they could be corrected by what he himself calls "strong" emendations. The question deserves to be studied afresh, since neither author has considered the argument in the light of cantus-firmus treatment, which has proved itself in this study to be a valuable tool of stylistic comparison.

Above all it must be stated that the cantus firmus has not been touched; it corresponds in all particulars of melody and rhythm to Ex. 4. In the general layout of sections the composition agrees, on the whole, with the Agnus of Obrecht. This is confirmed also by the C mode which the movements have in common. The tenor structure of the anonymous Angus, which should be compared with Table 3, gives the following scheme:

141 The documents proving Obrecht's early sojourn in Ferrara are somewhat equivocal; they mention only a certain Jacobo de Ulandia. Juten (*Annales de l'Académie R. d'Archéologie de Belgique*, LXXVII [1930], 441) is not quite certain that this name actually refers to Obrecht, as Gombosi is inclined to believe. However, even if this Jacobo is not Obrecht, the latter's indebtedness to Italian style remains undisputed.

TABLE 4

| Agnus | I/II | C(24) A 1–30 | (3) c/(3) | 31–42 (6) 43–70 |
| Agnus | III | ₵(12) B 1–32 | (4) 33–46 | 63–79 |

[phrase d not repeated]

The introductory and intermediary rests do not agree with those of Obrecht, which, as will be remembered, are patterned after Dufay. There are, in addition, some conspicuous deviations from the other Masses. The time signature of statement A is C, not O as one would expect. This duple meter seems to contradict our assertion that the rhythm of the cantus firmus has been adopted without change. Both statements are nevertheless correct: the composition as a whole proceeds in duple meter, but the original triple meter of the cantus firmus is superimposed on it. Two measures of the tenor take three measures of the composition, two dotted breves appear here in the guise of three undotted breves. There is consequently no change of relative rhythm but only a change in writing. At the beginning of Agnus II phrase c (m. 31–42) of the tenor is suddenly presented in augmentation, indicated in the diagram by dotted underscoring, for which no precedent exists in the other Masses. The augmentation of the original triple meter notwithstanding, the other voices continue in duple meter. In the last section of statement A the augmentation is abandoned as suddenly as it appeared, and, what is more, the switchback occurs in the middle of the movement without any formal subdivision.[142] The cantus firmus, which has so far been carried in the tenor, shifts for the Agnus III to the soprano and runs its course in a fashion similar to Obrecht's Gloria.

The tenor treatment of the anonymous Agnus permits us to draw several important conclusions. The peculiarities of the tenor rule out the possibility that either Dufay or Okeghem served as a model. This leaves only Obrecht, and there are indeed several points in favor of such an assumption. The idea of changing the pace of the cantus firmus, of making the change in the first statement, and of shifting it from one voice to another can be traced to Obrecht. Merely on the basis of the tenor treatment it therefore appears very likely that the

142 In Table 4 the numbers in parentheses indicate the inserted rests, not those that belong to the original rhythm of the cantus firmus; thus the total number of rests before the entry of the tenor is seven, but only six appear in the diagram because the last one belongs to m. 43 of the cantus firmus.

anonymous Agnus was modeled after him. Yet each of the ideas mentioned is realized in a singular fashion and in a very independent
spirit. The anonymous composer takes more liberties than Obrecht;
he is further removed from the borrowed voice, shifts it in the course
of a single movement, and submits only a small section of it to a
change of pace. Obrecht does not do this in his Mass; his artifices are
valid for the entire movement or at least an entire tenor statement.
The nature of the cantus-firmus treatment does not in itself preclude
Obrecht's authorship, but the greater distance to the borrowed voice
implies that, if he is the author, he must have written it later than the
complete *Caput* Mass.

We must now examine the stylistic evidence and see whether or
not it can be reconciled with the above findings. With regard to
general style, there exists an undeniable similarity between the anonymous Agnus and that by Obrecht. This can be seen especially in the
use of sequential and imitative counterpoint, the prevalence of typical
rhythmic patterns, and even in certain melodic resemblances.[143] On
the other hand, there are stylistic dissimilarities which ought not to be
ignored. Agnus III differs sharply from all movements of Obrecht's
Mass in that the voices enter in anticipatory imitation; they come in
one by one with the initial motive of the cantus firmus before the
treble presents the cantus firmus proper. This manner of integrating
all voices obliterates the distinction between structural and free voice.
Obrecht never employs anticipatory imitation in the *Caput* Mass,
although it was not unknown to him, as his late works attest. The
presence of anticipatory imitation would therefore again confirm that
the work in question, if it is by Obrecht, must be fairly late.

Even more important is the stylistic dissimilarity with regard to
harmonic periods. It is true that they serve here also as a means of
articulation, but they frequently merge and lack the clear definition
typical of Obrecht. The very first one is linked to the next (Agnus I,
m. 8) by a deceptive cadence in conjunction with the archaic ornamental sixth cadence in the treble—a very curious combination. The
harmonic progressions themselves, less forceful and assured than those
of Obrecht, include awkward steps, such as tritones in the bass.[144]

[143] M. 73–75 of the anonymous Agnus III should be compared with m. 74–75 (alto)
of Obrecht's Agnus III.

[144] See m. 57 and 62–63; the tritones could, of course, be eliminated by a *b*-flat and *e*-flat
respectively, but it is not clear whether they are intended here.

This tonal vagueness would not be impossible with Obrecht, but it would point to a work of his early period.

The dissonance treatment discloses further dissimilarities. The faulty progressions which Wolf has justly criticized cannot all be eliminated by emendations unless one does not shrink from actually rewriting certain passages. Several dissonances—e.g., m. 31 of the treble—are undeniably scribal errors (the notes should read a third lower). Others, however, recur consistently and cannot be reasoned away as mistakes, as they belong to the vocabulary of the time. Jeppesen has devoted some space to the treatment of suspensions in the fifteenth century and has cited a number of pertinent illustrations.[145] Dissonant preparations or resolutions of the suspension are quite common in the anonymous composition. A single case may be quoted here (Ex. 15). The outermost voices of our example form a strict and

Ex. 15. Anonymous: Excerpt from the Agnus Dei on *Caput.*

faultless counterpoint, but the sustained *d* of the cantus firmus clashes with the suspended *c*. While similar clashes do occur in the works of Okeghem, Obrecht, and Josquin, they are introduced there less clumsily and appear usually in four-part harmony where the harshness is considerably softened. This softer type of dissonance can be seen in Obrecht's Gloria (m. 30 and 36). Wolf has marked the passage with an exclamation point, but it is undoubtedly correct even though it introduces the dissonance by a skip. However, I have not found in Obrecht's Mass cases comparable to the bareness and harshness of Ex. 15.

The treatment of harmony and dissonance implies that Obrecht could have written the piece only at an early period, before his Italian journey. This conclusion, however, is incompatible with some of the other findings. Obrecht's authorship would inevitably involve a stylistic contradiction betweeen an advanced stage of imitation and cantus-firmus treatment and an early stage of harmony and dissonance

[145] Knud Jeppesen, *The Style of Palestrina and the Dissonance,* 2nd ed., 1946, 227 ff.

treatment. The paradox is resolved without difficulty by the assumption that the author is a contemporary of Obrecht, less gifted than the latter, but definitely a member of the Flemish school. He must have known Obrecht's Mass, though he did not slavishly imitate it. This assumption explains both the similarities and the dissimilarities of the two compositions. The composer displays the typical features and mannerisms of the Flemish school without possessing Obrecht's Italianate elegance. He emulates Obrecht but unites features that, on the evidence of the extant works, are mutually exclusive with Obrecht. While Gombosi is right in stressing general similarities, his categorical assertion of the authenticity of the work must be questioned because he does not consider the individual stylistic divergencies. Unless some new evidence should make a revision necessary, Wolf's rejection of Obrecht's authorship seems warranted.

7. SUMMARY AND POSTSCRIPT ON OTHER CANTUS FIRMI

We have come to the end of this long (but I hope not excessively long) study. If I have trespassed on the patience of the reader I have done so because of the methodological novelty of the discussion, which comprises not only two branches of musicology but also liturgiology, iconography, and the history of art. A musicological problem, the riddle of the *Caput* Masses, served as a starting point by posing the question of the origin of the *Caput* melisma. Its eventual identification prompted a more ramified investigation into related and also seemingly unrelated fields. However, without the aid of the latter fields it would have been impossible to understand the significance of the plainsong and to appreciate its peculiar position in the non-Roman liturgies. The musical and liturgical aspects of such problems cannot be divorced; and they call for the joint efforts of specialists in both fields.

While many questions concerning the liturgical and musical history of the antiphon *Venit ad Petrum* still remain unanswered,[146] there can be no doubt about the outcome as regards the history of the Mass cycle. We have seen that the *Caput* Mass is based on an unusual plainsong from the Sarum use; that Dufay (or possibly an unknown

---

[146] I hope that this study will induce historians of plainchant to delve into some of the unresolved problems.

English composer) gave it an arbitrary rhythmic shape, strictly retained in all subsequent compositions; that Okeghem took it over literally, so literally in fact that he contrived a "canon" to make this point quite clear; and that Obrecht brought the two models into a higher unity.

The three *Caput* Masses were composed within the short span of little more than two decades, between 1463 and 1483 (or 1485). They witness the rise of Renaissance music in Dufay, the last flowering of late Gothic mysticism in Okeghem, and the musical trend of the High Renaissance in Obrecht. They give us in utmost concentration a survey of the tremendous growth of musical style in the second half of the century. It is only regrettable that we do not have a *Caput* Mass by Josquin which would round out the picture. The significance of the compositions lies not only in their inherent artistic value but also in their disclosure of the existence of a firm tradition, manifested in the borrowing of a voice from the past which gives authority to the work of the present. Precisely because the composer was securely anchored in a tradition he dared to work out on the basis of the same structural voice a new composition which would be as distinct from the old one and as greatly contrasted with it as possible. The three *Caput* Masses differ from one another as clearly as do the Mixolydian, Dorian, and Ionian modes, which furnish the harmonization of the same plainsong in each case. The difference of modes is symbolical; it is only the outward symptom of a more significant inner divergence of style. In actual performance the identity of the underlying voice and of the formal structure is scarcely audible and is swept aside by the overpowering factors of style and idiom. They testify to the triumph of musical imagination over the mechanics of musical material.

At the beginning of this study it was pointed out that the correct identification of a cantus firmus is vital for the proper understanding and evaluation of a composition, and the discussion of a particular case will have driven this point home. It is fitting, therefore, to conclude our essay by way of a postscript with some additional identifications of hitherto unknown cantus firmi. They will facilitate future research and complement our subject, as they relate only to the three composers of *Caput* Masses.

Let us turn first to Dufay's Mass on *Ecce ancilla Domini,* which is based on the antiphon [147] of the same name, sung at the Feast of the Annunciation. Van den Borren has printed the full text of the tenor [148] but has read the second sentence *Beata es Maria* erroneously as *Gratare Maria*. In consequence he has overlooked that this is not the continuation of the first chant; it is an independent antiphon and pertains to another feast, the Visitation of the Virgin (July 2).[149] The cantus firmus actually comprises, therefore, two antiphons which appear always in the same order. Dufay's Mass cycle is related to a Mass of the same name by Regis, for a time secretary of Dufay. The beginning of the latter work is likewise founded on *Ecce ancilla* in conjunction with a second antiphon, in this case *Ne timeas Maria,* which belongs also to the Annunciation.[150] Regis evidently imitated Dufay, for he not only uses different chants, but modifies the beginning of *Ecce ancilla* in exactly the same way as Dufay does. Furthermore, the antiphons *Beata es Maria* and *Ne timeas* belong to the same melody type and mode and are therefore very similar melodically.[151] Regis differs from Dufay in one vital point: he employs the two antiphons as double cantus firmus in two voices simultaneously. In his independent attitude toward the borrowed voices he exercises the privilege of a later composer which we have already observed in the case of Obrecht.

The next work to be discussed here is Okeghem's Mass on *Ecce ancilla Domini,*[152] which carries the same title as the Masses of Dufay and Regis. The similarity of title is deceptive because Okeghem's cantus firmus has nothing to do with the antiphon just discussed. Plamenac has published the latter in his edition with the erroneous implication that it was the plainsong source.[153] Okeghem actually

[147] *Ant. Rom.*, 564. The Mass is as yet unpublished. Dufay follows the plainsong faithfully, but begins on g with a rising fourth, which does not appear in the known medieval or modern versions. This interesting melodic change may have been prompted by the desire to make the beginning similar to that of *Beata es Maria* (see notes 149 and 151).

[148] *Op. cit.*, 147.

[149] *Ant. Rom.*, 648. Dufay's plainsong agrees with the current version.

[150] *Ant. Rom.*, 563; for an analysis of the Mass and its numerous plainsongs see C. W. H. Lindenburg, *Het Leven en de Werken van Johannes Regis,* Amsterdam [1938]; also van den Borren, *op. cit.*, 203. Regis quotes in his Mass, among other plainsongs, *Beata es Maria.*

[151] It may be added that they stand in direct succession in the *Ant. Sar.*, Pl. 16, and belong here to the same service. Both begin with the turn g-c, as does also *Ecce ancilla* in the version that Dufay and Regis use.

[152] Complete edition, I, No. 6.

[153] This has already been questioned by Besseler (*Zeitschrift für Musikwissenschaft* XI, 13), but he could not identify the melody in the Gregorian repertory.

drew on the antiphon *Missus est [Angelus] Gabriel*,[154] which is sung in honor of the Virgin during Advent. The miniature of the Chigi Codex,[155] in which the piece is preserved, gives us a clue to the text. It depicts Mary's visitation by the Archangel Gabriel and thus refers, as miniatures frequently do, directly to the music. Although Okeghem uses the plainsong melody faithfully enough, the borrowed passage is hard to find because it belongs to the latter half of the chant. As in the case of the *Caput* melisma, the fact that the cantus firmus omits the beginning is the main obstacle to correct identification, and is in this particular case even a reason for confusion because the words suggest the beginning of another chant.

Okeghem's famous *Déploration* [156] on the death of Binchois, *Mort tu as navré,* is at least partially based on a cantus firmus. The final section of the tenor beginning with the words *Pie Jesu* is borrowed from the end of the sequence *Dies irae.* Okeghem quotes the melody quite emphatically and faithfully.

We turn now to Obrecht's Mass *Sicut spina rosam genuit,*[157] which belongs, together with his *Salve diva parens* Mass, among his most outstanding works. Wolf was unable to trace its plainsong in liturgical sources or Chevalier's *Repertorium Hymnologicum.* He could have saved himself the trouble of consulting Chevalier, because the text is not rhymed. The reason why it does not appear in any of the liturgical indices is that the cantus firmus is again only a fragment. It stems from the middle of the respond *Ad nutum Domini,*[158] which was set polyphonically as early as the Notre Dame school. According to medieval practice only the soloistic sections of the chant served as tenors for polyphonic compositions. Ignoring this restriction, Obrecht has chosen his cantus firmus from the choral section (between asterisk and *versus*). The selection of a choral passage implies that the distinction between soloistic and choral polyphony [159] was on the wane in Obrecht's day.

The Mass *Ave regina celorum* [160] by Obrecht may be mentioned by

---

[154] *Pal. mus.* XII, 200; *Proc. Mon.,* 246; the latter source contains a misprint: the notes for the syllables *[ec]ce* and *an[cilla]* should exchange places. The antiphons of the same title in *Ant. Rom., Ant. Mon.,* and LU are different and less elaborate melodies.

[155] See the facsimile in the complete edition, Vol. I.

[156] Marix, *Les Musiciens de la Cour de Bourgogne,* 83.

[157] *Werken,* I, No. 11.

[158] *Pal. mus.* XII, 365; *Ant. Sar.,* 523; *Proc. Mon.,* 187, etc.

[159] See our study "The Beginnings of Choral Polyphony."

[160] *Werken,* I, No. 12.

way of conclusion. In spite of its suggestive title, the composition is not founded on a Gregorian melody. Wolf's statement that its tenor is borrowed from Obrecht's motet of the same name [161] is correct but incomplete. Both the Mass and the motet go back in turn to a freely composed chanson motet by Walter Frye.[162] This work of the little-known English composer, who must have spent a considerable part of his life at the court of Burgundy,[163] was one of the most popular compositions of its kind. Obrecht borrows the tenor (transposed down by a minor third in the motet) and at times also sections of the treble. The cantus firmi of his Masses on *Ave regina* and *Caput* bespeak stronger indebtedness to Burgundian composers than is suggested in the Flemish style of his music.[164]

[161] Printed in the complete edition, and in Ambros, *Geschichte der Musik*, 1911, V, 20. The text is not that of the familiar Marian antiphon (*Ant. Rom.* 55) but a less-known one, also in honor of the Virgin (LU, 1864; *Proc. Mon.* 270) which has only the incipit in common with the first one. In the edition of Ambros-Kade the texts have been confused, and the more familiar version has been arbitrarily substituted for the original text.

[162] See Wolfgang Stephan, *Die burgundisch-niederländische Motette zur Zeit Ocke-ghems*, Kassel, 1937, 53, fn. 21. The composition has come down to us in more than a dozen manuscripts—*e.g.* Trent 1013, 1086; Chansonnier Laborde (incomplete); Munich, State Lib., MS mus. 3232, 37v, Seville, Colombina, 5-1-43, No. 29; etc. For the music see Vincent, *Revue Archéologique*, XIV (1857/1858), 679. Contrary to Stephan's assertion, Frye does not draw on the plainsong.

[163] See van den Borren, *op. cit.*, 210, and Bukofzer, "English Church Music of the XVth Century," in *The New Oxford History of Music*.

[164] The hope of completing this study without the addition of last-minute information has just been shattered. Only after the book had gone through the proofreading stage did I discover a portion of the *Caput* Mass by Dufay in an unknown English manuscript fragment of the Coventry Corporation. The English background to the *Caput* Mass is thus confirmed in a most unexpected manner. Particulars will be given in the *Journal* of the AMS.

List of Abbreviations

AMS	*American Musicological Society*
AMW	*Archiv für Musikwissenschaft*
Ant. Mon.	*Antiphonale Monasticum* (1934)
Ant. Rom.	*Antiphonale Romanum* (1919)
Ant. Sar.	*Antiphonale Sarisburiense*
DTOe	*Denkmäler der Tonkunst in Oesterreich*
Grad. Rom.	*Graduale Romanum* (1924)
Grad. Sar.	*Graduale Sarisburiense*
IMG	*Internationale Musikgesellschaft*
LU	*Liber Usualis* (1938)
MQ	*The Musical Quarterly*
Pal. mus.	*Paléographie musicale*
Proc. Mon.	*Processionale Monasticum*
Proc. Sar.	*Processionale ad usum Sarum*

MANUSCRIPT SYMBOLS

Ao	Aosta, Seminario, MS without signature
BL	Bologna, Liceo Musicale, 37
LoF	British Museum, Add. 40011 B
LoM	British Museum, Egerton 3307
ModB	Modena, Estense, lat. 471
O	Bodleian, Canonici misc. 213
OH	Old Hall MS
OS	Bodleian, Selden B 26

Pemb	Cambridge, Pembroke College, Incun. C. 47
Tr	Trent Codices, 87–93
TuB	Turin, Naz. J. II. 9
W_1	Wolfenbüttel 677
W_2	Wolfenbüttel 1206

List of Manuscripts

In the following list all manuscripts referred to are listed in alphabetical order according to the place where they are kept. Roman
numerals in brackets correspond to the number of the study in
which the source is mentioned; numerals in italics indicate extensive discussion.

Aosta, Seminario, MS without signature — [II, III, IV, V, VII]
Apt, Basilique de Sainte-Anne, 16 *bis* — [II]
Berlin, Staatsbibl., mus. 40098 — [IV]
Bologna, Liceo Musicale, 37 — [II, III, IV, V, VII]
     109 — [VI]
     143 — [VI]
Bologna, Bibl. Univ., 2565 — [VII]
Brussels, Bibl. Royale, 9085 — [VI]
Cambrai, Bibl. de la Ville, 6 — [V]
     11 — [V]
Cambridge, Caius College, 667 — [III]
     820/810 — [I]
Cambridge, Magdalen College, Pepys 1236 — [II, III, IV, V]
     Pepys 1760 — [VI]
Cambridge, Pembroke College, Incun. C. 47 — [III, VII]
Cambridge, Trinity College, B 11. 13 — [IV]
     O 3. 58 [1230] — [III, *IV*, V]
Cambridge, Univ., Add. 710 — [II]
     Add. 5943 — [III]
     Add. 6668 — [VII]
     M m II 9 (*Ant. Sar.*) — [I, II, III, IV, VII]
Cervera (Spain), Arch. Municipal, undesignated folio — [VI]

Douce 381	[III]
E Mus. 7	[I]
Hatton 81	[I]
lat. lit. b 8	[III]
lat. lit. e 7	[IV]
lat. theol. d 1	[III]
Selden B 26	[I, II, III, *IV*, V]
Oxford, Magdalen College, B II 3. 16, Fragm. C	[IV]
Oxford, New College, 362	[I]
Oxford, University College, B 192	[II]
Paris, Bibl. de l'Arsenal, 135	[VII]
Paris, Bibl. Nat., fr. 146 (Fauvel)	[I]
fr. 9346	[IV]
fr. 12744	[IV]
it. 476	[VI]
it. 568	[II, III]
it. 972	[VI]
it. 973	[VI]
lat. 903 (Grad. St-Yrieix)	[VII]
lat. 904 (Grad. Rouen)	[VII]
lat. 1112	[VII]
lat. 17311	[VII]
lat. 17325	[VII]
nouv. acqu. fr. 4379	[IV]
Perugia, Bibl. Comunale, 431	[VI]
Prague, Univ., XI E 9	[III]
Rome, Vaticana, Barb. lat. 171	[V]
Chigi C. VIII. 234	[VII]
Reg. 1146	[VI]
San Marino, Huntington Libr., EL 34 B 7	[VII]
Sens, Bibl. de la Ville, 46 (Office of Pierre de Corbeil)	[V]
Sevilla, Colombina, 5-1-43	[VII]
Trent, Castel del Buon Consiglio, 87-92	[II, IV, V, VI, VII]
Capitolare, 93	[II, IV, V, VI, VII]
Turin, Bibl. Naz., J. II. 9	[II, VII]
Venice, Marciana, it. IX. 145	[IV]
Washington, D.C., Library of Congress, Laborde Chansonnier	[VI, VII]
Wernigerode, Stolberg Libr., Zb 14	[III]
Whalley (Lancs.), Stonyhurst College, II	[III]
Wolfenbüttel, Herzogl. Bibl., 677	[I, IV]
1206	[I]

Worcester, Cathedral Libr., Add. 68   [I]
                     F 160 (Ant. Worc.)   [I, IV, VII]
Zwickau, Ratsschulbibl., uncatalogued fragment   [IV]

INDEX

Note: Page references in brackets indicate musical examples. The individual sections of the Mass (Gloria, Credo, etc.) have been indexed only if they appear as musical examples.

Index